Jud

Student's Book

3

CONTENTS

CONTENTS

Welcome!

WHAT KIND OF LANGUAGE LEARNER ARE YOU?

Which student are you more like: Carla or Carlos?

If you are more like Carla, read these statements. Are you more like Silvio or Silvia?

Carla

I'm learning English because I want to pass examinations.
I like grammar and I always learn the rules by heart.
I read a few pages of an English book every day, and I look up all the new words in my dictionary.
When I speak English, I try to use phrases from my coursebook.

Silvio

When I listen to English, I always want to understand every word.
A mistake is when you break grammar rules.
A good learner of English never makes any mistakes.
When I speak English, I always try to remember the rules.

Carlos

Why am I learning English? So I can communicate with people.
I never worry much about grammar – it's boring.
I don't often look up words – I guess the meaning and I'm usually right!
When I speak in class, I try to say things in different ways.

Silvia

We have English homework three times a week and I always bring it to school on time.
When I do an exercise, I choose my answers very carefully.
It's best when the whole class does the same thing – I don't like pair or group work.
Before I start an activity, I always want to know exactly what to do.

If you are more like Carlos, read these statements. Are you more like Leonie or Leo?

Leonie

I'm sometimes late with my homework – I'm not very organised!
I do exercises quickly – I don't spend a long time thinking about the answers.
I love it when we work in groups or play games.
I enjoy activities like projects because we can decide what to do.

Leo

When I listen, I want to understand what people mean – not every word they say.
A mistake is when people don't understand you.
I get things wrong in every English lesson – all learners do. It's nothing to worry about.
When I speak or write English, I say what I feel and forget about the rules!

Now look at the Learning Styles below. Read about the learning style of the student you are most like. Then read about the other students' learning styles. Are you sometimes like them too?

LEARNING STYLES

CONSTRUCTION
You ...

- enjoy grammar practice exercises.
- like working with the teacher.
- are good at homework and tests.
- enjoy writing more than discussion.
- don't like games or group work.

REFLECTION
You ...

- always want to know why and find rules for things.
- like working hard on your own and getting things right.
- prefer listening, reading and writing to speaking.
- sometimes don't finish work and are unhappy if it isn't perfect.

ACTION
You ...

- like listening and speaking more than reading and writing.
- enjoy fun activities and moving around the classroom.
- like doing lots of different things and working with other people.
- like games more than writing and grammar.

INTERACTION
You ...

- really enjoy learning languages.
- love group and pair work and prefer speaking to writing.
- don't like exercises and rules.
- like discussing personal things and feelings.

There are **Your Choice!** sections in every unit with activities for each learning style. Try different activities – it's good to know your own learning style, but it's also good to try out other ways of learning.

PREVIEW

COMMUNICATIVE AIMS
LEARNING HOW TO ...

1 Talk about states and regular activities

2 Talk about what's happening now

3 Talk about future arrangements

4 Describe past events

5 Talk about likes and dislikes

6 Agree and disagree

7 Talk about skills, abilities and ambitions

8 Describe a system

TOPICS AND VOCABULARY

Leisure activities

School subjects

Clothes

Feelings

Phrasal verbs with *get*

Films

Music and dance

Books

Phrasal verbs with *up*

World records

A

I love going to the cinema.

B

He plays in a band on Saturdays.

I can teach you to dance in a range of styles.

C

1 Match six of the communicative aims (1–8) with the pictures (A–F).

2 Write four more words for each of these categories.

Music and dance
breakdancing   jazz

Films
animation   comedy

Feelings
angry   cheerful

Each book is labelled with a unique ID number, and people are asked to report back to the website when they find a book.

I was thinking 'I hope the surf gets better soon' when suddenly I saw the shark.

It's raining again!

4 Do the questionnaire with three other students.

YESTERDAY
Questionnaire

1 Think of an international event that happened yesterday (politics, sport, the weather, an accident, etc.)
* What was it?
* In what country did it happen?
* How did you feel about it?

2 What about a national event – something that happened in your country?
* What was it?
* When and where did it happen?
* How did you feel about it?

3 What about a local event – something that happened in your town or city?
* What was it?
* When and where did it happen?
* How did you feel about it?

4 What about a personal event – something that happened to you or someone in your family? (a meeting, a conversation, a surprise)
* What was it?
* When and where did it happen?
* How did you feel about it?

What interesting or surprising things did you find out? Tell another group.

3 🔘 1.01 Listen to extracts 1–3 from Units 1 and 2. Match them with A–C below.

A An interview about regular activities
B A conversation between a mother and daughter
C A description of a picture

Believe it or not!

'Go!' is the shortest complete sentence in English.

1 How are you feeling?

Talking about states and regular activities
Talking about what's happening now
Talking about future arrangements
Present tense review
Adverbial phrases of frequency

1 OPENER

Read the *Teenage Life* questionnaire and think about your answers.

2 READING

Sophie Miller, 16, lives in Liverpool. Read her answers to the questionnaire and match them with the questions.

a Biology and Spanish.
b Half term – I'm spending a week in Spain on a school trip. I can't wait!
c School, TV, boys!
d A hoodie, a denim skirt and boots.
e I'm fed up with the weather – it's raining again!
f I want to be a doctor. And I'd like to travel round Latin America.
g I care about the environment and I work as a volunteer at our local park.
h Once or twice a month.
i A science fiction novel by Stephenie Meyer called *The Host*. It's brilliant.
j I work in a shoe shop every Saturday and I often go to clubs with my friends on Saturday night. Or we listen to music and play video games.
k Yes, he's 17, and he's a student at sixth form college.
l There's a lot of street crime round here. It's quite scary.

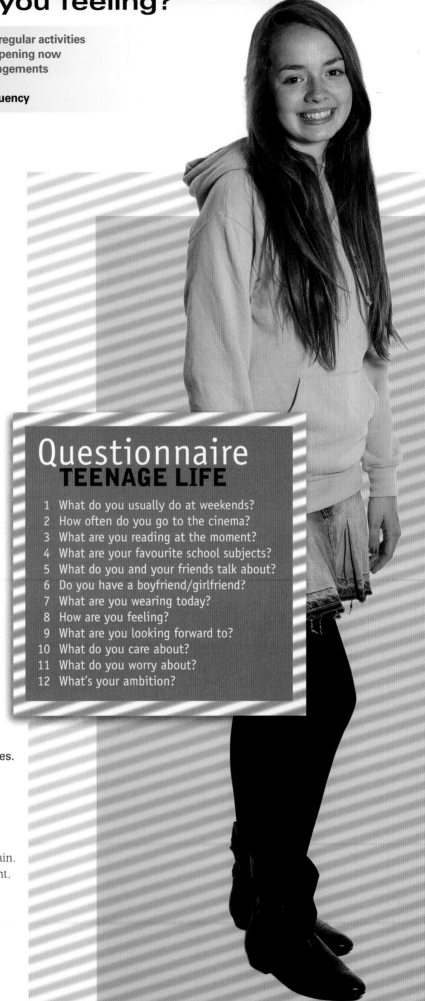

Questionnaire
TEENAGE LIFE

1 What do you usually do at weekends?
2 How often do you go to the cinema?
3 What are you reading at the moment?
4 What are your favourite school subjects?
5 What do you and your friends talk about?
6 Do you have a boyfriend/girlfriend?
7 What are you wearing today?
8 How are you feeling?
9 What are you looking forward to?
10 What do you care about?
11 What do you worry about?
12 What's your ambition?

🔊 1.02 Now listen and check.

3 AFTER READING AND LISTENING

True or false? Correct the false sentences.

1 Sophie has a part-time job.
2 She goes to the cinema every week.
3 She's reading a boring book.
4 She's learning Spanish.
5 She's feeling very cheerful.
6 She's looking forward to a week in Spain.
7 She doesn't care about the environment.
8 She worries about crime.

Your response What do you have in common with Sophie? In what ways is she different from you? Would you like to meet her?

4 LISTENING

🔊 1.03 Read the profile of Rob Flynn. There are eight mistakes in the text. Can you guess what they are? Then listen and see if you are right.

Now correct the mistakes in the text.

> Does he play the violin in a band?

> No, he doesn't. He plays the _____.

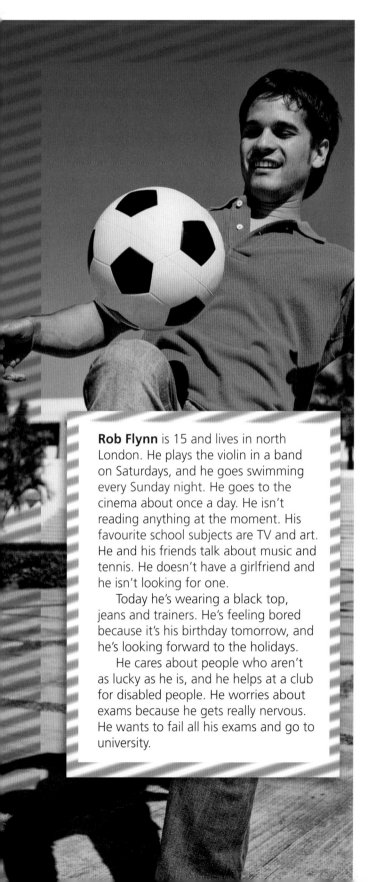

Rob Flynn is 15 and lives in north London. He plays the violin in a band on Saturdays, and he goes swimming every Sunday night. He goes to the cinema about once a day. He isn't reading anything at the moment. His favourite school subjects are TV and art. He and his friends talk about music and tennis. He doesn't have a girlfriend and he isn't looking for one.

Today he's wearing a black top, jeans and trainers. He's feeling bored because it's his birthday tomorrow, and he's looking forward to the holidays.

He cares about people who aren't as lucky as he is, and he helps at a club for disabled people. He worries about exams because he gets really nervous. He wants to fail all his exams and go to university.

5 PRONUNCIATION

🔊 1.04 Listen and repeat.

> college does London month novel
> often once want what worry

Now write the words under /ɒ/ or /ʌ/ in the chart. Then listen and check.

/ɒ/ job	/ʌ/ club

6 SPEAKING

Ask another student the questions in the *Teenage Life* questionnaire. Note down the answers.

> **Extension** What three questions would you ask to find out what someone is like? Choose from the questionnaire or think of your own questions.

7 WRITING

Write a profile of the student you interviewed in exercise 6. Use the profile of Rob to help you.

LANGUAGE WORKOUT

Complete.

Present simple
I _____ in a shop every Saturday.
She _____ in Liverpool.
We often _____ to clubs.
He _____n't have a girlfriend.
What _____ you care about?

Present continuous
She _____ learning Spanish.
He _____n't looking for a girlfriend.
What _____ you reading at the moment?
I _____ spending a week in Spain.

We use the present _____ to talk about states and regular activities.
We use the present _____ to talk about temporary events and what is happening now.
We can also use the present continuous to talk about future arrangements.

Adverbial phrases of frequency
How often?

every	day
	night
once a	week
twice a	month
three times a	year

▶**Answers and Practice**
Language File page 112

2 # Why didn't I enjoy it more?

Describing past events
Past simple review

1 OPENER

Look at the title of this lesson and the photo of the girl. How is she feeling? Why?

2 READING

1.05 Joni Freeman is 16. Read her blog about her holiday and find out what went wrong.

3 AFTER READING

Answer the questions.

1 Why were Sara and Joni excited?
2 Did they make the same friends on the first day?
3 What did Joni think of Sara's new friends?
4 What did Sara's friends think of Joni?
5 Did Joni and Sara spend any time together?
6 Why did Joni feel lonely?
7 Why did Joni try to sound cheerful on the phone?
8 Who was also on the phone?

Your response Can you remember a time when you didn't get on well with one of your best friends? What happened?

I've just got back from my first holiday without parents. My best friend Sara and I went on holiday together after our exams. We were really excited, but everything went wrong from the start …

We were on holiday in Newquay – it was a great place. The surfing was fantastic and the parties lasted all night. So why didn't I enjoy it more? Somehow it didn't mean anything to me – I was depressed and bored.

Sara and I both made new friends on the first day, but different friends. Sara's new friends were quite posh – they thought I wasn't good enough for them. I didn't care – I didn't like them anyway.

So Sara and I didn't spend any time together. I was with my new friends and Sara was with hers. I liked my new friends and we all wanted to have fun. But in fact I felt really sad and lonely because I missed Sara.

When Mum phoned, I was so pleased to hear her. To tell the truth, I nearly cried when I heard her voice. But I tried to sound cheerful – I didn't want her to know I was miserable.

Then I felt someone's eyes on me and turned round. It was Sara, and she was on her mobile too. She didn't look very happy – did she feel the same as me? Was she also on the phone home?

4 LISTENING

1.06 Listen to the phone conversation between Joni and her mother. Match Joni's activities yesterday with the times: morning (M), afternoon (A) or night (N).

> fall asleep on the beach   go for a swim in the sea
> go to a party   walk round the harbour
> dance for five hours   have a picnic
> meet her friends in a club   visit a fortune teller

5 SPEAKING

Ask and answer questions about Joni's activities yesterday.

> What did Joni do yesterday morning? Did she fall asleep on the beach?

> No, she didn't. She …

6 ROLE PLAY

Sara did the same things as Joni yesterday, but at different times. Act out a phone conversation between Sara and her father.

Sara	Father
Say hello.	
	Greet Sara and ask how she is.
Reply.	
	Ask what she did yesterday.
Reply.	
	Ask how everyone is at home.
Thank him for calling and say goodbye.	
	Tell her to enjoy the rest of the holiday.

7 PRONUNCIATION

Write the words under /θ/ or /ð/ in the chart.

> anything   maths   month   mother
> other   thought   weather   without

/θ/ both	/ð/ together

1.07 Now listen and check. Repeat the words.

8 VOCABULARY

Complete the chart with these adjectives. Which of the adjectives can you find in Joni's diary?

> **Word Bank** Feelings
>
> angry   bored   cheerful   depressed   embarrassed
> excited   happy   lonely   miserable   nervous
> pleased   sad   scared   tired   worried

☺	☹

Now tell each other when you had ☺ or ☹ feelings.

A I felt excited when I watched the World Cup Final.
B I was angry when my brother lost my MP3 player.

> **Extension** Describe an experience, but don't say how you felt. Can other students guess?
>
> I went to the dentist yesterday.
>
> Did you feel nervous?

9 WRITING

Imagine you went on holiday with a friend. Write your diary. Use Joni's blog to help you.

- Where did you go?
- Who were you with?
- Who did you meet?
- What did you do?
- How did you feel?

LANGUAGE WORKOUT

Complete.

Past simple of *be*: *was/were*
The surfing **was** fantastic.
We _____ really excited.
I _____n't good enough.
_____ she also on the phone home?

Past simple: regular verbs
The parties last____ all night.
I like____ my new friends.
I tr____ to sound cheerful.
I _____n't care.
Why _____n't I enjoy it more?

Past simple: irregular verbs
Everything **went** wrong from the start.
It _____n't mean anything to me.
_____ she feel the same as me?

Regular and irregular verbs both form the _____
and _____ in the same way.

▶**Answers and Practice**
Language File page 112

1 3 She was surfing

Describing what happened and what was happening
Past simple and past continuous

1 OPENER

What is unusual about the woman in the photo? What do you think happened to her?

2 LISTENING

1.08 Listen and complete the description of the film *Soul Surfer*.

Soul Surfer is about an accident which happened to ___1___-year-old surfer Bethany Hamilton. Amazingly, she got over the accident and was surfing again only four ___2___ later. Now she's no longer a teenager and she competes successfully in ___3___ surfing championships. Anna Sophia Robb plays Bethany in the movie, which also stars Jack Nicholson's ___4___ and Pierce Brosnan's ___5___.

3 READING

1.09 Read the text about Bethany's accident. What is the most surprising fact in it?

4 AFTER READING

Answer the questions.

1 What did Bethany and Alana often do?
2 What were Bethany's plans for the future?
3 What was she thinking when the shark attacked?
4 What happened to the sea around her after the shark bit her?
5 What was she repeating to herself after the attack?
6 What question did she ask everyone in hospital?

Your response What do you think about the way Bethany responded to the accident?

Tunnels Beach, Kauai Island, Hawaii

It was a beautiful morning. Bethany Hamilton was surfing with her best friend, Alana. The girls got on well together and frequently took part in surf competitions. Bethany hoped to become a professional surfer.

'I had no warning at all. The water was clear and calm. It was more like a swimming pool than the Pacific Ocean. I had my right hand on the board and my left hand in the cool water. We were waiting for the next big wave. I was thinking "I hope the surf gets better soon" when suddenly I saw the shark.

The attack happened so fast. The huge jaws of the 4½-metre shark covered the top of the board and my left arm. Then I watched in shock while the water around me turned bright red. I didn't scream. It's strange, but there was no pain at the time. But I knew I had to get back to the beach quickly. I started to paddle with one arm. I wasn't thinking about the shark, or trying to get away from it. Only one thought was repeating itself again and again in my head: "Get to the beach."'

While Bethany was recovering in hospital, she asked everyone the same question. 'When can I surf again?'

5 LISTENING

1.10 Listen to the radio broadcast and decide: true or false? Correct the false sentences.

Teenager punches crocodile
Darwin, Australia

1 Shane was helping his father, Clive, in the garden.
2 He decided to swim in the lake.
3 While he was swimming, he heard a splash.
4 He saw a small crocodile which was swimming towards him.
5 When Shane shouted 'Help!', his father thought he was joking.
6 The crocodile took Shane's leg and pulled him under the water.
7 When Shane kicked the crocodile, it closed its jaws.
8 When he stood up, he saw the crocodile right behind him.
9 When Shane and the crocodile were face to face, he punched it on the mouth.
10 When the crocodile swam away, Shane got out of the water as fast as he could.

6 SPEAKING

Student A Ask Student B questions 1–5.

Student B Close the book and answer the questions.

1 What was Shane doing in the garden?
2 Where did Shane go for a swim?
3 What did Shane hear while he was swimming?
4 What did Shane see when he turned?
5 What did Clive think when Shane shouted 'Help!'?

Now change roles. Ask and answer questions 6–10.

6 Where did the crocodile pull Shane?
7 What did the crocodile do when Shane kicked it?
8 What did Shane see after he stood up?
9 What did Shane do when he was face to face with the crocodile?
10 What did Shane do when the crocodile swam away?

Extension Role play the conversation between Clive and Shane on the way to hospital.

7 PRONUNCIATION

1.11 Listen and write the words in the correct column according to the pronunciation of the underlined letters.

championship change competition international ocean professional punch shark shout watch

/ʃ/ splash	/tʃ/ beach

8 VOCABULARY

Match the phrasal verbs with their meanings, and find them in this lesson.

Word Bank Phrasal verbs with *get*

get away   get back   get on   get out (of)   get over

1 be friends
2 recover from
3 escape
4 return
5 leave

Extension Write five new sentences using each of the phrasal verbs in the Word Bank.

9 WRITING

Write a short newspaper article describing what happened to Shane. Listen to the radio broadcast in exercise 5 again, and use the questions in exercise 6 to help you.

LANGUAGE WORKOUT

Complete.

Past simple and past continuous
Past simple
↓
Past continuous

She _____ _____ (wait) for the next big wave **when** she _____ (see) the shark.
She _____ (ask) everyone 'When can I surf again?'
while she _____ _____ (recover) in hospital.

We use the past _____ to describe an event or a short action in the past. We use the past _____ to describe a longer activity, to give the background to an event.

▶**Answers and Practice**
Language File page 113

4 Integrated Skills
Describing a significant event

1 OPENER

It all started on a bus

Rosa Parks, 42, was on her way home from her job in a department store in Montgomery, Alabama, USA on 1st December 1955. At 6pm she got on a bus for Cleveland Avenue, paid her fare, and sat down in the first row of 'black' seats.

In Alabama, as in most states in the USA at that time, there were laws to keep white and black people separate. For example, they could not eat in the same restaurants, sit in the same railway carriage or play pool together. White and black men could not even use the same toilets. And on the buses in Montgomery, the front four rows of seats were for whites and the seats behind them were for blacks.

After the third stop, all the 'white' seats on the Cleveland Avenue bus were full and a white man was standing. The bus driver told Rosa and three other black people to stand up so that the white man could sit down. The others did what they were told. Rosa moved – but only to the window seat in the same row.

In a TV interview years later, Rosa explained what happened next. 'When the bus driver saw me still sitting, he asked if I was going to stand up and I said, "No, I'm not." And he said, "Well, if you don't stand up, I'm going to call the police." I said, "You may do that." '

In her autobiography Rosa wrote, 'People always say that I didn't give up my seat because I was tired, but that isn't true. I was not tired physically, or no more tired than I usually was at the end of a working day. No, I was only tired of giving in.'

The police arrested Rosa Parks and she later had to pay a $10 fine. As a result of her arrest, black people refused to use the buses in Montgomery for 381 days. The boycott ended when the US Supreme Court decided that it was illegal to separate whites and blacks on buses.

One of the people who organised the boycott was a 26-year-old minister called Dr Martin Luther King, who won the 1964 Nobel Peace Prize for his work as leader of the American civil rights movement. Many historians believe that the movement began with Rosa Parks's action on the Cleveland Avenue bus.

READING

2 🔘 1.12 Read *It all started on a bus* and answer the questions.

1 Why did Rosa Parks get on the Cleveland Avenue bus?
2 In Alabama in 1955, what two forms of transport kept black and white people apart?
3 Where did Rosa move to when the bus driver told her to stand up?
4 Why didn't Rosa give up her seat?
5 What did the bus driver do when Rosa didn't give up her seat?
6 What was the result of the Montgomery bus boycott?
7 What did Rosa's action help to start?

3 Find the highlighted words in the text which mean:

1 not together *adj*
2 line of seats *n*
3 action when people refuse to buy or use something *n*
4 money you pay for a journey *n*
5 taken to a police station by the police *v*
6 religious leader *n*
7 basic rights which everyone in a society should have *n*
8 large shop with many sections *n*
9 doing what you don't want to do because you are told to *v*
10 money you have to pay for breaking the law *n*

4 LISTENING

(●) 1.13 Listen to two people describing significant events in their lives. Match their descriptions with two of the photos.

 **A**  **B**  **C**

1 I'll never forget the first time I was close to a wild animal. It happened when I was __1__. I was on a camping holiday with my __2__ on Vancouver Island in Canada. It was a fine night and we were sleeping in the open around the fire. Suddenly I woke up in the middle of the night. The stars were really beautiful and I felt so __3__. But what woke me? Then I realised something was sitting by the fire, only a metre away from us. It was a wolf! I was really __4__ – in fact I was terrified. Then the wolf stood up and slowly walked away. I couldn't believe it! And I couldn't go back to sleep. In the morning I was very __5__. But when I told my parents about the wolf, they didn't believe me!

2 I'll always remember when I first played for the school ice hockey team. It was November 23rd – I can't forget the __6__! I was 15 and I was wearing a new pair of skates I got for my __7__. It was a home game and lots of people were watching. I felt quite __8__ at the start, but I soon relaxed. The crowd were cheering and screaming. And when we scored a goal the noise got even louder. It was an __9__ experience. I didn't score a goal, but that didn't matter. I was part of the hockey team now – that was the __10__ thing.

Now listen again and complete the texts.

5 SPEAKING

Interview another student about a significant event in their life. It could be the first time they did something. Use these questions to help you and make notes.

Tell me about a significant event in your life:
● What was it? How old were you?
● What were you and other people doing at the time?
● What happened? How did you feel?

Use your notes to tell a new partner about the event.

6 GUIDED WRITING

Write about a significant event in your life. Use the texts in this lesson and the questions in exercise 5 to help you.

LEARNER INDEPENDENCE

7 Keep a *Learning Diary* about your English language learning. Use these headings to help you.

> *Date:* 13 September
> *What we did in class:* Unit 1 Lesson 4
> *Activities I enjoyed:* Talking about the first time I went to a gig.
> *Difficulties I had:* The past simple of some irregular verbs.
> *My plan:* Learn the list of irregular verbs on page 127!
> *What I did outside class:* I found the words of my favourite songs on the Internet. I looked up some of the difficult words in the dictionary.

8 Word creation: You can create new English words using prefixes and suffixes. Add the prefix *dis-* or *un-* to make the opposites of these words, and complete the sentences.

> agree appear comfortable friendly
> happy lucky popular usual

1 Joni didn't enjoy her holiday – she was *unhappy*.
2 It doesn't happen very often – it's very _____.
3 Joni _____ with Sara while they were on holiday.
4 I'm so _____ – I won the lottery but I lost my ticket.
5 No one wants to be his friend – why is he _____?
6 We didn't really enjoy the film because the cinema seats were _____.
7 Where's Tom? He _____ while I was on the phone.
8 I tried to talk to them but they were very _____.

9 (●) 1.14 **Phrasebook:** Find these useful expressions in Unit 1. Then listen and repeat.

> I can't wait!   I'm fed up with …
> once or twice a month
> Everything went wrong.   I didn't care.
> I'll never forget the first time I …
> I couldn't believe it!
> I'll always remember when …

Which expression means …?

1 It didn't matter to me.
2 I was very surprised.
3 I'm really looking forward to it.
4 I'm tired of …

Inspiration EXTRA!

LANGUAGE LINKS

There are nearly 1,000 living languages. But how many languages can a person speak? Read the text and find out.

FAMOUS POLYGLOTS

Hello Selam Hola Olá

Ciao Salut Hallo Ahoj

A polyglot is someone who is multilingual, who can speak several languages. In India, for example, 25% of the population know two languages and 8.5% know three. But some people can speak many more languages.

Ziad Youssef Fazah claims to speak 59 languages! He was born in Liberia in 1954 and moved to Beirut in Lebanon in 1964. 'I was 11 years old when I realised I had a gift for languages. I was starting to learn English in school. Within three months I learnt the language completely and was hungry to learn another. Within six months I learnt French, German and Armenian, and before the end of the school year I was fluent in all the Scandinavian languages as well.' Ziad now lives in Rio de Janeiro in Brazil and works as a language teacher.

Another famous polyglot is Professor Alexander Arguelles, an American who knows more than 34 languages, including Korean, Russian and Arabic.

But the prize for the most languages goes to an Englishman, Sir John Bowring, who was Governor of Hong Kong in the 19th century. He claimed to know 200 languages and speak 100!

Cześć Hej Jambo

How many languages do people in your country speak?

What languages do your parents speak? What about your grandparents?

SKETCH *The Mirror*

🔘 1.15   Read and listen.

MAN 1	Why are you looking at me like that?
MAN 2	I wasn't looking at you in any special way.
MAN 1	Oh yes, you were. I saw you. *Both men touch their noses.*
MAN 1	And stop copying me.
MAN 2	I wasn't copying you. *Both men touch their noses.*
MAN 1	Look! You did it again.
MAN 2	Did what?
MAN 1	Copied me. I touched my nose and you touched yours at the same time.
MAN 2	Did I? I didn't notice. I was thinking about something else.
MAN 1	Please stop copying me.
MAN 2	I can't help it. I'm a mirror, and I do what you do.
MAN 1	You're not a mirror – mirrors don't talk.
MAN 2	Well, I'm a talking mirror.
MAN 1	A talking mirror? No, you're not! You don't repeat what I say, do you?
MAN 2	Do you?
MAN 1	Sorry?
MAN 2	Sorry?
MAN 1	Look, I'm getting really angry now. Stop looking at me like that!
MAN 2	Stop looking at me like that!
MAN 1	Oh! Sorry.
MAN 2	Sorry.
MAN 1	That's better. *Both men smile.*
MAN 2	Better.
MAN 1	Bye. *Man 1 turns to leave.*
MAN 2	Bye. No, wait! *Man 2 climbs through the frame and follows Man 1.*

Now act out the sketch in pairs.

Game *Word Maze*

- Work in pairs to move from *BEAUTIFUL* to *CALM*.

- Move from line to line by finding pairs of opposites. For example, the opposite of *BEAUTIFUL* in the first line is *ugly*. Now find a word in the second line which is the opposite of one of the words in the first line.

- As you move through the Word Maze, write down all the pairs of opposites.

- The first two students to get to *CALM* are the winners.

BEAUTIFUL				
wrong	comfortable	happy	ugly	hungry
boring	lonely	terrified	lucky	sad
tired	interesting	better	great	hot
exciting	worse	first	right	surprising
easy	wild	left	old	brilliant
important	favourite	scared	fast	difficult
hard	slow	unusual	same	bright
fantastic	huge	nervous	cool	different
CALM				

REVISION

LESSON 1 Look at the profile of Rob Flynn on page 11. Write a similar profile of Sophie Miller using her answers to the questionnaire on page 10.

Sophie Miller is 16 and she lives in Liverpool. She works in a shoe shop every Saturday and often goes to clubs with her friends on Saturday night.

LESSON 2 Look at Joni's blog on page 12. Write five questions beginning with *Who ...?* and answer the questions. Use the past simple.

Who went to Newquay for a holiday?
Joni and Sara did.

LESSON 3 Look at Bethany's story on page 14. Retell the story of the shark attack from Alana's point of view.

Bethany and I were ...

EXTENSION

LESSON 1 Look at Rob's profile on page 11. Write a similar profile of yourself.

LESSON 2 Look at Joni's blog on page 12. Write the conversation between Joni and her mother about her holiday.

LESSON 3 Read Bethany and Shane's stories on pages 14–15 again. Imagine a shark attacked you when you were surfing and you escaped. A newspaper interviewed you about the attack. Write the newspaper article with the headline 'Teenage surfer escapes shark attack'.

YOUR CHOICE!

CONSTRUCTION Past simple or past continuous

Complete with the correct form of the verbs.

I remember the first time I __1__ (ride) a motorbike. It happened while I __2__ (stay) with my friend Mike. He __3__ (clean) his new motorbike outside his house and he __4__ (ask) 'Do you want a go?' Of course I __5__ (say) 'Yes!'. But while I __6__ (go) down the road on the motorbike, I __7__ (hear) someone shouting. Then I realised that Mike __8__ (shout) 'Stop now!' So I __9__ (put) on the brakes and I __10__ (fall) off!

REFLECTION Spelling rules

Complete.

Past simple

- Most regular verbs add _____ (example: _____).
- Verbs ending in *e* add _____ (example: _____).
- When verbs end in a consonant + *y*, the *y* changes to _____ (example: _____). But we don't change the *y* after a vowel (example: ___).

Past continuous

- We form the tense with _____/_____ + *ing* (example: _____).
- Verbs ending in *e* drop the *e* before *ing* (example: ____). But we don't make a change when _____ comes after *ee* (example: _____).

Doubling consonants

- For both tenses, most one-syllable words ending with a single vowel and a consonant (example: _____) double the consonant when adding _____ or _____ (example: _____, _____). But we don't double the consonants *w*, *x* or *y*.

ACTION Alphabet sentences

- Work in groups of four.
- Student A says a letter of the alphabet.
- Student B says a verb beginning with that letter.
- Student C says the past simple of that verb.
- Student D says a sentence using the past simple verb.

INTERACTION
Doing and feeling

- Work in a small group.
- Ask each other about last weekend.

  What were you doing at (time) on (day)?

  How did you feel? Why?

  A What were you doing at 8am on Saturday?

  B I was having breakfast in the kitchen. I felt tired because I went to bed late.

WOMEN IN THE WORLD

Women in the World QUIZ True or false?

WOMEN ...
- do 66% of the world's work.
- produce 50% of the world's food.
- earn 10% of world income.
- own 1% of the property in the world.
- make up 70% of the world's poorest people.
- make up 64% of the people in the world who are illiterate.

Answer: all the statements are true.

ACHIEVEMENTS

1963
Valentina Tereshkova of Russia became the first woman astronaut.

1975
Junko Tabei of Japan became the first woman to climb Mount Everest.

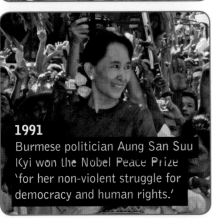

1991
Burmese politician Aung San Suu Kyi won the Nobel Peace Prize 'for her non-violent struggle for democracy and human rights.'

2000
Grandmother Jennifer Murray became the first woman to fly solo round the world in a helicopter.

DEMOCRACY AND THE VOTE

1893
New Zealand became the first country in the world where women could vote.

1906
Finland became the first European country to give women the vote.

1920
Women could vote in the USA – but not Native American women.

1931
Women got the right to vote in Spain.

1971
Switzerland gave women the vote in national elections.

1984
Liechtenstein became the last country in Europe to give women the vote.

2005
Kuwaiti women got the right to vote.

2010
Women still could not vote in Saudi Arabia.

POLITICS AND POWER

1960
Sirimavo Bandaranaike became the world's first female Prime Minister when she won the election in Sri Lanka.

1966
Indians elected Indira Gandhi as their first female Prime Minister.

1979
Margaret Thatcher became the UK's first female Prime Minister.

1988
Benazir Bhutto won the election in Pakistan and became the country's first female Prime Minister.

2010
Of the 192 countries in the United Nations, only 17 had a female head of state. Women had only 19% of the seats in parliaments around the world.

READING

1 🔘 1.16 How much do you know about the position of women in the world? Do the quiz and read the three texts. Which facts are the most surprising?

2 Answer the questions.

Where …
1 did the first woman in space come from?
2 did women first get the vote in Europe?
3 did the world's first female Prime Minster come from?
4 couldn't women vote in 2010?
5 did women get the vote in 1984?

Who …
6 won a prize for her work for human rights?
7 are the owners of 99% of the world's property?
8 was the first woman to climb Mount Everest?
9 became Pakistan's first female Prime Minister?
10 couldn't vote in the USA in 1920?

VOCABULARY

3 Match these words and phrases with their definitions.

1	income *n*	a	basic things that everyone should be able to have or do
2	property *n*	b	not able to read or write
3	illiterate *adj*	c	money that you get from working
4	struggle *n*	d	leader of a country
5	human rights *n*	e	official choice you make between people or ideas in an election
6	vote *n*		
7	election *n*	f	fight
8	head of state *n*	g	place in parliament
9	seat *n*	h	when people choose a new leader or government
		i	land and the buildings on it

4 MINI-PROJECT
Women in my country

Work with another student and make notes about the position of women in your country. Check your facts in the library or on the Internet.

- When did women get the vote?
- How many female members of parliament are there?
- Has your country had a female head of state?
- What are some great achievements of women from your country?
- Is there equal pay for women?
- How can the position of women be improved?

Work together and use your notes to write a report about the position of women in your country. Read your work carefully and correct any mistakes. Then compare your report with other students.

Women got the vote in my country in …

21

2 ARTS

1 You can't help laughing

Talking about likes and dislikes
Agreeing and disagreeing
Verb/Preposition + gerund
so/nor + auxiliary verbs

A

B

C

D

1 OPENER

Look at the film posters. What kind of films are they?
Choose from these words.

Word Bank Films

action film   animation   comedy   documentary   drama
horror film   musical   romantic film   science fiction film

2 READING

🔘 1.17   Read the descriptions of the films and match them with
the posters.

1 Teenager Bella
Swan meets
Edward Cullen, who's
incredibly intelligent
and good-looking. He's
also a vampire. At first
he avoids seeing Bella,
but they fall in love
with each other. When
more vampires appear,
Edward is afraid of
losing Bella. But it isn't
really a scary movie –
sometimes you can't
help laughing.

2 Things keep going
wrong for divorced
father Larry Daley,
and he's fed up with
looking for work. Then
he gets a job as a night
guard at the Museum
of Natural History. But
at night, everything in
the museum comes to
life …

3 In 2154, Jake Sully
joins a mining
expedition to Pandora
– a moon inhabited
by beings called the
Na'vi. His job is to
report information
about the Na'vi to his
human employers, but
he falls in love with a
beautiful Na'vi female.
Then Jake turns against
the humans and starts
fighting to protect
Pandora, the place he
now feels is home.

4 Captain Barbossa
kidnaps Elizabeth
Swann. He plans to use
her blood to remove the
curse on his ship, the
Black Pearl. Elizabeth
risks losing her life
– can her friend Will
Turner and pirate Jack
Sparrow succeed in
rescuing her?

5 Troy is captain
of the basketball
team. Gabriella is a
maths genius. They're
very different, but they
become friends. They're
both good at singing, so
they decide to audition
for their high school's
musical – but some
people want to stop
them taking part.

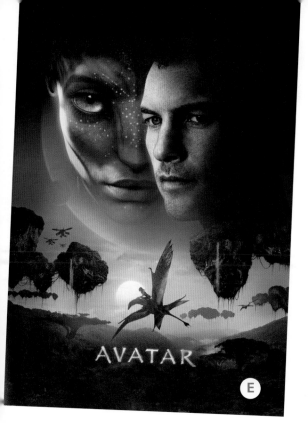

AVATAR

E

3 AFTER READING

True, false, or no information? Correct the false sentences.

1 Edward can't help falling in love with Bella.
2 Bella is scared of losing Edward.
3 Lots of things go wrong for Larry.
4 Larry doesn't mind looking for work.
5 Things in the museum start moving at night.
6 Jake tries to protect Pandora.
7 Jake succeeds in saving Pandora.
8 Elizabeth Swann's life is in danger.
9 Troy and Gabriella are good at dancing.
10 Troy wants to stop Gabriella taking part in the musical.

Your response Have you seen any of these films? If so, what did you think of them? What kind of films do you enjoy?

4 VOCABULARY

Complete the chart with these adjectives.

Word Bank Opinions
amazing awful boring brilliant disappointing excellent exciting funny interesting scary silly terrible thrilling

5 PRONUNCIATION

1.18 Listen and check your answers to exercise 4. Repeat the words and mark the stress.

6 LISTENING

1.19 Listen to five people talking about the films on the posters. Which adjectives from exercise 4 do they use to describe each film?

7 SPEAKING

Complete these sentences for yourself about films.

I love …   I'm not keen on …   I'm interested in …
I'm bored by …   I can't stand …
I'm scared of …   I don't mind …

Now read your sentences to another student. Do you agree or disagree?

A I love going to the cinema.
B So do I. OR Do you? I don't.

B I'm not keen on seeing musicals.
A Nor am I. OR Aren't you? I am.

> **Extension** Do a class survey. What are the three most popular kinds of film? Which is the most popular film at the moment?

8 WRITING

Write a short review of a recent film. Use the descriptions in exercise 2 and these questions to help you.

- What kind of film is it? What's it about?
- Who's in it?
- What's your opinion of the film?

> **Extension** Read out your review but don't say the film title. Can other students guess the film?

LANGUAGE WORKOUT

Complete.

Verb + gerund
You can't help laugh**ing**.
He avoids see___ Bella.
Things keep go___ wrong.
Jake starts fight___ to protect Pandora.
She risks los___ her life.

Preposition + gerund
Edward is afraid **of losing** Bella.
He's fed up _____ look___ for work.
Can they succeed _____ rescu___ her?
They're both good _____ sing___.

so/nor + auxiliary verbs
I love …   So do I.   I don't mind …   Nor do I.
I'm scared of …   So am I.   I can't stand … Nor can I.

▶**Answers and Practice**
Language File page 113

2.2 Promise to work together

Talking about skills, abilities and ambitions
Verb (+ object) + infinitive

1 OPENER

Look at the Star School web page. What kind of show is it about?
Are there shows like this on TV in your country?

STAR SCHOOL

In this great reality TV show, ten hopeful contestants spend nine weeks at the school. They learn to sing and each week they perform one of their own songs on TV. Viewers vote for the songs by phone and the contestant with the lowest number of votes leaves the show.

WHO'S WHO at STAR SCHOOL

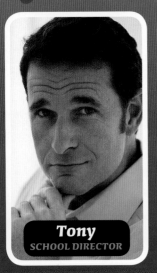

Tony
SCHOOL DIRECTOR

Jess
VOICE COACH

Adam
DANCE COACH

Rachel
SONGWRITING COACH

APPLY NOW - BEST OF LUCK!

2 LISTENING

🔘 1.20 You are going to hear Tony, Jess, Adam and Rachel talking to the new Star School contestants. Before you listen, read sentences A–J and guess who says what. Then listen and check.

A I can teach you to dance in a range of styles.
B Don't pretend to be a poet when you aren't one!
C Our teachers are great and they can help you to develop your talents.
D I want you to practise your songs hard and help each other.
E I'd like to welcome you.
F I hope to help you to find your special voice.
G The important thing is that you manage to fit the words to the music.
H Try out new dance routines and don't refuse to experiment.
I We expect you to obey the rules and attend all your classes.
J Promise to work together, because you can't learn to dance alone.

3 AFTER LISTENING

Answer the questions using the sentences in exercise 2 to help you.

1 What two things does Tony expect the contestants to do?
2 What does Tony say about the Star School coaches?
3 What does Jess hope to do?
4 What does Jess want the contestants to do?
5 What can Adam teach the contestants?
6 What does Adam ask them to promise?
7 What does Rachel tell the contestants not to do?
8 What does Rachel say is important?

Your response Would you like to go to Star School? Why/Why not?

What's your opinion of TV talent shows?
What happens to the contestants who win?
What about the ones who don't win? How do they feel?

4 PRONUNCIATION

Write the words in the correct column.

> attend expect hopeful manage obey perform
> practise pretend promise refuse special talent

■. ■	.■ ■
hopeful	*attend*

🔘 1.21 Now listen and check. Repeat the words.

5 LISTENING

🔘 1.22 Read the questionnaire and listen to Anna and Will's answers.

TRUTH QUESTIONNAIRE

1 Do you promise to tell the truth?
2 What new skill do you want to learn?
3 What would you like to teach your friends to do?
4 Is there something you pretend to like but don't really like?
5 Is there anything you refuse to eat?
6 What do your parents ask you to do which you don't enjoy?
7 What can you just manage to do but would like to do better?
8 What do you hope to do when you leave school?

Listen again and decide: true or false? Correct the false answers.

Anna
1 Yes.
2 Ballroom dancing.
3 To speak to me sometimes.
4 Salad.
5 Peas.
6 To do the washing up.
7 To use PowerPoint®.
8 To go to university.

Will
1 Yes.
2 To drive a bus.
3 Nothing.
4 Swimming.
5 Garlic.
6 To write thank-you letters.
7 To speak Spanish.
8 To get a job.

Extension Compare Anna and Will's answers.

> Both Anna and Will promise to tell the truth.

6 SPEAKING

Do the *Truth Questionnaire* with two other students and note down their answers.

7 WRITING

Write a paragraph comparing the students' answers to the *Truth Questionnaire*.

Sara wants to learn to do judo, and Lucy wants to learn to swim.

Extension Do a class survey. What new skills do other students want to learn? What do they want to do when they leave school?

LANGUAGE WORKOUT

Complete.

Verb + infinitive
I'd like **to welcome** you.
They learn _____ sing.
I hope _____ _____ you.
Promise _____ _____ together.
Don't refuse _____ _____.
Don't pretend _____ _____ a poet.
What can you just manage _____ _____?

Verb + object + infinitive
We expect **you to obey** the rules.
I want _____ _____ practise your songs.
I can teach _____ _____ dance.
They can help _____ _____ develop your talents.

▶**Answers and Practice**
Language File page 114

3 Books are left in public places

Describing a system
Present simple passive

1 OPENER

What was the last book you read? What did you think of it? Where did you get it from? Where else can you get books?

2 READING

 1.23 Read *Free books!* and find out why the books are free.

FREE BOOKS!

bookcrossing.com

'FREE BOOK! Take me home and read me!' says the note on the cover of *Casino Royale*. The paperback is lying on a café table. Is this a joke? No, it's an invitation. The book is registered at www.bookcrossing.com and you are invited to take it home and read it.

Ron Hornbaker, an American, came up with the idea of BookCrossing in 2001 and he set up the website. It's visited by around one million members in over 130 countries around the globe, from Afghanistan to Zimbabwe. 'Our goal is to make the whole world a library,' says Hornbaker. BookCrossing is particularly popular in the US, the UK, Germany, Canada and Spain.

How does BookCrossing work? Books are left in public places – on buses, in museums, in cafés, on park benches – and they are found by other people. Each book is labelled with a unique ID number, and people are asked to report back to the website when they find a book.

So why not try it? The next time you finish a good book, register it at the website with some enthusiastic comments and label it with its BookCrossing ID number. Then leave it in a public place for someone else to pick up and enjoy. Who knows? – your book may turn up on the other side of the world!

This is a really cool website!
Montse, Barcelona

Sharing books is a great idea!
Jonas, Zurich

It's fun, it's green and it's free!
Sofie, Denmark

3 AFTER READING

Answer the questions.

1 What is the title of the paperback?
2 What are you invited to do?
3 Whose idea was BookCrossing?
4 Who is the website visited by?
5 Where are books left?
6 What are finders of books asked to do?
7 'So why not try it?' Try what?

Your response In what other public places could you leave a book? Which of your books would you choose?

4 PRONUNCIATION

1.24 Listen and repeat.

> **Linking: consonant sound + vowel**
> It's_an_invitation.
> Take_it home_and read_it.
> Books_are left_in public places.
> Each book_is labelled with_a unique_ID number.
> Leave_it_in_a public place for someone_else to pick_up_and_enjoy.

5 VOCABULARY

Match the phrasal verbs with their meanings. Which of the verbs can you find in *Free books!*?

> **Word Bank** Phrasal verbs with *up*
>
> come up with   give up   grow up   look up
> pick up   set up   stand up   turn up

1 appear, be found
2 become an adult
3 find in the dictionary
4 lift, collect
5 rise to your feet
6 stop
7 start, create
8 think of

> **Extension** Complete these sentences with verbs from the Word Bank.
> 1 _____ your clothes – don't leave them on the floor!
> 2 He should _____ smoking at once.
> 3 I can't find my watch but I expect it will _____.
> 4 My brother wants to be a pop star when he _____
> 5 She's hurt her foot so she can't _____.

6 LISTENING

🔘 1.25 Listen and complete the text with these words.

> borrowed bought grown done
> made produced published read
> registered said sold taken

BOOKS: The Inside Story

Books are __1__ of paper, and most of the world's paper is __2__ from pine trees. These trees are __3__ in countries such as Canada, the USA, Sweden, Finland and Japan.

A book is __4__ somewhere in the world every 20 seconds – that's over 1.5 million books a year! Many books are __5__ by town bookshops, but now increasing numbers are __6__ online through virtual bookshops like Amazon.

In the UK, about 60% of the population is __7__ with a library. About one third of the books which are __8__ out of libraries are __9__ by children. More books are __10__ by girls than boys, and most reading is __11__ in bed.

It's __12__ that a good book is the best of friends. So find a new friend today!

7 SPEAKING

Ask and answer the questions.

1. What book would you like someone else to read?
2. Who's it written by?
3. What's on the cover of the book?
4. What's it about?
5. Which is your favourite character? Why?
6. Why did you enjoy the book?

8 WRITING

Write a short review of a good book, using the questions in exercise 7 to help you. Put your review inside the book or on the class noticeboard. Then start BookCrossing – exchange books with other students in your class.

9 SPEAKING

Make the questions in the *World Records Quiz* and choose the best answer, A, B or C.

A Where are the most newspapers sold?
B I think it's …

🔘 1.26 Now listen and check.

> **Extension** Write one or two similar quiz questions – make sure you know the right answers. Then give your questions to your teacher and have a class quiz.

World Records Quiz

1 where/the most newspapers/sell?
A China
B Germany
C the UK

2 where/the most films/make?
A France
B India
C the USA

3 where/the most cars/sell?
A Australia
B China
C Japan

4 where/the most coffee/produce?
A Brazil
B Kenya
C Mexico

5 where/the most coffee/drink (per person)?
A Italy
B Poland
C Scandinavia

6 where/the most tea/produce?
A Canada
B China
C India

7 where/the most tea/drink (per person)?
A France
B Switzerland
C Turkey

8 where/the most bananas/grow?
A Brazil
B India
C Mexico

9 where/the most rice/grow?
A China
B Japan
C Vietnam

LANGUAGE WORKOUT

Complete.

Present simple passive
The book _____ registered at www.bookcrossing.com
You _____ invited to pick it up.
Each book _____ labelled.
The books _____ found **by** other people.

We form the present simple passive with the present tense of _____ + past participle.

▶**Answers and Practice**
Language File page 114
Irregular Verbs page 127

Describing a picture

1 OPENER

Look at the pictures and match them with three of these art styles.

> realism   impressionism   surrealism
> expressionism   pop art

Which picture do you like most and why? Is there one you don't like? Why?

What's your favourite picture?

A

1 I don't really have a favourite picture, but there's a painting which means **a great deal** to me. It's a picture of a woman who's crying. She's holding a handkerchief to her face, but you can see from the **expression** in her eyes that something terrible has happened. And in fact this painting is a response to the horrors of **war**. It's quite shocking, with dramatic black lines and strong colours – the woman has a red hat and her hands are green. It makes me feel sad, but it's a brilliant picture.

2 My favourite picture? I have a different one every day – it depends on how I'm feeling. But this is one of my favourites. It shows an **attractive** girl with blonde hair and a dark-haired man who's turned away from her. He's probably her boyfriend, but he's upset and angry. And she has an expression on her face which shows that something is very wrong. I **wonder** what's happened – it's obviously a painful moment. I like the fact that the picture suggests a story and it looks like an image from a comic book.

3 This is definitely my favourite picture! It shows a group of friends who are enjoying lunch together. They're in a restaurant with a river in the **background**. Some of the people are sitting at tables, eating and drinking, while others are standing chatting behind them. In the **foreground**, a woman is holding a dog and there are two boatmen in white vests and straw hats. It's an impressionist painting which shows beautiful treatment of light and colour, but it's quite **realistic**. What I like about it are the questions it asks: What are the friends talking about? What are they going to do next?

B

C

FORGET IT! FORGET ME! I'M FED UP WITH YOUR KIND!

READING

2 ⊙ 1.27 Read and match the pictures with the texts. Then listen and check.

Do you agree with the opinions?

3 Find the highlighted words in the texts which mean:

1 nice to look at *adj*
2 true to life *adj*
3 ask myself *v*
4 fighting between countries or groups of people *n*
5 back of the picture *n*
6 look *n*
7 a lot *n*
8 front of the picture *n*

4 What do the words in italics refer to?

Text 1
1 *It's* quite shocking …
Text 2
2 I have a different *one* every day.
Text 3
3 *They're* in a restaurant …
4 What I like about *it* …

5 **Linking words**: *which* and *who*

We use the relative pronouns *which* for things and animals and *who* for people. Find three examples of each in the texts in exercise 2. Which words do they refer to?

6 LISTENING

⊙ 1.28 Listen and choose the correct answer.

Do you have a favourite picture, or one which means a lot to you?

Yes, there are several pictures which I like a lot, but there's one in particular.

What kind of picture is it?
It's a painting/poster on my bedroom/kitchen wall.

Can you describe it?
It's a picture of a sunset in the Greek islands. There aren't any people or boats/cars in it, just the sea, the sky and the islands. I don't know who painted it but there's a date on it – 57/75. So I think it's from 1957/1975.

Why is it important to you?
It reminds me of holidays in Greece. I love travelling around the islands.

How does it make you feel?
Happy and relaxed. The colours are fantastic – the sea is black/blue and grey, some of the islands are green and blue, but the mountains in the background are pink/red. And the sky is yellow and blue.

7 SPEAKING

Ask another student about their favourite picture or a picture which means a lot to them. It could be a photo, an album cover, a painting or a poster. Use the questions in exercise 6 to help you.

8 GUIDED WRITING

Write a short description of your favourite picture or a picture which means a lot to you. Use the texts in exercises 2 and 6 to help you.

LEARNER INDEPENDENCE

9 Classroom English: Match the questions with the answers.

1 How is *island* pronounced?
2 Can you teach us to read phonetic script?
3 Excuse me. How is /ɪk'spreʃn/ spelt?
4 Do you want us to finish the writing for homework?
5 What's this called in English?
6 What's a good way to practise speaking?

a Poster.
b E-X-P-R-E double S-I-O-N.
c Yes, please.
d Of course. Let's have a look at the pronunciation guide at the back of the book.
e Have phone conversations in English with a friend.
f /'aɪlənd/

10 Word creation: Add the suffix *-ful* or *-less* to these words to make adjectives, and complete the sentences.

care (x2)   colour (x2)   hope (x2)
pain (x2)   success   truth

1 He was very _____ and dropped the picture.
2 My foot hurts a lot – it's _____.
3 You can trust her – she's always _____.
4 His clothes are usually very _____.
5 There are ten _____ contestants at Star School.
6 Please be _____ with the new TV.
7 It doesn't hurt at all – it's _____.
8 I feel depressed – everything seems _____.
9 Water is _____.
10 The team win all their matches – they're very _____.

11 ⊙ 1.29 **Phrasebook**: Find these useful expressions in Unit 2. Then listen and repeat.

You can't help laughing.
Best of luck!
The important thing is …
Do you promise to tell the truth?
Why not try it?
Who knows?
It depends.
I wonder what's happened.
I like the fact that …
It reminds me of …

Now write a five-line dialogue using three of the expressions.

Inspiration EXTRA!

PROJECT *Two-minute talks*

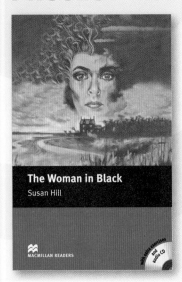

The Woman in Black
Susan Hill

MACMILLAN READERS

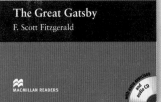

The Great Gatsby
F. Scott Fitzgerald

MACMILLAN READERS

Disney TRON LEGACY

1 Work in a group and make a list of films you have seen and novels you have read recently. Then choose one film and one novel which you would like to talk about.

2 Research: Make notes under these headings, using books or the Internet to check details where necessary.

Description
- *Genre* – What kind of film/novel is it? (eg thriller, science fiction) What is it about?
- *Setting* – Where and when does it take place?
- *Characters* – Who are the main characters?
- *Plot* – How does the story begin? What happens and how does it end?

Your opinion
- What is your opinion of the film/novel?

3 🔘 1.30 Listen to an example of a two-minute talk about a film. Can you guess the title?

4 Work together and prepare the talks. Use this structure:
- *Introduction* – Say what you are going to talk about (film or novel) but don't say the title.
- *Description* – Describe the film/novel (see 2 above).
- *Opinion* – Say what you and others think of it (see 2 above).
- *Conclusion* – Summarise what you have said.

5 Take turns to practise giving the talks in two minutes. Choose two speakers to give the talks to the other groups, who try to guess the titles of the film and novel.

Poems

Write another verse for each poem.

YES/NO POEM

Peace

Yes to listening and understanding.
No to shouting and arguing.
Yes to meeting and talking.
No to fighting and killing.
It's peace, peace, peace.

Yes to ____.
No to ____.
Yes to ____.
No to ____.
It's ____. (x3)

HELLO/GOODBYE POEM

FUN

Hello to smiles and laughter.
Goodbye to feeling sad.
Hello to holidays and happiness.
Goodbye to empty days and loneliness.
It's fun, fun, fun.

Hello to ____.
Goodbye to ____.
Hello to ____.
Goodbye to ____.
It's ____. (x3)

Give your poems to your teacher and listen. Can you guess who wrote each poem?

REVISION

LESSON 1 Look at the Word Bank on page 22. Write a list of at least one film for each kind.

Animation
Shrek ...

LESSON 2 Look at Language Workout on page 25. Write sentences about Star School using six of the verbs.

Jess helps the contestants to find their special voice.

LESSON 3 Look at the World Records Quiz on page 27. Write the answers to the quiz questions.

1 The most newspapers are sold in China.

EXTENSION

LESSON 1 Read the review you wrote in exercise 8 again. Now write another review of the same film giving the opposite opinion.

LESSON 2 Write a paragraph giving your answers to the Truth Questionnaire.

LESSON 3 Complete with the verbs in the present simple passive.

Do you know how paper is __1__ (make)? Trees __2__ (cut) down and __3__ (send) to a paper factory. There the wood __4__ (chop) into tiny pieces and these __5__ (mix) with water to make pulp. Then the water __6__ (remove) and the pulp __7__ (dry) between heated rollers. During this process, the pulp __8__ (turn) into paper.

YOUR CHOICE!

CONSTRUCTION Present simple active or passive?

Complete with the correct form of the verbs.

When you __1__ (buy) a laptop computer, you are buying something which __2__ (design) in one country and __3__ (build) in another country with parts which __4__ (come) from all over the world. Workers in Malaysia __5__ (build) laptops with hard drives which __6__ (make) in Singapore, microprocessors which __7__ (produce) in Costa Rica and batteries which __8__ (come) from Mexico. The laptop __9__ (fly) to the USA, it __10__ (put) in a bag which __11__ (make) in China, and then it __12__ (sell) on the Internet.

ACTION Game: *Guess the person*

● Play in two teams.

● Each team thinks of popular books, songs, and films. For books or songs, think of who they are written by or sung by. For films, think of who the film is directed by.

● The teams ask each other questions. When a team answers correctly, they ask the next question.

A Who are the Twilight books written by?

B Who is *Avatar* directed by?

REFLECTION Infinitive or gerund?

Complete.

Verbs which take only one form

● *ask*, *decide* and *promise* all take the _____:
I promised _____ (phone) her.

● *dislike*, *enjoy* and *keep* all take the _____:
I kept _____ (phone) her.

Verbs which take either form with same meaning

● Some verbs take either the _____ or the _____ with no change in meaning. For example, *start* and *continue*:
Suddenly it started to rain.
Suddenly it started _____.

INTERACTION Childhood memories

● Work in a small group.

● Think about your favourite activities and people when you were a child. Make a list of activities and people. For example:

Favourite activities: *I enjoyed eating ..., drinking ..., playing ..., watching ..., sitting in ..., hiding in ..., listening to ...*

Favourite people: *friend, relative, teacher, neighbour ...*

● Take turns to ask and answer questions about your favourite childhood activities and people. For example:

A What did you enjoy eating?

B Who was your favourite friend?

1 Read and complete. For each number 1–10, choose word or phrase A, B or C.

TEENAGERS AND MONEY

A recent survey of 10,000 British teenagers shows that while they have less money than in the past, they save more. When they __1__ how much money they get from their parents, teenagers __2__ that they get between 15% and 18% less than a year ago. It isn't true that teenagers are __3__ at saving: 33% of boys and 24% of girls save all or most of their money.

But you can't help __4__ surprised at their ideas about how much things cost. They __5__ that the average price of a house is £75,000, when in fact the average house __6__ over £160,000! And how much __7__ to go to university? More than one third of the young people who __8__ to go to university expect __9__ £10,000. In fact the average amount students __10__ is double that – £20,000.

1	**A** ask	**B** are asked	**C** are asking
2	**A** say	**B** to say	**C** saying
3	**A** hopeless	**B** hoping	**C** hopeful
4	**A** be	**B** being	**C** to be
5	**A** think	**B** are thinking	**C** were thinking
6	**A** costs	**B** is costing	**C** was costing
7	**A** costs	**B** is it costing	**C** does it cost
8	**A** hope	**B** hopes	**C** hopeful
9	**A** borrow	**B** borrowing	**C** to borrow
10	**A** borrow	**B** borrowing	**C** to borrow

2 Complete with the present simple or present continuous of the verbs.

1 'What _____ you usually _____ on Saturday nights?' (do) 'I _____ to the cinema.' (go)
2 'How _____ you _____ at the moment?' (feel)
3 Sophie _____n't _____ French, she _____ Spanish. (learn)
4 'What _____ you _____ about?' (care) 'I _____n't _____ about anything.' (care)
5 'How often _____ you _____ to parties?' (go) 'It depends. I _____ to two parties next weekend!' (go)
6 Sophie _____ boots because it's cold. (wear)
7 Rob _____ forward to the holidays. (look) But the exams are first and he always _____ nervous about them. (get)
8 'Why _____n't Rob _____ a girlfriend?' (have) 'Because he _____n't _____ for one at the moment.' (look)

3 Complete with the past simple of these verbs.

cry go hear like make
miss spend want try

1 The holiday _____ wrong from the start.
2 Joni _____n't _____ to stay in Newquay.
3 Joni and Sara both _____ new friends.
4 Joni _____n't _____ Sara's new friends.
5 Joni and Sara _____n't _____ any time together.
6 Joni _____ her family.
7 Joni nearly _____ when she _____ her mother.
8 Joni _____ to sound cheerful on the phone.

4 Write sentences using the past simple or past continuous.

Bethany (surf) with Alana because they (get) on well together.

Bethany was surfing with Alana because they got on well together.

1 The girls (wait) for a big wave when the shark (attack).
2 Bethany (think) about the surf when she (see) the shark.
3 Bethany (not scream) or (feel) pain at the time.
4 What question (she/ask) everyone while she (recover) in hospital?
5 She (feel) very happy when she (surf) again for the first time.

5 Complete with the gerund of these verbs.

borrow go have laugh listen make watch

1 Sometimes when a film is really bad, it's funny and you can't help _____.
2 Walt Disney was famous for _____ animated films.
3 I'm fed up with _____ to people talking in the cinema.
4 When I feel like _____ to the cinema, there's nothing on I want to see!
5 How about _____ a DVD and _____ it at home?
6 She dreams of _____ her own cinema at home.

6 Complete with the infinitive of these verbs.

become dance go help practise sing

1 Star School teaches contestants _____ and dance.
2 The director expects them _____ to all their classes.
3 The school helps them _____ better singers.
4 Jess wants the contestants _____ their songs hard.
5 She also expects the contestants _____ each other.
6 Adam can teach them _____ in lots of different styles.

7 Gerund or infinitive: match the beginnings with the endings.

1 Sophie's parents want her
2 But Sophie feels like
3 She promises
4 Her parents want to avoid
5 So they allow her
6 She's dreaming of

a to phone her parents every night.
b having an argument with her.
c to go on holiday with them.
d having lots of parties when her parents are away.
e to do what she wants.
f staying at home and being with her friends.

8 Complete with the present simple active or passive of the verbs.

Books of the past, present and future

You want to buy a book? Simple! Or is it? In the past you only bought books in bookshops. But today many books __1__ (sell) in supermarkets and other shops. Lots of people __2__ (buy) books on the Internet and the books __3__ (send) to them by post. In fact many people don't read paper books any more. Lots of books __4__ (record) and people __5__ (listen) to them on MP3 players. And there are e-books which __6__ (download) onto computers and __7__ (read) or __8__ (listen) to by people on the bus or train.

VOCABULARY

9 Complete with ten of these words.

avoid bench calm captain denim documentary handkerchief library politics scream trip *n* upset warning

1 Blue jeans are made of _____.
2 If you are _____, you feel worried and unhappy.
3 'Be careful!' is a _____.
4 People _____ when they are hurt.
5 When water is _____, it doesn't move very much.
6 You use a _____ to blow your nose.
7 A _____ is a film/TV programme about real events.
8 You _____ something by staying away from it.
9 You can borrow books from a _____.
10 A _____ is a long seat, usually made of wood.

10 Match these words with their definitions.

ambition enthusiastic genius illegal obey paperback recover terrified

1 against the law
2 very very frightened
3 extremely intelligent person
4 get better after an accident or illness
5 do what someone tells you to do
6 someone who trains people
7 book which hasn't got a hard cover
8 very interested, keen or excited

11 Match the verbs in list A with the words and phrases in list B.

	A	B
1	fail	in love
2	fall	the truth
3	go	a website
4	obey	examinations
5	perform	rules
6	tell	a song
7	visit	boots
8	wear	wrong

12 Find the odd word.

1 awful brilliant disappointing terrible
2 bored excited interested keen
3 hopeful nervous scared terrified
4 attractive beautiful good-looking intelligent
5 ballet ballroom salsa routine
6 break make produce grow

LEARNER INDEPENDENCE
SELF ASSESSMENT

Look back at Lessons 1–3 in Units 1 and 2.

How good are you at …?	✓ Fine	? Not sure
1 Talking about states and regular activities Workbook p2 exercises 1 and 3	☐	☐
2 Talking about what's happening now Workbook p2 exercise 2	☐	☐
3 Talking about future arrangements Workbook p3 exercise 5	☐	☐
4 Describing past events Workbook pp6–7 exercises 1–3	☐	☐
5 Describing what happened and what was happening Workbook pp8–9 exercises 1–3	☐	☐
6 Talking about likes and dislikes Workbook p15 exercise 5	☐	☐
7 Agreeing and disagreeing Workbook p14 exercise 4	☐	☐
8 Talking about skills, abilities and ambitions Workbook p16 exercises 1–4	☐	☐
9 Describing a system Workbook pp18–19 exercises 3–5	☐	☐

Not sure? Have a look at Language File pages 112–114 and do the Workbook exercise(s) again.

Now write an example for 1–8

1 She goes to parties every Friday night.

PREVIEW

COMMUNICATIVE AIMS
LEARNING HOW TO ...

1 Make logical deductions and discuss possibility
2 Express obligation and prohibition
3 Give advice
4 Describe what you can see and hear
5 Make predictions, promises and offers
6 Talk about plans and intentions
7 Talk about future possibility

TOPICS AND VOCABULARY

Space
The solar system
Rules and regulations
School life
Teenage problems
Phrasal verbs with *down*
Sounds
Superstitions
Phrasal verbs with *out*
Memory

1 Match five of the communicative aims (1–7) with the pictures (A–E).

2 Put the words into categories.

Space		Sounds

Rules and regulations

astronomer arrested
illegal forbidden
cheer police star
scream planet
universe shout world
laugh allowed

moon clap law whistle

Are you going to stay in bed all day?

You mustn't use a mobile while you are driving.

She saw furniture moving and heard voices talking.

D

We can't be the only planet in the universe where there is life.

E

You'd better tell a teacher or your parents.

4 Work with three other students. Look at the two lists below and think about things that you did or that happened to you in the last week. Choose one from each list to talk about.

Stories of my week

★ Something that made me happy

★ Something that made me angry

★ Something that made me change my opinion

★ Something that embarrassed me

★ Something that made me feel good

★ A surprise (what was it?)

★ An argument (what about?)

★ A discussion (what about?)

★ A problem (how did you solve it?)

★ A success (what was it?)

Now take turns to tell each other two stories about your week

What interesting or surprising things did you find out? Tell another group.

3 🔘 1.31 Listen to extracts 1–3 from Units 3 and 4. Match them with A–C below.

A Statements about energy
B An extract from a short story
C A discussion about laws

Believe it or not!

The sentence 'The quick brown fox jumps over the lazy dog' is a pangram – it uses every letter of the alphabet.

35

1 There could be tens of billions of planets

Making logical deductions and discussing possibility
must and *can't*
could, may and *might*

1 OPENER

Put these parts of the universe in order of size, from the biggest to the smallest.

> galaxy   planet   solar system   star

2 READING

🔘 1.32 Read *We are not alone*. What is the most surprising fact in the article?

3 AFTER READING

True, false, or no information? Correct the false sentences.

1 There may be lots of other planets like Earth in the universe.
2 Up to a quarter of the stars in the universe have Earth-like planets.
3 Many of these Earth-like planets may be at the right temperature for life.
4 Some of these Earth-like planets are in our solar system.
5 It's possible to see planets outside our solar system with a telescope.
6 Gliese 581 g is twice as big as Earth.
7 Gliese 581 g might have air like Earth.
8 Gliese 581 g is 20 years away from Earth.

Your response What do you think life is like on another planet in the universe? Would you like to visit a planet where there is life?

4 SPEAKING

Look at *The Solar System* and discuss the answers to these questions.

Which planet …
1 is nearer to Earth: Mercury or Mars?
2 is nearly twice as far from the Sun as Jupiter: Saturn or Neptune?
3 is closer to Earth: Mars or Venus?
4 is almost twice as far from the Sun as Saturn: Uranus or Neptune?
5 is nearly twice as far from the Sun as Mercury: Earth or Venus?

> It can't/must be … because …

> **Extension** Write four statements about distances in the solar system. Ask another student to check whether the statements are true or false.

We are not alone
One in four stars may have Earth-like planets in orbit around them

The universe is full of planets which can support life, according to a new report. After studying stars similar to the Sun, astronomers found that almost one in four of the stars might have small, rocky planets just like Earth. Many of these planets may be in regions which are neither too hot, nor too cold, for liquid water and life. We know that there are no other planets where there is life in our solar system. But there could be tens of billions of planets like Earth in our galaxy – and trillions of such planets in the whole universe.

Astronomers now claim they have discovered the most Earth-like planet ever found. It's a rocky world three to four times the size of Earth. They think it might have an atmosphere and gravity like ours, and could have water on its surface. The planet, named Gliese 581 g, is 20 light years (or nearly 200 trillion kilometres) away from us. In other words, light from the planet's star takes 20 years to reach Earth.

We can't be the only planet in the universe where there is life. Gliese 581 g is a possibility and scientists are sure there must be others. So we are not alone.

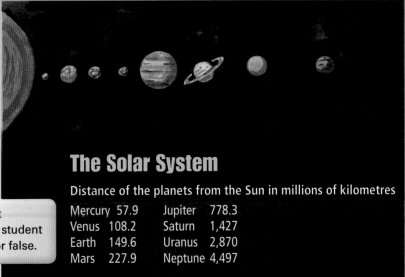

The Solar System

Distance of the planets from the Sun in millions of kilometres

Mercury	57.9	Jupiter	778.3
Venus	108.2	Saturn	1,427
Earth	149.6	Uranus	2,870
Mars	227.9	Neptune	4,497

5 VOCABULARY

Match the definitions with six of these words.

> **Word Bank** Space
>
> atmosphere galaxy gravity orbit planet solar system star universe

1 the Sun and the planets which go around it
2 the power that makes something fall to the ground
3 the mixture of gases around a planet
4 space and everything that exists in it
5 extremely large group of stars and planets
6 movement of a planet around a star

6 SPEAKING

Look at photos 1–6 and discuss what they show. Choose from these words.

> a biscuit a cake a camera clouds a gun a mirror the Moon
> a pen a pencil a plane a robot a rocket the sea a star
> snow a space helmet a telescope a torch a TV a UFO

> It could/may/might be …

> It must/can't be … because …

7 PRONUNCIATION

Cross out the silent letters in these words.

> biscuit could light might
> scientist white whole

🔘 1.33 Now listen and check.

8 LISTENING

🔘 1.34 Listen to the definitions and identify the items.

It could/may/might/must/can't be …

9 WRITING

Write definitions of five other things. Give your definitions to two other students and ask them to guess the words.

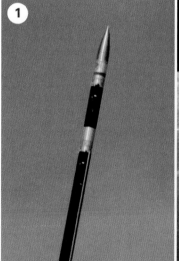
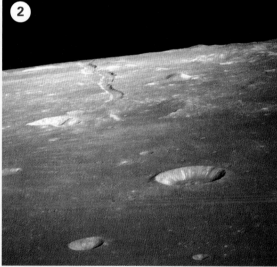

LANGUAGE WORKOUT

Complete.

must* and *can't
We _____ be the only planet where there is life.
Scientists are sure there _____ be others.

We use _____ to show that we are sure that something is true.
We use _____ to show that we are sure that something is not true.

could, may* and *might
We use *could*, *may* and *might* to show we think something is possibly true.

▶**Answers and Practice**
Language File page 114

2 When can you drive a car?

Expressing obligation and prohibition
must and *mustn't/can't*
have/has to and *don't/doesn't have to*
Reflexive pronouns

1 OPENER

What are the people in the photos doing? Do you think what they're doing is wrong? Are you allowed to do these things in your country?

2 SPEAKING

Look at the chart. Discuss when you can you do these things in your country – how old do you have to be? Complete the first column of the chart.

> You can drive a car when you're ...

> You can't drive a car until you're ...

> You have to be ... to drive a car.

When can you ...	Age in my country	Age in the UK
drive a car?		
get married?		
join the army?		
vote in an election?		
live by yourself?		
buy a pet?		
leave school?		
buy a lottery ticket?		
fly a plane?		
get a part-time job?		

Do you agree with these laws?

3 LISTENING

🔘 1.35 Listen to two British people talking about the laws and complete the chart for the UK.

> **Extension** What are the differences between your country and the UK?

4 SPEAKING

Discuss five other laws in your country, for example:

When can you get a full-time job?
How old do you have to be to ride a motorbike?
Do you have to wear a seat belt in a car?
Are people allowed to smoke in restaurants?
Must you buy a TV licence if you have a TV?

5 READING

1.36 Read *Partners in Crime*. Which phrase describes the photo?

PARTNERS IN CRIME

Two British men plan to spend their summer holiday crossing the USA. But they have to avoid the police because they aim to break as many American laws as possible.

Americans don't have to worry, because Richard Smith and Luke Bateman only want to break silly laws. Smith, who came up with the idea, said 'There are thousands of stupid laws in the United States, but we are limiting ourselves to about forty-five.' Smith enjoys himself more on holiday when he has a purpose. He doesn't want to spend all his time sitting by a pool.

The pair intend to start their law-breaking holiday in Los Angeles – riding a bike underwater in a swimming pool. They also want to go whale-hunting in Salt Lake City, Utah (1,500 km from the ocean), and cross the road on their hands in Hartford, Connecticut.

The men had to plan their 28,000 km journey across the continent carefully. It will take about two months – as long as they don't get themselves arrested on the way!

Other laws that Smith and Bateman hope to break include:

▼ You mustn't fall asleep in a cheese factory in South Dakota – you must stay awake.
▼ You aren't allowed to play golf in the streets of Albany, New York.
▼ You can't take a lion to the cinema in Baltimore.
▼ It's illegal to go fishing in your pyjamas in Chicago.
▼ It's forbidden to sleep on top of a refrigerator in Pennsylvania.
▼ You mustn't drive round the town square in Oxford, Mississippi more than 100 times.

6 AFTER READING

Match the questions with the answers. There are two wrong answers.

1 Why do Smith and Bateman have to avoid the police?
2 How many laws do they hope to break?
3 Does Smith enjoy sitting by a pool?
4 What's the strange law in Los Angeles?
5 What mustn't you do in Salt Lake City?
6 What can't you do in Hartford, Connecticut?

a Cross the road on your hands.
b About two months.
c They don't want to get themselves arrested.
d Crossing the USA.
e Go whale-hunting.
f About 45.
g You mustn't ride a bike in a swimming pool.
h Not really.

Your response What do you think of the men's holiday plans? Do you know of any 'silly' laws in your country?

7 PRONUNCIATION

Write the words in the correct column.

> allowed arrest asleep avoid factory himself include intend journey limit ocean partner purpose ticket

■■	■■
factory	*allowed*

1.37 Now listen and check. Repeat the words.

8 WRITING

Write ten more laws for your country, including two 'silly' laws.

You must/have to …
You mustn't/can't …
You can …
You don't have to …

You have to wear a helmet when you're cycling.
You mustn't eat eggs on Mondays.

Now compare your laws with other students. Can you identify the 'silly' laws?

LANGUAGE WORKOUT

Complete.

must* and *mustn't/can't
You _____ stay awake in a cheese factory.
You _____ fall asleep.
You _____ take a lion to the cinema.

have to* and *don't/doesn't have to
They _____ _____ avoid the police.
Americans _____ _____ _____ worry.

You must/You _____ to = It's obligatory.
You mustn't/You _____ = It's not allowed.
You can = It's allowed.
You don't _____ to = It's not necessary.

The past tense of both *must* and *have to* is *had to*.
The men _____ _____ plan their journey carefully.

Reflexive pronouns

myself	ourselves
yourself	yourselves
himself/herself/itself	themselves

▶**Answers and Practice**
Language File page 115

3 You should calm down!

Giving advice
should/ought to and *shouldn't*
had better (not)
Adjective + infinitive

www.teenageproblemssolved.com

TEEN PROBLEM PAGE

PROBLEMS

It's about my best friend. Her mood changes so quickly. One minute she's happy and cheerful, and the next she's really sad and depressed. It's hard for her to concentrate for long – she often lies down on her bed and falls asleep. I don't want to panic, but I'm really worried about her. What should I do?   **Lara 15**

I get good marks at school, so my friends all want to copy my homework. But I spend a lot of time working while they're having fun. It's not fair and I'm getting fed up with it. But how do I tell them they can't copy my work? I don't want to lose my friends – help!   **Sam 16**

Two older boys at my school are bullying me. Every time I see them they say something rude. They tell other people lies about me and they send me horrible text messages – the last one said: 'Everyone hates you'. I don't want to go to school because I can't take it any more. What should I do?   **Joe 15**

I know lots of people would like to have my 'problem', but I'm so upset and miserable. I'm really thin and I can't put on weight. It doesn't matter how much I eat, I still stay the same. I'm too embarrassed to talk to my friends about it – they'll just think it's funny.   **Abbie 16**

ADVICE

A You'd better tell a teacher or your parents about the text messages at once – cyber bullying is very serious. But try not to show the bullies that you are upset or angry – I know it's difficult, but you should try to ignore them.

B Your friends ought to know that they shouldn't copy your work. It's cheating and they'd better not do it any more. The next time they ask, say 'No' nicely but firmly. Explain that they have to do the work themselves or they won't learn anything. If they don't understand, they aren't real friends.

C Take it easy and don't worry so much! It's silly to get stressed about something you can't change. Of course, it's sensible to make sure that you eat a balanced diet. But for some people it's more or less impossible to put on weight.

D I think you should calm down! It's quite normal for teenagers' moods to change rapidly. It doesn't always mean that something is wrong. It's helpful to talk about things, so why don't you sit down with her and have a chat? If she doesn't want to talk, perhaps you ought to have a word with her parents.

1 OPENER

Which of these words do you expect to find in the messages on the *Teen Problem Page*?

bullying cheating comedy concentrate diet
embarrassed factory marks mood panic shark

2 READING

🔘 1.38 Read the messages and match the problems with the advice. Then listen and check.

3 AFTER READING AND LISTENING

Answer the questions.

Who ...
1 wants to stop going to school?
2 should discuss things with her friend?
3 ought to say 'no' to his friends?
4 should try to ignore the bullies?
5 had better talk to their teacher or parents?
6 shouldn't worry?
7 spends a lot of time doing homework?
8 thinks her friends will laugh at her?

Your response Which do you think is the most serious problem? Do you agree with all the advice? If not, what advice would you give?

4 PRONUNCIATION

🔘 1.39 Listen and repeat.

/æ/ sad	/e/ said
and	end
bad	bed
had	head
sand	send
sat	set

Now listen and write the words you hear.

5 SPEAKING

Tell another student your opinions. Use adjectives from the Word Bank and these phrases.

> keep a secret   feel nervous about exams
> tell lies   listen to the teacher   learn English
> concentrate in a noisy place   talk to friends
> break a promise   talk to my parents
> make a revision timetable   laugh at people
> wear uncomfortable shoes

A I think it's difficult to keep a secret.
B So do I. OR Do you? I think it's easy.

Which things do you both feel the same about?

Word Bank Adjective + infinitive

We can use *to* + infinitive after these adjectives.

difficult   easy   good   hard   helpful
important   (im)possible   normal
rude   sensible   silly   wrong

▶ Language File page 115

6 VOCABULARY

Complete the sentences with verbs from the Word Bank. Which of the phrasal verbs can you find in the *Teen Problem Page* messages?

Word Bank Phrasal verbs with *down*

calm down   lie down   sit down   slow down
turn down   write down

1 You're driving too fast – please _____!
2 If you don't feel well, you'd better go and _____.
3 The music is very loud – you ought to _____ it _____.
4 I know you're upset and angry, but you should try to _____.
5 Please would you _____ your mobile number?
6 Come in and _____. Would you like a cup of coffee?

Extension Can you think of some more phrasal verbs with *down*?

7 SPEAKING

What should you do in these situations? Tell each other what you think.

1 A friend of yours steals a DVD from the supermarket.
2 A friend of yours says 'Do you like my new jacket?' You think it's awful.
3 You find a 50-euro note in the street. There's no one else around.
4 Your aunt gives you a sweatshirt for your birthday. You don't like the colour.
5 Your friend Maria doesn't know that her boyfriend is going out with another girl.

8 WRITING

Write a note describing a problem and ask for advice.

Now exchange notes with another student. Write a reply giving your partner some helpful advice.

LANGUAGE WORKOUT

Complete.

should/ought to* and *shouldn't
You _____ try to ignore them.
They _____ copy your work.
What _____ I do?

We can use *ought to* instead of *should*.
You _____ _____ have a word with her parents.

had better (not)
You'd _____ tell a teacher or your parents.
They'd _____ _____ do it any more.

We can use *had better* when something is important **now**.

▶**Answers and Practice**
Language File page 115

4 Integrated Skills

Discussing facts and opinions

1 OPENER

Do the *World Facts Quiz*: choose A, B or C.

WORLD FACTS QUIZ

1 What is the population of the world today?
A 3 billion   **B** 5 billion   **C** 7 billion

2 What will be the population of the world in 2050?
A 5 billion   **B** 7 billion   **C** 9 billion

3 How many children in the world live in poverty?
A 100 million   **B** 500 million   **C** A billion

4 How many 5 to 14-year-olds in the developing world work for a living?
A 50 million   **B** 100 million   **C** 150 million

5 How many children get no primary education?
A 50 million   **B** 75 million   **C** 100 million

6 What percentage of all illness in the world is caused by dirty drinking water?
A 20%   **B** 40%   **C** 80%

🔘 1.40   Now listen and check. Which fact is most surprising? Which is most shocking?

READING

2 🔘 1.41   Read *Global Issues*. For each of the four topics, decide which statement is a fact and which is an opinion.

Global Issues

Income

'At least 80% of the people in the world live on less than $10 a day. However, in developing countries the figure is much higher – 95% live on less than $10 a day.'

'I agree that it's an imperfect world – the problem is that the poor get poorer and the rich get richer. I think people from rich countries ought to give more of their income in aid.'

Water

'We must all try to use less water, especially people living in the USA, because they use an incredible amount of water.'

'However, at least a billion people in the developing world can't get enough water and over two and a half billion don't have proper toilets.'

Children

'In my opinion, the Chinese policy of one family, one child has been very successful. Other countries should think about doing the same – I believe in population control.'

'In fact, 24,000 children a day die because of poverty, many of them in poor villages in remote parts of the world. And eight million children under the age of five die every year from diseases which we can treat.'

Energy

'A quarter of the world's population live without electricity, including over 500 million people in Africa alone.'

'However, there's lots of sun in Africa and it's free, so people ought to use its energy. The developing world should use more solar power.'

3 Are you surprised by any of the facts in the text? Why? Do you agree with any of the opinions? Why?

4 Compare the language in the facts and opinions. In which do you find:

Pronouns like *I* and *we*?   Verbs like *should* and *ought to*?
Statistics?   Words like *agree*, *believe* and *think*?

5 **Linking words**: *however* and *and*

Find examples of *however* in *Global Issues*. Then complete this text with *however* and *and*.

It is true that more aid is now given to the poorer countries ___1___ more is promised in the future. ___2___, what is needed is both more aid ___3___ fair trade. Developing countries should get a fair price for their exports. ___4___, it's not just about money and prices. It's also important for people in poor countries to develop new skills. As the Chinese proverb says: 'Give a man a fish ___5___ he will eat for a day. ___6___, if you teach a man to fish, he will eat for the rest of his life.'

6 **LISTENING**

🔘 1.42 Listen and complete the text.

YOU CAN MAKE A DIFFERENCE!

How can *you* make a difference to the world? You can SAVE ENERGY!

1 Switch off the lights when you leave a _____.
2 When you make hot drinks, just boil the water you need. In a _____ you can save enough energy to light your house for a _____.
3 Run the washing machine at 40°C, not 60°C, and use a _____ less energy.
4 Turn down the heating in your house by 1°C – it will cost _____ less!
5 Turn your TV, radio or DVD player off at the wall. When you leave them on standby, it uses 10 to _____ % more electricity.
6 Walk, cycle or, if you must, take the _____ to school. Don't let your parents drive you – be impolite and say 'no'!
7 Buy local food, not fruit or vegetables from the other side of the _____.
8 Think before you fly. A New York–Paris return flight gives out about _____ tonnes of CO_2 (a greenhouse gas) per passenger.

7 **SPEAKING**

Make questions from the statements 1–8 in exercise 6 and interview two other students about how they save energy.

> Do you switch off the lights when you ...?

8 **GUIDED WRITING**

Write a paragraph about how people can save energy. Use the phrases in the box and the text in exercise 6 to help you.

> **Expressing opinions**
> We should/ought to/must ...   In my opinion, ...
> I believe in ...   I agree/disagree (that) ...
> I think (that) ...

LEARNER INDEPENDENCE

9 Learning contracts: These are important classroom rights.

1 The student's right to learn
2 The teacher's right to teach
3 Everybody's right to safety, dignity and respect

It is a good idea for the class and teacher to discuss these rights and the responsibilities which go with them. Together you can make an agreed list of rules.

Students
We should listen to each other and respect each other's views.
We must be punctual.

Teacher
I should discuss each week's learning plan with you.
I must mark your homework within three days.

10 Word creation: Add the prefixes *il-*, *im-* or *in-* to make the opposites of these adjectives, and complete the sentences.

> correct   credible   legal   logical
> perfect   polite   possible   visible

1 It's against the law. It's _____.
2 I can't believe it. It's _____.
3 We can't see black holes. They're _____.
4 I can't do it at all. It's _____.
5 It's not right, it's wrong. It's _____.
6 It doesn't agree with the facts. It's _____.
7 When you are rude you are _____.
8 It's not how it should be. It's _____.

11 🔘 1.43 **Phrasebook**: Find these useful expressions in Unit 3. Then listen and repeat.

> In other words ...
> You aren't allowed to ...
> What should I do?
> It's not fair.
> I'm getting fed up with it.
> I can't take it any more.
> Take it easy.

Which expression(s) ...?
1 means 'Relax.'
2 is a request for advice.
3 mean 'I've had enough.'
4 means 'It's forbidden.'

LANGUAGE LINKS

Here are five headings in different languages for sections of menus. Group together the headings which mean the same.

English
Starters   Fish   Meat   Vegetables   Desserts

French
Desserts   Hors d'œuvres   Légumes   Poissons   Viandes

German
Fishgerichte   Fleischgerichte   Gemüse   Nachspeisen   Vorspeisen

Italian
Antipasti   Carne   Contorno   Dolci   Pesce

Spanish
Carnes   Entremeses   Pescados   Postres   Verduras

Now match the food words in the box with the headings for each language. For example:

English

Starters	Fish	Meat	Vegetables	Desserts
soup	trout	ham	potatoes	ice cream

Eis   ice cream   gelato   glace   helado
ham   jambon   jamón   prosciutto   Schinken
Forelle   trota   trout   trucha   truite
minestra   sopa   soup   soupe   Suppe
Kartoffeln   patatas   patate   pommes de terre   potatoes

Every time you look at a menu with English translations, learn some more English words for food!

SKETCH *Sign language*

🔊 1.44   Read and listen.

OFFICER   Excuse me, sir. What are you doing?
MAN   I'm taking photographs.
OFFICER   Yes, I know. But you can't do that.
MAN   Yes, I can. I'm very good at taking photos.
OFFICER   No, sir, I mean you aren't *allowed* to do that.
MAN   It's not against the law to take pictures.
OFFICER   Not usually, sir, but you can't take pictures *here*.
MAN   Why not?
OFFICER   Look at the sign – it says: Police No Entry.
MAN   Oh, that's OK. I'm not a police officer.
OFFICER   Exactly. That's why you shouldn't be here.
MAN   No, that's why *you* shouldn't be here.
OFFICER   I beg your pardon?
MAN   You're a police officer, so you shouldn't be here.
OFFICER   Are you trying to be funny?
MAN   Certainly not! The sign says that police mustn't come in here.
OFFICER   No, it doesn't!
MAN   You don't have to shout.
OFFICER   Sir, that is a *police* sign. It says *no one* can come in here.
MAN   No one?
OFFICER   That's right.
MAN   Then you're breaking the law. You'd better leave before I take a photo of you!

Now act out the sketch in pairs.

PUZZLE

Look at the chart on the right. The five people all have different jobs:

artist   nurse   politician   reporter   scientist

They all have different pets:

cat   dog   goldfish   rabbit   snake

They all like different activities:

dancing   riding   skiing   surfing   swimming

Work in pairs. Discuss the clues and complete the chart.

> He must be a reporter.
> He can't have a snake.
> She can't like swimming.

Name	Job	Pet	Activity
Alice			
Ben			
Claudia			
Dave			
Elena			

Clues
Elena likes skiing.
Ben works in a hospital.
Claudia doesn't like horses or water sports.
The woman with a snake likes riding.
One of the men is a reporter.
The scientist has a rabbit and likes dancing.
Alice isn't a politician.
The nurse has a dog and likes swimming.
Dave doesn't have a goldfish.

REVISION

LESSON 1 What are these things? Write sentences with *must/can't* using the words in brackets.

1 It's round and red. (orange/tomato).
2 It has 1,250 pages. (dictionary/newspaper)
3 It's a large animal. (elephant/mouse)
4 It has two wheels. (car/motorbike)
5 It can fly. (helicopter/train)

1 It must be a tomato.
It can't be an orange.

LESSON 2 Look at the six laws at the end of the text in exercise 5 on page 39. Rewrite all of them using *mustn't, can't* and *have to*. For example, in the first law, replace *mustn't* with *can't*.

You can't fall asleep in a cheese factory in South Dakota.

LESSON 3 Look at the *Teen Problem Page* advice on page 40. Rewrite some of the advice using *should(n't)* and *ought to*.

A You shouldn't show that you are upset or angry. You ought to try to ignore them.

EXTENSION

LESSON 1 Look at exercise 6 on page 37 and write two sentences about each photo.

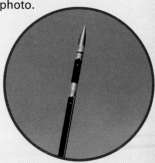

It could/may/might be …
because …
It must/can't be …
because …

Photo 1
It could be a pen because it's long and thin.
It can't be a pencil because it's all made of metal.

LESSON 2 Write sentences about things you must and mustn't/can't do:

on a plane   in a church   in a museum   in a shop
You can't carry a knife on a plane.

LESSON 3 Read this message from *Teen Problem Page* and write some helpful advice.

I'm at a new school because we've moved to another town. I had lots of friends at my old school but now I feel very lonely. What can I do to make new friends?

I think you should …

YOUR CHOICE!

CONSTRUCTION *must, mustn't* or *don't have to?*

Complete with *must, mustn't* or *don't have (to)*.

Travelling in other countries is exciting, but if you really want to enjoy your trip, you __1__ make some plans in advance. To enter most countries, you __2__ have a passport. Maybe you __3__ to get a visa, but you __4__ check before you leave. And you __5__ take enough money. You __6__ to spend a lot, but you __7__ find yourself without enough money for food and a place to stay. You __8__ to organise everything in advance, but you should book somewhere to stay on the first night. And you __9__ take the right clothes for the climate. But remember, if you're flying, you __10__ take more luggage than the airline allows.

ACTION Game: *What is it?*

● Work in a small group.
● Take turns to choose an imaginary object. Don't say what it is! Pick up your object and use it. You can mime and make sounds, but don't say anything.
● The rest of the group try to guess what your object is.

A It could be a box.
B It can't be a computer.
C It must be a TV!

REFLECTION Modal auxiliary verbs: *must* and *can*

Match the examples a–e with language functions 1–5.

1 *must* is used to express obligation.
2 *can* is used to express permission.
3 *can* and *can't* are used to talk about ability.
4 *must* and *can't* are used to make deductions.
5 *mustn't* and *can't* are used to express prohibition.

a He can swim but he can't dive.
b You must listen to me.
c You must be joking – it can't be true!
d We can't talk during the exam.
e You can borrow my bike.

INTERACTION Your ideal holiday

● Work in a small group.
● Plan your ideal fortnight's holiday. Discuss where you should go, how to get there, where to stay, and what you want to do on your holiday. Think about when you should go and what you should take with you.

A I think we should go to the UK so we can practise speaking English.
B But the weather isn't great there – I think we ought to go to Australia!

Good reads

1 READING

🔵 1.45 The teenagers below are all looking for a book to read. Look at the book covers A–D and read the texts. Decide which book would be most suitable for each teenager.

Alesha likes books with lots of exciting dramatic action.

Maria enjoys romantic novels and she likes reading classics.

Kazuo prefers non-fiction and he is interested in politics.

Paolo likes detective stories and he is keen on history.

A

Gandhi had an extraordinary power to make people follow him. He showed that non-violence was a great and strong force for change. Gandhi gave his life to help the people of India. He lived in love, peace and truth, and his beliefs still continue to change people's lives.

Gandhi was one of the most influential leaders and civil rights campaigners that the world has ever known. This biography tells the story of Gandhi's life and achievements, from the policy of non-violent action that led India to independence from British control, to his work on reducing poverty, improving women's rights and the building of religious and ethnic unity.

MACMILLAN BIOGRAPHIES

Gandhi
Rachel Bladon

MACMILLAN READERS

audio download available

JAMES BOND

Live and Let Die
Ian Fleming

MACMILLAN READERS

B

'Breathe, Solitaire, breathe!' Bond shouted, as they started to speed through the water once more. They were only about thirty metres from the reef now. Now twenty … ten … Suddenly the breath was knocked from his body. Solitaire and Bond went right up out of the sea before falling back again. The sky lit up with the huge explosion.

Bond finds himself in Jamaica investigating the underworld criminal 'Mr Big'. As usual, Bond gets caught up in many dangerous situations. He also falls in love with Mr Big's girlfriend, the mysterious and beautiful Solitaire.

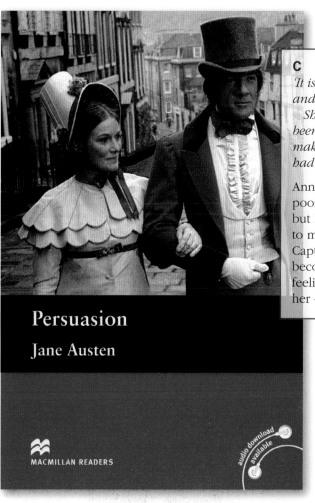

Persuasion
Jane Austen

MACMILLAN READERS

audio download available

C

'It is over! It is over!' Anne said to herself again and again. 'The worst is over!'
She had seen him. They had met. They had been in the same room once more! She tried to make herself feel calm. It was eight years since it had all ended between them.

Anne Elliott falls in love with a handsome but poor young captain, Frederick Wentworth, but her father and friends persuade her not to marry him. Eight years later, Anne meets Captain Wentworth again to find he has become rich and successful. Anne still has feelings for Wentworth, but he is angry with her – and possibly in love with another woman.

2 LISTENING

🔊 1.46 Listen to extracts from three of the books A–D. Which book is each extract from?

3 SPEAKING

Which of the four books would you most like to read? Tell each other why.

4 MINI-PROJECT
Reading Survey

Do the survey with three other students.

READING SURVEY

1 **How many books do you read in a month?**

2 **What kind of books do you like?**

    action/adventure stories
    horror/ghost stories
    science fiction stories
    romantic novels
    detective stories and thrillers
    historical novels
    graphic novels
    non-fiction
    travel books

    Which kind of book is your favourite?

3 **Who is/are your favourite author(s)?**

Tell another group about the results of your survey.

D

'I'm afraid,' said Miss Morstan.
'What should I do, Mr Holmes?'
Holmes jumped up excitedly.
'We shall go tonight to the Lyceum Theatre – the three of us – you and I and Doctor Watson. We'll meet your unknown friend. And we'll try to solve the mystery.'

Sherlock Holmes helps Mary Morstan find out the truth about her father and the man who has been sending her pearls.

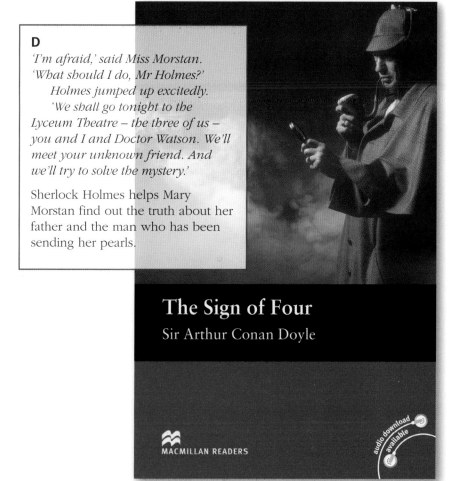

The Sign of Four
Sir Arthur Conan Doyle

MACMILLAN READERS

audio download available

1 She saw furniture moving

Describing what you can see and hear
Verbs of perception + present participle
can/could + verbs of perception

1 OPENER

Look at the newspaper headline and picture.
Which of these words do you expect to find
in the newspaper article?

> bruise code family fish fly fright
> haunted hear investigate move
> psychic strange train video

Knock twice for terror!

From the outside it looked like any other house. But the
people who investigated the strange happenings there
knew differently. Psychic investigators and the police
came to the same conclusion. The house in north London
where Mrs Peggy Hodgson and her teenage children lived
was haunted.

It all began when Peggy's daughter, Janet, heard
someone walking around in her bedroom. Four loud
knocks followed and Janet saw a large chest of drawers
moving across the room on its own. Then a hairbrush flew
through the air, hitting Janet's brother on the head and
giving him a nasty bruise.

Fright soon turned to terror when the teenage girl
began to speak in a strange voice. 'I could hear a voice
coming from Janet, my daughter,' Peggy told the police,
'but it was an old man's voice. And I couldn't see her lips
moving – I'm absolutely sure it wasn't her voice.'

A police officer watched a chair flying through the air.
'I saw the chair rising from the floor, moving sideways and
then floating back to its original position,' she said. 'I was
so scared that I didn't dare move.'

One expert brought in video equipment to record
the events. She saw furniture moving and heard voices
talking. But when she tried to play the video back there
was nothing there. 'I could see things happening,' she told
a newspaper reporter, 'but I couldn't record them.'

A psychic investigator, Maurice Grosse, tried to
communicate with the 'thing'. He used a code of one
knock for 'No' and two knocks for 'Yes.'

'Did you die in this house?'

Two knocks.

'How many years did you live here? Knock once for
each year.'

Fifty-three knocks.

Later that day Peggy called Grosse. 'Come quickly,'
she said. 'I can hear Janet talking in an old man's voice
again.'

Grosse ran into the room.

'My name is Bill Hobbs,' the voice was saying. 'I'm 72
years old and I have come here to see my family. But they
are not here now. I'm going away and won't come back.'

And after this, the haunting ended.

2 READING

🔘 2.01 Read *Knock twice for terror!* and check your
answers to exercise 1.

3 AFTER READING

Choose the best answer.

1 The opinions of people who investigated the Hodgsons'
   house were
   A the same. **B** different. **C** strange.
2 When Janet was in her bedroom, she heard someone
   A knocking. **B** flying. **C** singing.
3 A hairbrush hurt
   A Peggy. **B** Peggy's daughter. **C** Peggy's son.
4 Peggy heard Janet
   A talking to an old man. **B** speaking strangely.
   C telling the police.
5 When the chair rose into the air, the police officer
   A moved. **B** was very frightened.
   C went back to her original position.
6 The expert with video equipment couldn't
   A see things moving. **B** hear people talking.
   C record what happened.
7 'My name is Bill Hobbs,' said
   A the ghost. **B** Peggy. **C** Grosse.
8 The ghost lived in the house for
   A two years. **B** seventy-two years. **C** fifty-three years.

Your response Do you believe in ghosts?
Why/Why not?

4 SPEAKING

Look at the picture and say what you can see.

A I can see a girl flying a kite.
B I can see a man juggling.

5 LISTENING

2.02 Listen to the sounds and say what you can hear. Use the words and phrases in the box to help you. What do you think is happening?

A I can hear people running.
B I can hear a car starting.

> bells ring   car start   car stop   cheer   clap
> door close   door open   drive off   music play   run

Extension Work in pairs and write a paragraph saying what happened.

6 PRONUNCIATION

2.03 Listen and repeat.

/eə/ **hair**	/ɪə/ **hear**
air	ear
chair	cheer
dare	dear
pair	pier
wear	we're

Now listen and write the words you hear.

7 WRITING

Close your eyes. Imagine you are at home. It's Saturday evening and you are with your friends. What can you hear? What can you see?

Now write five sentences beginning *I could hear/see …*

I could hear my friends laughing.

LANGUAGE WORKOUT

Complete.

Verbs of perception + present participle
Janet heard someone walking around in her bedroom.
She saw furniture mov____.
A police officer watched a chair fly____ through the air.

We can also use this construction with *notice, listen to, smell* and *feel.*

can/could + verbs of perception
I can _____ Janet talking.
I could _____ things happening.

We can also use *can/could* before *feel, smell* and *taste.*

▶**Answers and Practice**
Language File page 116

2 I'll keep my fingers crossed!

Making predictions, promises and offers
Talking about plans and intentions
Future review: *will/won't, shall* **and** *going to*

1 OPENER

Here are some UK superstitions. Which do you think are for good luck and which bring bad luck?

Breaking a mirror
Catching a falling leaf in autumn
Crossing your fingers
Opening an umbrella indoors
Throwing a coin into a fountain
Walking under a ladder

Do you have these superstitions in your country?

2 READING

🔘 2.04 Read and answer the questionnaire.

3 AFTER READING

Work out your score and compare it with other students. Do you agree with the description for your score?

Your response Are some superstitions more reasonable than others? How many students in the class are superstitious? Who are more superstitious: boys or girls?

> **Extension** What other superstitions do you have in your country? Make a list of three or four superstitions and compare them with other students.

How superstitious are you?

Are you down to earth, or on another planet? Find out here!

1 A friend says 'Shall I read out your horoscope?' Do you ...
A say yes, listen carefully and follow all the advice?
B say yes, but only believe it if it says something good?
C ask your friend to read out the sports results instead?

2 You know that tomorrow is Friday 13th. What are you going to do?
A Stay in bed all day.
B Go out, but be very careful.
C Take no notice – it makes no difference anyway.

3 You see a painter up a ladder on your way to school. Will you ...
A walk round the ladder to avoid bad luck?
B walk under the ladder to prove it's not unlucky?
C walk round the ladder because it's safer?

4 You accidentally break a mirror. What do you say?
A 'Oh dear, I'll have seven years' bad luck!'
B 'I won't be unlucky, touch wood.'
C 'Never mind – I'll buy another one.'

5 A friend has a summer job interview tomorrow. What do you say?
A 'Don't worry – I'll lend you my lucky charm.'
B 'Good luck – I'll keep my fingers crossed!'
C 'Shall I role play the interview with you?'

6 It's evening and the sky is red. What do you say?
A 'Oh, that's lucky – the weather is going to be great tomorrow!'
B 'I hope it won't rain tomorrow.'
C 'I'm going to check the weather forecast.'

Now turn to page 121 to find out your score.

4 LISTENING

🔘 2.05 Read and listen to the beginning of a short story.

A doctor is driving home along a quiet country road. It's late at night and it's raining hard. Suddenly he sees a girl walking along the road. She looks like a student.

What do you think the doctor will do?
Now listen to the rest of the story. Continue to make predictions, and then find out if you predicted correctly.

> **Extension** Do you think this is a true story? Why/Why not?

5 SPEAKING

Make promises in response to statements 1–5.
Use *I'll/I won't* ... with these phrases.

> be away for long   phone once a week   drive carefully
> forget anything   look at the map

1 Remember your passport.
2 Have a safe journey.
3 Don't get lost!
4 Please keep in touch.
5 Come back soon.

Now make offers in response to statements 6–10. Use *I'll* ... and *Shall I ...?* with these phrases.

> close the window   turn down the heating
> carry it for you   lend you one   turn off the lights

6 I want to go to sleep.
7 I don't have a pen.
8 It's quite cold in here.
9 I'm feeling rather hot.
10 My suitcase is heavy.

6 PRONUNCIATION

🔘 2.06 Listen and repeat.

/æ/ bad	/ʌ/ luck
cat	cut
cap	cup
match	much
ran	run
sang	sung

Now listen and write the words you hear.

7 VOCABULARY

Match the phrasal verbs with their meanings. Which of the verbs can you find in this lesson?

> **Word Bank** Phrasal verbs with *out*
>
> find out   go out   look out   read out
> take out   try out

1 be careful
2 read aloud
3 discover
4 opposite of *stay in*
5 experiment with
6 remove

> **Extension** Complete the sentences with verbs from the Word Bank.
>
> 1 Are you going to _____ tonight?
> 2 You can _____ more details on our website.
> 3 Please _____ your answers to the questions.
> 4 Let's _____ this new computer game.
> 5 _____! There's a car coming.

8 WRITING

Write a paragraph about next week. Say what you *know* is going to happen because you have decided to do it, or because it is planned. You can also say what you *think* or *hope* will happen.

LANGUAGE WORKOUT

Complete.

will/won't
We use *will/won't* to say what we predict or hope for the future.
I**'ll** have seven years' bad luck.
I hope it _____ rain tomorrow.

We also use *will/won't* for offers, promises and decisions made at the time of speaking.
I _____ lend you my lucky charm.
I _____ keep my fingers crossed!
Never mind – I _____ buy another one.

shall
We can also use *Shall I ...?* to make offers.
Shall I read out your horoscope?

going to
We use *going to* to talk about plans and intentions.
I _____ _____ to stay in bed all day.
Are _____ _____ to go out?

We also use *going to* to predict the future from present evidence.
The weather _____ _____ to be great tomorrow!

▶**Answers and Practice**
Language File page 116

3 If you follow this advice ...

Talking about future possibility
First conditional

1 OPENER

What kind of things do you need to remember? How easy is it to remember them?

What do you do to help you remember things?

When did you last forget something important? Why do you think you forgot?

2 READING

Read *Memory Power* and match these headings with paragraphs 1–5.

Go to bed early
Make connections
Pay attention
Put it in writing
Say it aloud

🔘 2.07 Now listen and check.

3 AFTER READING AND LISTENING

Answer the questions.

According to the article …
1 Why is it a good idea to say things aloud?
2 What kind of things can you write down?
3 In what ways can you personalise new information?
4 Why is it important to listen carefully and read thoughtfully?
5 What will happen if you sleep well?

Your response Which piece of advice do you think is most helpful? Do you already follow any of this advice? Do you have any other tips?

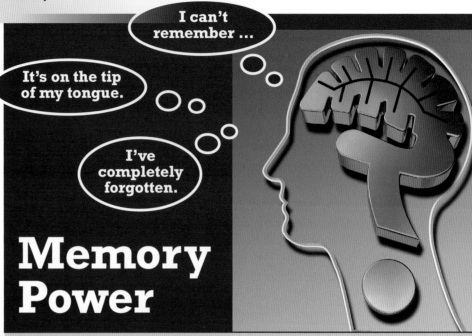

I can't remember …

It's on the tip of my tongue.

I've completely forgotten.

Memory Power

Do you sometimes forget phone numbers or online passwords, miss friends' birthdays, or forget where you put things? You're not the only one – we all have memory problems. But here are some useful tips to increase your memory power – if you follow this advice, your memory will improve!

1 _____ If you repeat things, they'll stay in your memory longer. Repeat phone numbers, directions to places, and the names of people when you first meet them. It's said that if you put something in a 'safe place', you'll forget where you put it. But if you say aloud what you're doing – 'I'm putting my keys in my coat pocket' – it will help you to remember.

2 _____ If you write things down, you won't forget them so easily. Write down things you have to do in your diary or on a calendar, make lists of things you need to buy, and note down words and phrases you want to learn. Then you can organise longer lists in categories to help you remember.

3 _____ You'll find it easier to learn new information if you link it with something you already know. If you want to remember a person's name, think of someone you know with a similar name. And it will be easier to recall a series of things if you make connections between them. For example, you can associate new facts with landmarks on your way to school, and put new words together in a sentence or short story. If you personalise new information, it will be more memorable.

4 _____ Listen carefully and read thoughtfully. You won't remember new things if you don't concentrate. That's why most people find it easier to learn in a quiet place.

5 _____ Research shows that sleep improves consolidation of information in the brain. If you get a good night's sleep, it will help to process new information and fix it in your memory.

4 LISTENING

Murphy's Law says: 'If something can go wrong, it will'. Match the beginnings and endings of these sentences about school.

1 If you are early,
2 If you are late,
3 If you want a book from the library,
4 If you do homework on a computer,
5 If you forget your calculator,
6 If you copy someone else's homework,
7 If you lend friends your notes,
8 If you have to decide between two answers,

a it won't be on the shelves.
b they will lose them.
c you will choose the wrong one.
d it will crash before you save your work.
e the school bus will be late.
f the teacher will find out.
g you will have a maths test.
h the school bus will be on time.

2.08 Now listen and check.

5 SPEAKING

What do you think the people are saying? Complete their sentences.

If we don't hurry, we'll …

If you drop any, you'll …

I'll lend you my new top if you …

You'll find your MP3 player if you …

We won't let you go to the party if you …

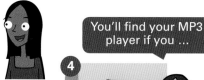

If you don't turn the music down, I'll …

6 PRONUNCIATION

Mark the stress. Which words are stressed on the first syllable?

> calendar concentrate connection improve information memorable memory organise personalise process remember similar

2.09 Now listen and check. Repeat the words.

7 SPEAKING

Use the questionnaire to interview two other students. Note down their answers.

Questionnaire
What will you do if …?

1 What will you do at the weekend if the weather is bad?
2 What will you say if your family asks you to cook dinner tonight?
3 What will you do if you can't sleep tonight?
4 What will you do if you forget your bag when you go home today?
5 What will you do if you find someone's wallet in the street on the way home?
6 What will you do tonight if you don't have any homework?
7 What will you say if a classmate asks to copy your work?
8 What will you reply if a friend invites you to the cinema after school?

8 WRITING

Use your notes from the questionnaire to write sentences comparing the two students.

If the weather is bad at the weekend, Ana will watch TV and Bruno will go to the gym.

Extension Write your answers to the questionnaire.

LANGUAGE WORKOUT

Complete.

First conditional If + present simple, future simple
_____ you **follow** this advice, your memory **will improve**!
If you _____ things down, you _____ forget them so easily.

The *if* clause can follow the main clause.
You _____ remember things if you _____ concentrate.
What _____ you do if you _____ sleep tonight?

We use the first conditional to talk about the possible future.

▶**Answers and Practice**
Language File page 116

4 Integrated Skills
Telling a story

Rebecca
Daphne du Maurier

1 OPENER

Rebecca is a novel by Daphne du Maurier. In the book, Maxim de Winter marries again after the death of his first wife, Rebecca. Maxim never talks about Rebecca, but other people talk about her ...

What problems do you think Maxim's new wife will have when they return to his home?

2 READING

🔘 2.10 Read the first part of the story and answer the questions.

1 Where did Maxim de Winter meet his second wife?
2 Who was Rebecca?
3 What did people say happened to Rebecca?
4 Where did Maxim de Winter live?
5 Why didn't the second Mrs de Winter feel confident?
6 What was Mrs Danvers like?
7 Why didn't Maxim want his wife to go to the cottage?
8 Who often stayed in the cottage?

SPEAKING

3 🔘 2.11 Look at the pictures and tell each other what happened in the second part of the story. Then listen and check.

A shy young girl of 21 was working for an American woman in Monte Carlo when she met Maxim de Winter, a rich and handsome Englishman. People said that Maxim couldn't get over the death of his beautiful wife, Rebecca, who drowned in a boating accident. But Maxim asked the young girl to marry him. After a honeymoon in Italy, Maxim took his new wife back to his beautiful home, Manderley, on the south-west coast of England.

But when she arrived at Manderley, the second Mrs de Winter didn't feel at all confident in her new role. She found herself in charge of a huge house with lots of servants, including the unfriendly housekeeper, Mrs Danvers. She soon realised that Mrs Danvers adored Rebecca. In fact, Rebecca seemed to haunt the house, and her presence was everywhere. But Maxim never talked about her.

One afternoon, Maxim and his wife went for a walk on the beach with their dog. When she followed the dog to an empty cottage, Maxim called her back. He was quite cross, and explained impatiently that the cottage held bad memories. Later, she discovered that Rebecca often stayed there.

The second Mrs de Winter wanted to be the perfect wife at Manderley's annual fancy dress ball.

4 Before you listen to the third part of the story, discuss the possible answers to these questions about it.

1 Why was Maxim so angry about his wife's dress?
2 Why did Mrs Danvers suggest the white dress?
3 What did Mrs de Winter say to Mrs Danvers the next day?
4 What did Mrs Danvers reply?
5 What did a diver find in the sea that night?
6 What did Maxim confess to his wife?
7 Did anyone else know what really happened to Rebecca?
8 Did Maxim ever love Rebecca?

5 LISTENING

🔘 2.12 Listen and check your answers to exercise 4.

6 Read these phrases from the last part of the story. How does it end?

inquest into Rebecca's death … verdict was suicide … Rebecca's diary … a doctor in London … the day she died … the next day … went to London … asked the doctor about Rebecca … very ill … only six months to live … never have a child … later … dinner in a restaurant … Rebecca wanted me to kill her … laughing when she died … wife didn't reply … all over now … looked very worried … suddenly … must drive back to Manderley … something's wrong … early hours of the morning … reached the top of the hill … sky above their heads was black … sky above Manderley was red

🔘 2.13 Now listen to the last part of the story and check.

7 GUIDED WRITING

Write the last part of the story using the phrases in exercise 6.

There was an inquest into Rebecca's death, and the verdict was suicide.

Tell me about your costume.

It's a secret! You won't know it's me – you'll have the surprise of your life.'

Go and change immediately! It doesn't matter what you put on.

8 When you come across a new word, try to guess what it means.

- What could the word mean in the context?
- What part of speech is it?
- Has it got a prefix or suffix?
- Is it like another English word you know?
- Is it like a word in your language?

Look at the text in exercise 2 again. Could you guess the meanings of the new words?

9 Word creation: Complete the two charts with words from Unit 4.

Noun	Adjective
cheer	
fright	
importance	
luck	
memory	
superstition	

Verb	Noun
calculate	
conclude	
differ	
investigate	
paint	
predict	

10 🔘 2.14 **Phrasebook:** Find these useful expressions in Unit 4. Then listen and repeat.

Take no notice.
It makes no difference.
Touch wood.
I'll keep my fingers crossed!
Have a safe journey.
Don't get lost!
Keep in touch.
Come back soon.
You're not the only one.
It's a secret!

Which expression means …?

1 Stay in contact.
2 You aren't alone.
3 It doesn't change anything.
4 Pay no attention.

Inspiration EXTRA!

PROJECT *Mystery report*

1 Work in a group and make a list of mysteries or unusual events which you have heard about. For example, animal or bird migration, levitation (people who can float in the air), sightings of 'ape-men' like the Yeti, or occasions when frogs and fish have fallen out of the sky like rain. Then choose one to write about.

2 Research: Find out information about the mysteries or events using the Internet or a library:

- What happens/happened?
- When and where does/did it happen?
- How do we know about it?
- What explanations are there for it?
- What is your opinion?

3 Work together and write about the mystery. Read your work carefully and correct any mistakes. Draw pictures or find photographs from magazines or online. Show your report to the other groups.

Bird Migration

Every year millions of birds fly huge distances across the world, often returning to the same place year after year. The Arctic tern, for example, flies south from the far north of North America and Europe to Antarctica and back again. In other words, from the North Pole to the South Pole and back. The total distance is around 70,000 kilometres and the birds fly between 330 and 520km a day.

People have tracked the Arctic tern's migration, so we know it happens. But no one knows for sure why the bird migrates or how it finds its way.

There are a number of different explanations. It's possible that the terns use the stars or the position of the sun in the sky. It's also possible that they use changes in temperature and smells to guide them. Some people claim that the birds remember the way.

We think that they find their way by using the position of the stars.

Game   *Where am I?*

- Imagine you're somewhere outside the classroom. You could be in a town, in the country, by water … . Think about these questions and make notes.

Questions
What time of day is it?
What's the weather like? Is it hot, warm, cold, wet?
What can you see around you?
Are there any people or animals? What are they doing?
What sounds can you hear?
What can you smell?
How do you feel – happy, relaxed, …?

- Now describe your experience to other students. Can they guess where you are?

It's the afternoon, it's a beautiful day, and it's quite warm. I can see hundreds of people all around me, and we're all watching animals running. I can hear people cheering and clapping and I can smell the grass. I feel excited!

REVISION

LESSON 1 Write five sentences beginning *I could see/hear someone/something* ... and use these verbs.

cry fall knock laugh run shout

I could hear someone crying.

LESSON 2 Write ten predictions for another student about the next 24 hours.

Greg will help cook dinner this evening.

Tomorrow, give your predictions to the student. How many of your predictions were correct?

LESSON 3 Complete these superstitions from different countries.

1 If you _____ (look) in a broken mirror, things _____ (go) wrong. (Russia)
2 You _____ (be) well all year if you _____ (eat) an apple at Christmas. (USA)
3 If you _____ (leave) your bag on the floor, you _____ (lose) all your money. (Spain)
4 You _____ (be) unlucky if you _____ (point) at the moon. (Taiwan)
5 If there _____ (be) a rabbit on a ship, it _____ (bring) bad luck. (France)

EXTENSION

LESSON 1 Think about your journey to school today and all the sounds you heard. Write a paragraph describing the journey.

While I was waiting at the bus stop, I heard the birds singing.

LESSON 2 Look at the Language Workout on page 51 and then write:

1 Three predictions with will
2 One offer with shall.
3 One promise with will.
4 One future plan with going to.
5 One prediction from present evidence with going to.

Tomorrow will be your lucky day.

LESSON 3 Complete these sentences.

1 If there's nothing good on TV tonight, I …
2 If I can't understand today's homework, I …
3 If I lose my house key, I …
4 If my parents tell me to go to bed early, I …
5 If I'm really lucky and win the lottery, I …

YOUR CHOICE!

CONSTRUCTION Words beginning with *re-*

In this unit find words beginning with *re-* which mean:

1 the opposite of *forget* v
2 say something again v
3 answer v
4 someone who writes news stories n
5 understand something that you didn't know before v

What other words beginning with *re-* do you know? Check in the Word List.

REFLECTION *will/won't, shall* or *going to*?

Complete the rules.

- We use _____ to talk about future plans and intentions.
  I _____ go shopping after school.
- We use _____ or _____ to make offers.
  I _____ get it for you. _____ I phone the doctor?
- We use _____ to say what we hope or predict.
  She _____ get better soon.
- We use _____ for promises.
  I _____ be home before midnight.
- We use _____ to predict the future when we can see that something is likely to happen.
  It _____ to rain – look at those clouds.

ACTION Speed dictation

- Work in teams of three, A, B and C.
- Student A goes to the other side of the classroom and chooses a paragraph from this unit.
- Student B crosses the room and Student A reads out the first sentence of the paragraph. Student B repeats the sentence and then returns.
- Student B says the sentence to Student C, who writes it down. Then Student B goes across to Student A for the next sentence. At the end compare Student C's paragraph with the book.

INTERACTION Celebrity memories

- Work in a small group.
- Imagine that you met a famous person who is dead! Imagine what happened, what you did and what you said.
- Ask and answer questions about the celebrities.
  Who did you meet and where?
  What was he/she wearing?
  What did he/she say?

1 Read and complete. For each number 1–12, choose word or phrase A, B or C.

Mystery in the sky

Many people see strange things in the sky and think they __1__ be UFOs. It's certainly difficult __2__ what happened to a young Australian pilot in 1978.

At 6.19pm on 21 October, 20-year-old Frederick Valentich took off in a Cessna 182 from Melbourne. He __3__ to fly over the sea to King Island, between Australia and the island of Tasmania.

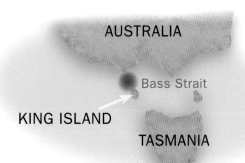

AUSTRALIA

Bass Strait

KING ISLAND

TASMANIA

At 7.06pm, Valentich contacted Steve Robey at Air Traffic Control in Melbourne, because he __4__ see a large aircraft __5__ over him. Robey was very surprised – he knew there __6__ be any other aircraft in the area. But the small Cessna wasn't alone. Valentich watched the UFO flying above __7__. The object was long and very fast with a green light. It __8__ like metal, but it wasn't a plane. Then it disappeared from the sky.

At 7.11pm, when Valentich was still 30 minutes from land, he reported engine problems. 'I'm going __9__ to reach King Island,' he told Robey. Suddenly he shouted 'I __10__ see that strange thing above me again, and it's not an aircraft!' Robey __11__ a strange noise over the radio, and then there was silence.

The Cessna 182 never reached King Island; the plane and pilot completely disappeared. We __12__ probably never know what happened to Frederick Valentich.

1	**A** can	**B** could	**C** mustn't
2	**A** to explain	**B** explain	**C** explained
3	**A** must	**B** have	**C** had
4	**A** can	**B** could	**C** did
5	**A** to fly	**B** flying	**C** flew
6	**A** ought	**B** should	**C** shouldn't
7	**A** him	**B** his	**C** himself
8	**A** saw	**B** watched	**C** looked
9	**A** try	**B** to try	**C** trying
10	**A** can	**B** could	**C** might
11	**A** listened	**B** heard	**C** sounded
12	**A** will	**B** won't	**C** can't

2 Write responses using *must* and *can't*.

It's next to Spain. *Germany or Portugal?*
It can't be Germany — it must be Portugal.

1   He comes from South America. *Brazilian or Italian?*
2   It lives in Antarctica. *A parrot or a penguin?*
3   They're made of glass. *Curtains or windows?*
4   She works in a hospital. *A pilot or a doctor?*
5   It's white and very cold. *Snow or rain?*
6   They're long and yellow. *Cucumbers or bananas?*
7   They perform on stage. *Actors or reporters?*
8   It has wings. *A plane or a helicopter?*

3 Complete the sentences with *must* or *mustn't*.

SCHOOL RULES

1   You _____ shout or make unnecessary noise.
2   You _____ run in the school building.
3   You _____ arrive on time for lessons.
4   You _____ listen to the teacher.
5   You _____ copy other students' work.
6   You _____ use mobile phones in class.

4 Rewrite the sentences replacing the words in *italics* with the correct form of *have to*.

1   *Must we* go to school every day?
2   *You don't need to* work all weekend.
3   *It's necessary for you to* hand in homework on time.
4   *He must* do some revision before the test.
5   *It was necessary for us to* answer 20 questions.
6   *They didn't need to* look up any words.

5 Choose the correct object or reflexive pronoun.

1   I'm teaching me/myself yoga from a book.
2   You have to believe in you/yourself.
3   He gave her/herself a glass of orange juice.
4   Look – we can see us/ourselves on TV!
5   We're going out with them/themselves tonight.
6   Well done! You must be pleased with you/yourselves!
7   It's so noisy I can't hear me/myself think!
8   It's hard to understand him/himself.

6 Complete with *'d better (not)* where possible. Otherwise write *should(n't)*.

1   You _____ always wash your hands before meals.
2   His leg is broken – we _____ call an ambulance.
3   You _____ go out in this awful weather.
4   Everyone _____ eat lots of vegetables.
5   If you want to pass the exam, you _____ do some work!
6   I don't think people _____ break promises.

7 Write sentences using *It's* + adjective + infinitive.

impossible/walk round the world
It's impossible to walk round the world.

1   hard/remember dates
2   good/see you again
3   rude/stare at people
4   important/tell the truth
5   wrong/cheat
6   nice/meet you

8 Complete with the present participle of these verbs.

burn eat play run sing wait

1 I can hear someone _____ the piano.
2 Is there a fire? Can you smell something _____?
3 Did you notice anyone _____ at the bus stop?
4 She felt the rain _____ down her neck.
5 Please don't watch me _____ lunch – I'm embarrassed!
6 I like listening to the birds _____.

9 Complete the phone conversation with *'ll/won't* or *(be) going to*.

JACK   Hi, Tim, what are you doing?
TIM   I __1__ wash my father's car.
JACK   Oh, there's no point – it __2__ rain. Come to the cinema with me instead.
TIM   But I haven't got any money.
JACK   No problem, I __3__ pay for you.
TIM   OK, I __4__ wash the car tomorrow. I'm sure Dad __5__ (not) mind. Just a minute – I __6__ tell him. Dad, I __7__ see a movie with Jack.
FATHER So you __8__ (not) wash my car today.
TIM   I promise I __9__ wash it tomorrow – I __10__ (not) forget. Jack, I __11__ meet you at the cinema in 15 minutes. Er, Dad, could you …?
FATHER I don't believe it – you __12__ ask me to give you a lift to the cinema!

10 Write sentences using the correct form of the verb: present simple or *will*.

1 I (cook) dinner tonight if you (like).
2 If we (not hurry), we (miss) the plane.
3 My sister (be) a doctor if she (pass) her exams.
4 If the team (score) another goal, they (win) the game.
5 We (not get) lost if we (look) at the map.
6 If it (rain) tomorrow, we (not have) a barbecue.
7 You (sleep better) if you (open) the window.
8 If I (not finish) my project, I (be) in trouble!

VOCABULARY

11 Complete with ten of these words.

army bruise clap concentrate communicate
election electricity factory haunted
honeymoon horoscope ladder planet poverty

1 There's going to be an _____ for a new prime minister.
2 The music is very loud – it's hard for me to _____ on my work.
3 I don't believe in ghosts, but they say the house is _____.
4 After the wedding, they had a _____ in Spain.
5 We should turn off the lights to save _____.
6 He wanted to be a soldier, so he joined the _____.
7 Whales can _____ with each other over very large distances.
8 A firefighter climbed up a _____ to the roof of the house.
9 Tell me your star sign and I'll read out your _____.
10 I had a bad _____ on my leg after the football match.

12 Match these words with their definitions.

adore forbidden ignore improve increase v
lie n mood nasty purpose recall

1 not allowed
2 opposite of *nice*
3 become better
4 become larger
5 remember
6 how someone is feeling
7 aim or goal
8 something that isn't true
9 take no notice of
10 love very much

13 Match the verbs in list A with the words and phrases in list B.

	A	B
1	boil	asleep
2	break	lies
3	fall	attention
4	switch off	the law
5	pay	the lights
6	tell	water

LEARNER INDEPENDENCE
SELF ASSESSMENT

Look back at Lessons 1–3 in Units 3 and 4.

How good are you at …?	✓ Fine	? Not sure
1 Making logical deductions and discussing possibility Workbook pp26–27 exercises 1–3	☐	☐
2 Expressing obligation and prohibition Workbook pp28-29 exercises 1–3	☐	☐
3 Giving advice Workbook pp30-31 exercises 1–3	☐	☐
4 Describing what you can see and hear Workbook pp38–39 exercises 1–4	☐	☐
5 Making predictions, promises and offers Workbook p40 exercises 1–3	☐	☐
6 Talking about plans and intentions Workbook p41 exercises 4 and 5	☐	☐
7 Talking about future possibility Workbook p42–43 exercises 1–3	☐	☐

Not sure? Have a look at Language File pages 114–116 and do the Workbook exercise(s) again.

Now write an example for 1–7

1   My alarm clock is ringing – it must be 7.30.

COMMUNICATIVE AIMS
LEARNING HOW TO ...

1 Talk about what has and hasn't happened
2 Talk about experiences
3 Talk about achievements and important events
4 Describe a sequence of past events
5 Talk about past habits and states
6 Talk about inventions

TOPICS AND VOCABULARY

Countries

Phrases with *go, learn* and *ride*

Sport

Geographical features

Disability

Recycling

Household items

Materials

Inventions

Phrases with *do* and *make*

A

They didn't use to have electric light.

1 Match four of the communicative aims (1–6) with the pictures (A–D).

2 Complete the words and put them into categories.

[Sport] [Materials]

[Household items]

car_et co_ton c_cling
cu_board cu_tains gla_s
ic_ho_key m_tal mirr_r
plas_ic p_per r_nning sai_ing
sa_cepan s_iing su_fing
va_uum cle_ner wo_l

B

They haven't reached the USA yet.

3 🔊 2.15 Listen to extracts 1–3 from Units 5 and 6. Match them with A–C below.

A An extract from an autobiography
B A description of an invention
C Information about a new sport

C

The car, which was sketched by da Vinci in 1478, runs by clockwork.

4 Play *What kind of person?*

Work in pairs and make notes describing four other students under these headings.

What kind of person?

Colour

....

Day of the week

....

Month of the year

....

Place

....

Clothes

....

Household item

....

Food

....

Animal

....

D

Ruth had planned to go to university, but instead she left school and started her own business.

Take turns to read out your descriptions to another group. Can they guess who the people are?

This person is red. She is Monday. June. And a beach. She is a pair of blue jeans. A phone. Pizza. And a cat.

Believe it or not!

Who is the world's greatest inventor? Many people think that Thomas Edison registered the most inventions – he had over 1,000 patents, including the light bulb. But Dr Yoshiro Nakamatsu from Tokyo has 3,200 patents, including the floppy disk! Although he's 78, he's still going strong, so that number will probably increase.

1 Has she learnt first aid yet?

Talking about what has and hasn't happened
Present perfect with *just, already, yet*

1 OPENER

Look at *10 things to do before you're 20*.
Tick the things that you have already done.

LISTENING

2 ⊙ 2.16 Listen to Lisa and Steve.
Write *L* (Lisa) and *S* (Steve) for
the things they've already done.

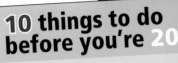

10 things to do before you're 20

1 Go to a gig
2 Learn first aid
3 Perform in a play
4 Ride a horse
5 Write a poem
6 Go camping with friends
7 Organise a birthday party
8 Go skiing
9 Learn to drive
10 Hold a baby

3 SPEAKING

Check your answers to exercise 2.

A Has Lisa been to a gig yet?
B Yes, she's already been to lots of gigs.

B Has she learnt first aid yet?
A No, she hasn't done that yet.

Now ask another student questions
about *10 things to do before you're 20*
and note down the answers.

4 WRITING

Write sentences about the student you
interviewed in exercise 3.

Pedro hasn't been to a gig yet, but he's
already learnt first aid.

Extension Write your own list of
10 things to do before you're 16 and
use it to interview another student.

5 READING

2.17 Read the newspaper report, and look at the route of the journey. How many countries have McGregor and Boorman been to so far?

Long Way Round

Actors Ewan McGregor and Charley Boorman have just arrived in Kazakhstan on a 20,000-mile motorcycle trip. The pair are on their way round the world – they've already travelled across Europe, but they haven't completed a quarter of their journey yet.

McGregor (famous for films such as *Star Wars*) and Boorman are spending more than three months travelling on motorbikes from London through Europe, Asia, Canada and the USA. It's a long and challenging journey – fortunately they haven't had any accidents yet.

McGregor and Boorman are making a film about the trip and are highlighting the work of UNICEF. They've already visited the Chernobyl Children's Project in Ukraine, and they're going to call in at a youth centre in Kazakhstan. They are also planning to visit a project which helps street children in Mongolia.

Route of the journey

14 April – Belgium
15 April – Germany
16 April – Czech Republic
19 April – Slovakia
21 April – Ukraine
27 April – Russia
1 May – Kazakhstan
16 May – Russia
19 May – Mongolia
2 June – Russia
1 July – USA (Alaska)
8 July – Canada
17 July – USA
29 July – New York City

6 AFTER READING

It's 1st May. Look at the route of the journey and ask and answer questions about McGregor and Boorman's trip.

A Have they been to Germany yet?
B Yes, they've already been to Germany.

1 go to Germany?
2 reach Alaska?
3 go to Russia
4 cross Mongolia?
5 travel through Ukraine?
6 arrive in Canada?

Make three more true statements about McGregor and Boorman's journey so far, using *just, already* or *yet*.

A They've just left Russia.
B They've already been to Belgium.
A They haven't visited the street children project yet.

Your response How would you like to travel round the world – on a motorbike or bicycle, on foot, by car, by boat or by plane? Who would you like to go with?

7 VOCABULARY

Complete the word maps with these words and phrases.

a bicycle   camping   on holiday   a horse
an instrument   a language   first aid
a motorbike   skiing   to drive   to a gig

GO   LEARN   RIDE

8 PRONUNCIATION

2.18 Listen and repeat.

/eə/ where		/eɪ/ way	
bear	pair	bay	pay
dare	stare	day	stay
hair	their	hey	they

Now listen and write the words you hear.

9 WRITING

Write a list of ten things you'd like to do in the future. Then exchange lists with another student. Write sentences about the things on your partner's list that you've already done and haven't done yet.

Meet a famous person   Travel round the world
Appear on television

I've already met a famous person – I've just met Ewan McGregor!

Extension Find a different partner and write three true and two false sentences about things that you've already done and haven't done yet. Can your partner guess which are false?

LANGUAGE WORKOUT

Complete.

Present perfect with *just, already, yet*
They have _____ arrived in Kazakhstan.
They have _____ travelled across Europe.
They haven't completed a quarter of their journey _____.
Have they crossed Asia _____?

We can use the present perfect with _____ to talk about *very* recent events.
We use the present perfect with _____ to emphasise that something has happened.
We can use the present perfect with _____ to show that we expect something to happen.

▶Answers and Practice
Language File page 117

Have you ever wondered ...?

Talking about experiences
Present perfect with *ever* and *never*
Present perfect and past simple

1 OPENER

Look at the photos and describe what the people are doing.

2 READING

🔊 2.19 Read the text and match the extreme sports with the photos. Then listen and check.

A

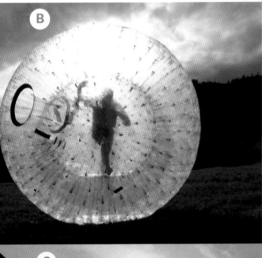

B

C

D

Zorbing

Zorbing – or sphereing – started in New Zealand in the mid-1990s. What's it like? It's like bungee jumping, it's like floating, it's like going on a roller coaster, and it's unlike anything you've ever done before! Imagine being inside a giant bouncy beach ball rolling down a steep hill at up to 50km an hour. You're strapped into the two-metre sphere and pushed over the top of a hill.

'I didn't have a clue what was going on,' says someone who has tried it. 'I saw colours whizzing by: blue sky, green grass, blue sky, green grass, and I could hear myself laughing uncontrollably.'

Have you ever wondered what it's like inside a washing machine? Well, try Hydro-Sphereing, where you roll down the hill in a sphere containing 30 litres of water!

Kite surfing

Kite surfing started in France in the 1980s and has recently become very popular worldwide. You use a small surfboard and a large kite on 30-metre lines. The kite pulls you through the water and you can steer with the lines. You can just speed through the water, or you can do jumps as high as a house. 'I've never had so much fun,' says a kite-surfer. 'It's much more exciting than water-skiing behind a boat.'

Para-skiing

Have you ever wanted to ski off a mountain and fly? If you like skiing and paragliding, then this is the sport for you, because it combines skiing and flying!

The way to do it is to ski straight down the hill with the parachute wing behind you. Then let the parachute come up in the air behind you and whoosh! Suddenly you're flying.

Free running

This sport is also known as parkour in France, where it began, and there are lots of videos of it on the Web. It involves free running through the city, climbing walls, crossing roofs and jumping from building to building. 'It's about getting from point A to point B in the most efficient way,' a free-runner explains. 'It's not just about exercise – it's about finding new ways to do things and new ways of looking at life. I've never done anything like it before.'

3 AFTER READING

Answer the questions.

Which sport(s) …
1 gives you a new view of a city?
2 is like going on a roller coaster?
3 is more enjoyable than water-skiing?
4 makes you look at things differently?
5 do you do on water?
6 makes you laugh so much that you can't stop?
7 needs no equipment?
8 came from France?
9 use the wind?

In which sport do you …
10 do nothing?
11 start very high up?
12 steer with lines?

Your response Which of these extreme sports would you most and least like to try? Why/Why not?

4 PRONUNCIATION

2.20 Listen and repeat the compound nouns. Mark the main stress.

bungee jumping   ice hockey   kite surfing
paragliding   roller coaster   water-skiing

5 SPEAKING

Ask other students questions and complete the chart.

Activity	Name	When	What it was like?
Go on a roller coaster			
Try bungee jumping			
Go water-skiing			
Play ice hockey			
Go sailing			
Do aerobics			
Win a race			
Ride a motorbike			

A Have you ever been on a rollercoaster?
B Yes, I have.
A When did you do it and what was it like?
B I did it on holiday last year. I was really scared on the ride, but I felt great afterwards.

Compare your chart with three other students.

Extension Make another chart with five more activities and complete it with three other students.

6 WRITING

How many of the activities in exercise 5 have you tried? Write a paragraph saying what you have tried, when, and what it was like.

7

Make a word map for sport. Use words from this lesson, and add other words you know.

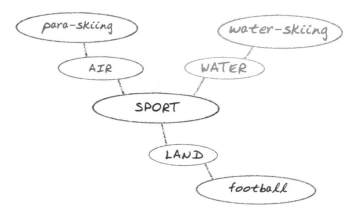

8 SPEAKING

Ask each other questions using *Have you ever wanted to …?* and these phrases.

change your name   move to another town
live in another country   visit …   meet …
learn to …   try …

A Have you ever wanted to change your name?
B No, I haven't.
A Why not?
B Because I'm happy with it!

9 WRITING

Write a paragraph about five things you've always wanted to do but have never done. Say why you've never done them.

LANGUAGE WORKOUT

Complete.

Present perfect with *ever* and *never*
Have you _____ wondered what it's like?
Have you _____ wanted to ski off a mountain?
I've _____ had so much fun.
I've _____ done anything like it before.

We use *ever* and *never* with the present perfect to talk about the time up to now. We mainly use _____ in questions and _____ in statements.

Present perfect and past simple
Kite surfing **started** in France **in the 1980s** and **has recently become** very popular worldwide.

We can use the _____ _____ to talk about an indefinite time in the past.
We use the _____ _____ to talk about a specific time in the past.

▶**Answers and Practice**
Language File pages 117–118

We've been friends ever since we met

Talking about achievements and important events
Present perfect with *for* and *since*

1 OPENER

Look at the photo of Usain Bolt. How is he feeling? What has he done?

2 READING

🔘 2.21 Read the text and match six of these headings with quotations 1–6.

Something I'd like to change
What I do at a race
Drugs
The future
Someone I rely on
Winning
Charity work

Usain Bolt: 9.58

Usain Bolt was born in Trelawney, Jamaica in August 1986. At the 2008 Olympics® in Beijing he won three gold medals (100 metres, 200 metres and 4x100 metres relay). He set a new world record in each event. In 2009 at the World Championships in Berlin he set new world records in both the 100 metres (9.58 seconds) and 200 metres (19.19 seconds). In his autobiography, *Usain Bolt: 9.58*, he talks about his life.

1 _____

'I've won hundreds of medals since I was at school. It's special when you win your first one, but after a while the novelty wears off. It's not the piece of metal that matters, it's the achievement itself. I don't need to see the medals to know I won, and I don't have to show them to anyone to prove it. Everybody knows.'

2 _____

'My best friend in the world is still NJ, or Nugent Walker Junior. We've been friends ever since we met on the first day at primary school and I can't remember ever falling out with him. We hit it off straight away and now he's my personal assistant, someone I can turn to at any time of day or night, who is always, always there for me.'

3 _____

'I don't worry about who I'm racing against or what's going to happen. I just go out there, entertain the crowd and win.'

4 _____

'I'd like to cut out the habit of looking around me as I run, because I know it would improve my times. It's a bad habit I've had since high school.'

5 _____

'My fame gives me an opportunity to help those who are less fortunate and assist other charitable agencies. I've been involved in a number of projects including work in the health, education, community development and sports sectors.'

6 _____

'My attitude to drugs has always been to stay away from them. I tried a cigarette when I was 13 years old, but I've never touched one since. I've had to do drug tests for years – I had my first drug test in Miami just before I was 17. I'm tested after every race, and every day I have to tell the authorities where I'm going to be in case they want to do a test.'

3 AFTER READING

Match the questions with the answers. There are two wrong answers.

1 How many medals did Usain Bolt win at the 2008 Olympics®?
2 How many medals has he won since he was at school?
3 How long has he known his personal assistant?
4 Why would he like to get rid of a bad habit?
5 What does being famous give him a chance to do?
6 What happens to him after every race?

a For three years.
b So he could run faster.
c He's tested for drugs.
d More than a hundred.
e Since they were at primary school.
f Help people who are less lucky than him.
g Travel around the world.
h Three.

Your response What do you admire about Usain Bolt? What does it take to be a successful athlete? What problems can fame and success cause?

4 VOCABULARY

Complete with the correct preposition: *about, at, in, to, with.*

1 be _____ the Olympic® Games
2 show something _____ someone
3 worry _____ something
4 fall out _____ someone
5 be involved _____ something
6 be _____ a class
7 be _____ school
8 live _____ a house

5 PRONUNCIATION

Mark the stressed syllable.

achievement attitude
authorities community
development entertain
fortunate novelty
opportunity primary

2.22 Now listen and check. Repeat the words.

6 SPEAKING

Make questions and interview another student. Note down the answers.

How long/you/be/at this school?
A How long have you been at this school?
B For three years./Since September 2010.

When/you/get/to school today?
A When did you get to school today?
B At eight o'clock.

1 How long/we/have/this coursebook?
2 When/you/start/learning English?
3 Who/you/know/the longest in this class? When/you/first/meet/them?
4 Which friend/you/have/the longest? How long/you/be/friends?
5 What's your favourite band? When/you/first/hear/them?
6 What's your favourite sport? How long/you/play/it?
7 How long/you/live/in this town?
8 How long/you/live/in the same house or flat?
9 What colour are your favourite shoes? When/you/get/them?
10 Has your family got any pets? How long/you/have/them?

Now tell another student about the most interesting answers.

Extension Ask another student to interview you. Give some true and some false answers to the questions. Your partner has to guess which answers are false.

7 WRITING

Look at questions 3–10 in exercise 6 again. Write a paragraph about yourself answering some of the questions.

LANGUAGE WORKOUT

Complete.

Present perfect with *for* and *since*
I've won hundreds of medals _____ I was at school.
I've had to do drug tests _____ years.

We can use the present perfect with *for* and *since* to talk about the unfinished past.
We use _____ to say *how long* something has lasted.
We use _____ to say *when* something started.

▶**Answers and Practice**
Language File pages 117–118

4 Integrated Skills
Describing personal experiences

1 OPENER

How much do you know about Peru? Do the quiz: choose A or B.

1	Peru is on the … coast of South America. **A** Atlantic **B** Pacific
2	Its capital is … **A** Lima **B** Santiago
3	It shares a border with … **A** Bolivia **B** Paraguay
4	The Andes … runs through Peru. **A** river **B** mountain range
5	The … built Machu Picchu. **A** Aztecs **B** Incas

READING

2 Students Julie and Simon are backpacking round South America. Read and complete Julie's blog with phrases a–f.

a and rises to over 4,000 metres in some places

b which tastes a bit like beef

c it was the capital of the Inca empire

d it's 3,809 metres above sea level

e for a hot shower and a rest before dinner

f on the edge of the mountain

🔘 2.23 Now listen and check. Which words in the phrases helped you to complete the text?

We've been busy since we arrived in Peru from Ecuador a week ago! It's our fourth country so far. First we took a bus from Lima, the capital, to Cuzco (24 hours!). Somewhere on the journey I lost my watch, but it wasn't **valuable**, so it didn't really matter. Cuzco is a beautiful old town surrounded by the Andes mountains – __1__. We spent a night in a **hostel**, and the next morning we started to walk the Inca trail to the city of Machu Picchu. The trail is often very **steep** __2__, so lots of people suffer from **altitude** sickness. I've been lucky because I haven't felt ill, but Simon has had a bad headache for a couple of days.

The trek along the Inca **trail** took four days and it was **exhausting**. But it was well worth it. On the last day, we got up at 4am to reach Machu Picchu in time for sunrise. When we got there, the city was **invisible** because it was covered in cloud. But suddenly the cloud lifted, and there was Machu Picchu __3__. It was magic!

We spent several hours **wandering** round the site – what an incredible place! Then back to Cuzco by bus and train __4__. We've had some interesting food in Peru. I've already tried llama, __5__. A local speciality in Cuzco is roast guinea pig, but I couldn't face it!

Tomorrow we're going to Lake Titicaca, on the border between Peru and Bolivia. It's the largest freshwater lake in South America and one of the highest in the world – __6__. The weather has been great – let's hope it stays that way.

3 Find the highlighted words in the text which mean:

1 cheap hotel *n*
2 height *n*
3 walking in a relaxed way *v*
4 path through the countryside *n*
5 rising quickly *adj*
6 very tiring *adj*
7 worth a lot of money *adj*
8 something you can't see *adj*

4 Linking words: *so* and *because*.

Find examples of *so* and *because* in the text. Then complete these rules.

We use _____ to talk about reason or cause.
We use _____ to talk about consequence or result.

Now complete these sentences with *so* or *because*.

1 They were tired _____ the bus journey took 24 hours.
2 Cuzco is surrounded by mountains, _____ it gets very cold at night.
3 We got up early _____ we wanted to see the sunrise.
4 Lots of people visit Machu Picchu _____ it's very beautiful.
5 I haven't got much money, _____ I can't go on holiday this year.

5 LISTENING

🔘 2.24 Listen to Julie and Simon talking to Rod, an American backpacker in Cuzco. Follow their route on the map and number the countries in the order they're visiting them.

SPEAKING

6 Look at your answers to exercise 5. Use the map and tell each other which countries Julie and Simon have already visited, and which countries they haven't visited yet.

7 Plan a backpacking trip with another student. Choose a country or group of countries, and decide which places you want to visit. Plan your itinerary.

8 GUIDED WRITING

Imagine you are on the road! Write a blog about the backpacking trip you planned in exercise 7. Use the text in exercise 2 to help you and include this information.

● Where are you now?
● Where is it exactly, and what's it like?
● How did you get there?
● Where have you already been?
● What have you done?
● Where are you going next?

LEARNER INDEPENDENCE

9 Self assessment: Look back over this unit, think about what you've learnt and make a list.

Information I've found out more about South America.
Grammar I've learnt how to use 'already' and 'yet' with the present perfect.
Vocabulary I've learnt new words for sports.

If there are any areas where you have problems, look back at the lesson again and refer to the Language File.

10 Word creation: Make nouns ending in *-ity* from these adjectives and complete the sentences.

active   electric   national   popular
possible   real   responsible   special

1 Seafood is a _____ in this restaurant.
2 Reading is my favourite leisure _____.
3 There's a _____ of rainstorms later today.
4 The _____ of backpacking holidays has grown recently.
5 Where are you from? What's your _____?
6 Parents have a _____ to look after their children.
7 If we turn off the lights, we'll save _____.
8 Snowboarding looks difficult, but in _____ it's quite easy.

11 🔘 2.25 **Phrasebook**: Find these useful expressions in Unit 5. Then listen and repeat.

I didn't have a clue.
Have you ever wondered what it's like?
I've never had so much fun.
I've never done anything like it before.
It didn't really matter.
It was well worth it.
It was magic!
What an incredible place!
I couldn't face it.
Let's hope it stays that way.

Now write a five-line dialogue using three or more of the expressions.

Inspiration EXTRA!

LANGUAGE LINKS

Try to write eleven English words for colours. Then read *The Language of Colours.*

THE LANGUAGE OF COLOURS

English, like most languages, has eleven words to describe colours: white, black, red, green, yellow, blue, brown, purple, pink, orange and grey.

However, the Japanese word *awo* can mean *green*, *blue* or *pale* depending on what it is used to describe (for example, vegetables, sea, clouds).

In Hanunóo, a language which is spoken by 7,000 people on the island of Mondoro in the Philippines, there are just four words for colours: black, white, red and green. The Native American language Navaho uses the same word for blue and green, but has two words for black: one for the black of darkness, and one for the black of objects like coal.

Dani, a language spoken in Papua New Guinea, has only two words for colours: one is for 'cool' colours, like black, green and blue, and the other is for 'warm' colours, including white, red and yellow.

Find out what these colours are. Which two are colours of the rainbow?

beige   khaki   indigo   maroon   turquoise   violet

SKETCH *The Interview*

🔘 2.26   Read and listen.

WOMAN   Are you ready?

MAN   Yes, sorry. Right. Er. Now. Which job have you applied for?

WOMAN   Deep-sea diver.

MAN   And what experience have you got of diving?

WOMAN   Well, none, really, but I …

MAN   I'm sorry. Let me ask you again. Have you ever been underwater?

WOMAN   Oh yes, lots of times.

MAN   I see. So you have dived.

WOMAN   No, I haven't. Not in the sea, that is.

MAN   Then where have you dived?

WOMAN   Do I have to answer that?

MAN   Come on. Answer the question! Where have you dived if you haven't dived in the sea?

WOMAN   You've already asked me that.

MAN   I know I have! And what's the answer?

WOMAN   In the bath at home.

MAN   That's not deep-sea diving!

WOMAN   I know. But you see – there's a problem. I can't swim.

MAN   So why have you applied for a job as a deep-sea diver?

WOMAN   Why? Because it's very well paid and there's lots of foreign travel.

MAN   Well paid! Travel! Stop wasting my time and get out! You've failed to get the job! The interview is over.

WOMAN   No, I'm sorry, but you're the one who has failed. We were looking for a good interviewer and you were terrible. Goodbye. Next!

Now act out the sketch in pairs.

Game *Help!*

- Work in small groups.
- One group member is a tourist on holiday in a country where he/she doesn't speak the language. The other members are people who live in that country.
- The tourist has a problem and needs help. But because the tourist doesn't speak the language he/she has to mime the problem. The other group members try to guess what the problem is.
- The group member who guesses the problem becomes the tourist, and the game is played again.

> Your plane goes at ten o'clock, but you've lost your watch and don't know what the time is.

> There's a crocodile in your room and it's eaten your bag.

REVISION

LESSON 1 Look at *10 things to do before you're 20* on page 62. Use your answers to exercise 2 to write eight sentences about Lisa and Steve.

Lisa's already been to lots of gigs. She hasn't learnt first aid yet.

LESSON 2 Look at exercise 8 on page 65. Write six sentences about the student you interviewed.

Helena has never wanted to change her name because she likes it.

LESSON 3 Write five sentences using these phrases.

> last four days last Wednesday I got up
> a couple of minutes summer

She's only been here for a couple of minutes.
I haven't felt well since I got up.

EXTENSION

LESSON 1 Look at exercise 5 on page 63. Imagine it is 17 July. Write eight questions about McGregor and Boorman's trip using verbs from the text in the present perfect and *yet*. Answer the questions using *just*, *yet*, or *already*.

Have they been to the Czech Republic yet?
Yes, they've already been there.

LESSON 2 Look at the chart you completed in exercise 5 on page 65 and write a paragraph about the students you interviewed.

Kris and Stephanie haven't been water-skiing, but Nadia has. She went water-skiing when she was on holiday in Spain last summer.

LESSON 3 Look at exercise 2 on page 66. Imagine you are interviewing Usain Bolt. Choose some of the questions 4–10 in exercise 4 and write his answers.

YOUR CHOICE!

CONSTRUCTION Present perfect or past simple?

Complete with the present perfect or past simple of the verbs.

Zorbing is quite a new sport and many people __1__ (not try) it yet. Dwane van der Sluis and Andrew Akers __2__ (invent) zorbing in New Zealand in the 1990s. The inventors __3__ (want) to design a ball so that people could 'walk' on water, but it __4__ (not work) very well. Then they __5__ (try) rolling it down a hill with great success. Now zorbing centres __6__ (open) around the world and soon everyone will know someone who __7__ (try) the sport. 'Once you __8__ (have) a go, you want to do it again and again,' a teenage zorber said.

REFLECTION Present perfect

Choose the correct rule.

- We use *for* to refer to
  A a period of time.   B a point in time.
- We use *since* to refer to
  A a period of time.   B a point in time.
- We use the present perfect with just to talk about things that
  A happened a long time ago.   B happened very recently.
- We use the present perfect with *already* to talk about things that
  A have happened.   B haven't happened.
- We use the present perfect with *yet* to talk about things that
  A we expect to happen.   B have happened recently.
- We usually use *ever* in
  A questions.   B negative statements.
- We use *never* in
  A affirmative statements.   B negative statements.

ACTION Make yourself look good!

- Work in groups of four. Use these verbs: go, kiss, meet, see, talk, win.
- Student A makes a sentence using one of the verbs in the present perfect.
  I've been to India.
- Student B repeats the sentence and adds to it.
  I've been to India and China.
- Student C repeats Student B's sentence and adds to it.
  I've been to India, China and Egypt.
- Student D repeats Student C's sentence and adds to it.
  I've been to India, China, Egypt and Antarctica.

INTERACTION The present I've always wanted

- Work in a small group.
- We are given presents on our birthdays and at other times of the year. Imagine it's one of those days and you can choose the present.
- What present have you always wanted but never got? It could be a thing, or an event, or a skill you'd like to have, or something you'd like for someone else.
- Take turns to tell each other about the present you've always wanted and why it has been such an important wish.

TOURISM

A

Wait until the guys back home see this!

Do you think we should give them money?

Great! I wanted to get a picture of the Masai jump dance!

B Tourism: who gets the money?

Many tourists believe that much of the money they spend on a holiday to a poor country benefits the local community. But how much of the cost of this kind of holiday really goes to the country you visit?

Let's take a family in Europe who go on holiday somewhere in Africa. Some of their money goes to the travel agent who sells the holiday, and to the tour company that organises it. More money goes to the European airline that flies the family there and back. The resort is owned by a European company. The manager and top staff at the resort are European, and most of their salary is paid into banks back home. The tourists travel from the airport to their hotel in an imported coach and the hotel furniture is all made in Europe. The waiters, cooks and cleaners are local, but they don't earn very much money. And the food and drink which they serve is almost all imported.

As a rule, less than a third of the money paid for this kind of holiday goes to the country which is visited.

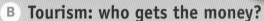

C How tourism can help developing countries

So is it always wrong to visit poor countries as a tourist? Not at all – it depends on the kind of holiday you take. Responsible tourists use their visit to learn about the culture and language of the country they are in. They interact with the locals and ask questions – rather than believing that they know all the answers! They travel by public transport and eat the local food. The souvenirs they buy are locally-made, not imported. And everyone benefits. The responsible tourist has a great holiday and the money that is spent stays in the country.

D The good news about tourism

Tourism is big business in Europe and provides at least 10 million jobs across the continent. Spending by tourists is vital for the economies of many European countries, providing a high percentage of their income. Croatia gets 25.5% of its income from tourism, Malta 23% and Greece 17.2%. Tourism is also important for Spain (17.2%) and Switzerland (12.6%).

E THE TOURISTS ARE COMING
Benjamin Zephaniah

Tell them to be careful
If they're not give them an earful
The tourists are coming
The tourists are coming.

They may want to party nightly
But tell them they must be tidy
The tourists are coming
The tourists are coming.

They must respect what we've planted
They should not take us for granted
The tourists are coming
The tourists are coming.

They should practise what they preach
When they're lying on our beach
The tourists are coming to play.

Because our land is sunny
They come here with their money
The tourists are coming
The tourists are coming.

2.28 Listen and choose the correct answer.

Are tourists destroying the famous places they visit?

Let's look at some well-known tourist sites around the world and see what's happening.

Machu Picchu
This Inca site in Peru receives about 100,000/ 1,000,000 visitors a year. There are so many tourists that you can only walk along the Inca Trail to the site if you are in a group/on your own.

Angkor Wat
More and more tourists come to Cambodia to visit the Angkor Archaeological Park. One way of reducing/increasing numbers is to have two prices for entry: Cambodians go free but foreigners pay $10/$20 for a day ticket.

Pompeii
The Roman town is one of the best-known sites in the world but it is also one of the ones which is in most danger. In 1981, 86,300/863,000 visitors came to see what life was like in Roman times, but now the numbers have increased to two/ten million people a year.

Taj Mahal
The Taj Mahal is the most popular tourist site in India – every year it has 300,000/3,000,000 visitors – and you are never alone there. One plan is to close the Taj Mahal completely and only let visitors look at it from a distance.

1 READING

2.27 Read texts A, B, C, D and E and answer the questions.

1 Which text(s):
- gives advice on responsible tourism?
- tells local people and tourists how to behave?
- gives facts and figures about money and tourism?
- shows the attitudes of tourists to local people?

2 In general, how much of the money that tourists spend on a holiday to a poor country benefits the local community?

3 In *The Tourists Are Coming* the poet tells the tourists to do four things. What are they?

4 In your opinion, how valuable is the income from tourism to your country? What can people do to increase it?

5 Have any of the texts made you change your ideas about tourism?

6 What do you think the Masai's attitude to tourists and tourism is?

2 VOCABULARY

Match these words with their definitions.

1	resort *n*	a	tell people what to do
2	benefit *v*	b	show you think something is important
3	community *n*	c	place where people go for a holiday
4	respect *v*	d	people who work for a business or organisation
5	salary *n*	e	bring into a country from abroad
6	staff *n*	f	what you earn each month from a job
7	import *v*	g	group of people who live in a place
8	preach *v*	h	help

4 MINI-PROJECT
Responsible tourism

Discuss these topics with another student. Use the texts in this lesson to help you.

- Ways in which tourism could become more responsible: money, jobs, respect for the environment and local people.
- Problems which more responsible tourism could face: numbers of people, accommodation, travelling to and from remote places.

Work together and write two paragraphs giving your views on responsible tourism. Read your work carefully and correct any mistakes. Then compare your report with other students.

He had won awards

Describing a sequence of past events
Past perfect

1 OPENER

Look at your hands. How many things can you do with them? What makes human hands unique?

2 READING

2.29 Read *Teenage Inventors* and match the inventions with the photos. Then listen and check.

TEENAGE INVENTORS

From school project to successful business

When Ruth Amos created a design for a handrail as part of a school project, her main aim was to get a good mark. The 16-year-old didn't realise that she had invented something which might make her rich. Her teacher had asked her to design a product to help old or disabled people go up and down the stairs. Ruth's StairSteady is a metal bar which slides on a metal rail. People with limited mobility can push the bar along the rail to help them balance. Ruth had planned to go to university, but instead she left school and started her own business. 'I can't believe how successful the StairSteady has been,' said Ruth. 'It's doing really well.'

The glove that translates

Ryan Patterson found the inspiration for his invention in a fast food restaurant. 'There was a group of deaf people who needed help to order their food,' Ryan remembers. Although deaf people can use sign language to communicate, many people don't understand it. Ryan had been fascinated by electronics as a child and had won awards for designing robots by the time he was 16. Now, at the age of 18, he used his skills to invent a Sign Language Translator – a glove which translates sign language into letters. All the deaf person does is put on the glove, make a sign, and the letter appears on a computer screen.

The waterbike

Californian Krysta Morlan was 16 when she invented a special waterbike. She thought of the idea when she was doing exercises in the swimming pool. She had spent a lot of time in hospital and needed to do exercises to recover her strength. 'I loved cycling, but I hadn't ridden a bicycle for a long time,' she explained. 'The idea of the waterbike was to have fun and still get the advantage of a workout in the pool.' Anyone can have fun on Krysta's invention, whether they are disabled or not.

Braille

In 1824, when he was 15, Louis Braille invented a way for blind people to read. Louis himself had been blind since the age of three. When he was 10, he went to a school for the blind in Paris. Two years later, an old soldier called Charles Barbier visited the school. Barbier told Louis about something he had learnt in the war called 'night-writing'. It was a way for soldiers to communicate in the dark so that the enemy did not hear them speak. However, night-writing was hard to learn because it used 12 raised dots on a page. For three years Louis simplified the system that Barbier had told him about. Louis's system uses only six dots, and blind people read by moving their fingers over the dots.

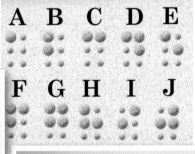

C

A

B

D

3 AFTER READING

Answer the questions. Whose invention(s) …

1 is the oldest?
2 are to do with language?
3 helps people with walking difficulties?
4 is to do with cycling?
5 uses computers?
6 helps people who cannot see?
7 helps people who cannot hear?
8 is fun whether you are disabled or not?
9 are to do with hands?

Your response Whose invention is useful to the greatest number of people? Why? Which inventions were for personal use? What would you like to invent?

4 PRONUNCIATION

Mark the stress. Which words are stressed on the first syllable?

advantage balance bicycle communicate disabled
electronics enemy inspiration invention mobility
realise recover simplify translator university

🔘 2.30 Now listen and check. Repeat the words.

SPEAKING

5 Tell each other why things happened. Use *because* and the phrases in the box to complete the sentences.

forget her number leave my books at school
win the match not eat anything all day tickets sell out
not sleep all night lose the key pass the exam

1 I didn't do my homework …
2 She was exhausted …
3 He didn't call her back …
4 She couldn't get into the house …
5 They were really happy …
6 I was hungry …
7 We couldn't go to the gig …
8 The players were delighted …

6

Interview two other students about recent new experiences.

When was the last time you …
- tried a kind of food that you'd never eaten before?
- talked to someone who you'd never talked to before?
- discovered a singer who you'd never heard before?
- visited a place that you'd never been to before?
- got a present that you'd always wanted?
- did something that you'd always wanted to do?

Extension Write sentences about the students you interviewed.
Kurt had never eaten curry before, but he tried it last month and he liked it.

7 WRITING

Make a list of things you did yesterday after you had come home from school. Think about:

have something to eat have a shower watch TV
play football do my homework phone a friend
listen to music go shopping read a magazine
clean my teeth go to bed

Now write sentences using *after* with the past perfect and past simple.

After I'd come home from school, I phoned Alexis.
After I'd phoned Alexis, I went for a walk.

Extension Interview another student about what they did yesterday after they had come home from school.

LANGUAGE WORKOUT

Complete.

Past perfect

Past perfect	Past simple	NOW

She **had spent** a lot of time in hospital and needed to do exercises.
Ryan _____ _____ awards by the time he was 16.
Louis Braille _____ _____ blind since the age of three.

We form the past perfect with _____ + past participle.
Contractions: _____/you'd/he'd/she'd/we'd/they'd
We use the _____ _____ to describe the earlier of two past events.

▶**Answers and Practice**
Language File page 118

75

People didn't use to throw things away

Talking about past habits and states
used to + infinitive

1 OPENER

Look at photos 1–5. They are all examples of recycling. What are they? And what do you think they are made from?

2 READING

2.31 Read *Recycle now!* Check your answers to exercise 1.

3 AFTER READING

Answer the questions.

1 Why did we use to buy fewer clothes?
2 Why did we use to buy fewer shoes?
3 Why do we produce more rubbish now?
4 Which kinds of rubbish are recycled in the TV ads?
5 What example shows that the UK is now recycling more?
6 What recycled materials did Oliver Heath use in the home he designed?

Now say what the items in photos 1–5 used to be.

Your response Do you recycle more now than you used to? What things do you recycle? What things do you use that are made from recycled materials?

Recycle now!

People didn't use to throw things away. We used to mend our clothes and we used to wear shoes until they wore out. And we didn't use to buy so much in the first place.

But now we consume more and so we produce more rubbish. The UK used to be one of the worst recyclers in Europe, but the Recycle Now campaign has made a big difference. It has an annual Recycle Week and has made TV commercials showing the recycling of metal cans, glass bottles and paper into interesting new everyday items. One ad showed a town with cars, trains, buildings and even planes made of metal cans. Now the UK recycles around 3.5 billion cans a year, almost twice as many as 10 years ago. And supermarkets have reduced their use of plastic bags by nearly 50% in the last five years.

Top UK designer Oliver Heath is a strong supporter of the campaign – he designed the first home constructed entirely from recycled materials, including yoghurt pots and glass bottles. And he is excited by the imaginative recycling of waste. 'There's an awful lot of exciting design stuff out there. I like all the new uses for ordinary products – glass bottles turned into bricks, rubber car tyres into pencil cases and carpets, plastic cups into pencils.' You can also buy pens made from recycled computer printers, T-shirts made from plastic bottles, and jewellery made from plastic bags.

So don't throw things away! All the items you recycle are valuable resources and can be made into something useful, even stylish and fun. In the USA they've made chairs from old books, plant pots from shoes and even a house from a jumbo jet. The possibilities are endless!

4 SPEAKING

Look at the picture of a sitting room 200 years ago and say what's wrong. Use *They used to …/They didn't use to …* and these phrases.

> have electric light   have vacuum cleaners   light candles
> make phone calls   paint pictures   play cards
> take photos   watch TV   write letters

> They didn't use to have electric light.

> **Extension**   Make a list of ten other differences between life now and life 200 years ago. Compare your list with another student.
> *People didn't use to have computers.*

5 VOCABULARY

Ask and answer questions about what these things are made of.

> **Word Bank** Household items
>
> a carpet   a computer   a cupboard   curtains   a desk
> envelopes   a hot water bottle   keys   a magazine
> matches   a mirror   a saucepan   a vacuum cleaner

A   What's a carpet made of?
B   It's made of wool. What's a computer made of?
A   It's made of …

> **Word Bank** Materials
>
> cotton   glass   metal   paper   plastic   rubber   wood   wool

6 PRONUNCIATION

🔊 2.32   Listen and repeat.

/eɪ/ waste	/e/ west
later	letter
pain	pen
paper	pepper
saint	sent
tale	tell
wait	wet

Now listen and write the words you hear.

7 SPEAKING

How have you changed since you became a teenager? Tell other students about your likes, dislikes, feelings, clothes, possessions and hobbies. Make notes about changes in their lives.

A   I used to like Eminem but I don't any more.
B   I didn't use to like mushrooms but I do now.
A   I used to be afraid of the dark, but I'm not now.
B   I used to play the piano but I don't any more.

8 WRITING

Write about how you and other students have changed in the last few years. Use your notes from exercise 7.

> **Extension**   Write about how life has changed in your town in the last few years.

> **LANGUAGE WORKOUT**
>
> Complete.
>
> **used to + infinitive**
> It _____ _____ be a car tyre.
> We _____ _____ mend our clothes.
> We _____n't _____ to buy so much.
> Why _____ we _____ to buy fewer shoes?
>
> We can use *used to* when we talk about past habits and states.
>
> ▶Answers and Practice
> Language File page 118

The first car was invented by him

Talking about inventions
Past simple passive

Leonardo da Vinci – ahead of his time

Leonardo da Vinci was not only a great artist, he was also a brilliant inventor. And believe it or not, the first car was invented by him over 500 years ago!

It's no secret that da Vinci drew plans for a car. Several attempts were made in the last century to build the vehicle, but without success. However, a team of computer designers, engineers and carpenters have finally put da Vinci's plans into practice. They spent eight months building a replica of da Vinci's car – and it works! The car, which was sketched by da Vinci in 1478, runs by clockwork.

'It was – or is – the world's first self-propelled vehicle. It is highly sophisticated, a work of genius – and Italian,' said Paolo Galuzzi, director of the Institute and Museum of the History of Science in Florence, where the model is on display.

'It is a very powerful machine,' said Professor Galuzzi. 'It could run into something and do serious damage.'

Da Vinci's other inventions

Flying machine He designed several flying machines, including a helicopter. The first successful powered flying machine was built and flown by Orville and Wilbur Wright in 1903.

Parachute In 1485, da Vinci sketched a design for a parachute. No one knows whether he ever tested a full-scale model. The first reported successful parachute jump was made in 1797.

Robot He produced what are thought to be the first ever designs for a human-like robot in 1495. The robot was designed to wave, sit up, move its head, and open and shut its mouth. The first robot, Steam Man, was created by John Brainerd in 1865.

Scuba diving He sketched an air chamber to allow a diver to swim underwater without connection to the surface. In 1943 the aqualung was invented by Jacques-Yves Cousteau and Emilie Gagnon.

1 OPENER

Complete these questions about inventions with *What, When* or *Who*. Then try to match the questions with the answers.

1 _____ was the first car invented by?
2 _____ was built and flown in 1903?
3 _____ was the first successful parachute jump made?
4 _____ was the first robot created?
5 _____ was invented in 1943?

a The first real aeroplane.
b In 1865.
c The aqualung.
d Leonardo da Vinci.
e In 1797.

2 READING

2.33 Read and listen to the text, and check your answers to exercise 1.

Your response Which fact about da Vinci's inventions is most surprising?

3 SPEAKING

Complete the quiz questions. Then ask and answer the questions.

> When was the first telephone call made?

General Knowledge Quiz

1 **When _____ the first telephone call _____? (make)**
  A 1876   B 1928
2 **When _____ the zip _____? (invent)**
  A 1893   B 1938
3 **Who _____ *The Last Supper* and *Mona Lisa* _____ by? (paint)**
  A Raphael   B Leonardo da Vinci
4 **Who _____ *Hamlet* _____ by? (write)**
  A Charles Dickens   B William Shakespeare
5 **When _____ the Pyramids of Giza _____? (build)**
  A Over 4,000 years ago.   B Over 5,000 years ago.
6 **When _____ X-rays _____? (discover)**
  A 1895   B 1955
7 **Who _____ *The Marriage of Figaro* _____ by? (compose)**
  A Bach   B Mozart
8 **Who _____ the Simpsons _____ by? (create)**
  A Matt Groening   B Walt Disney

⊙ 2.34   Now listen and check.

> **Extension**   Write your own five-question quiz about inventions, using the Internet or library to check your facts.

4 READING

Read and complete the text with these words.

> television   phones   light bulb   bombs   bicycle   bags

Best and worst inventions

In a recent radio survey, the __1__ was chosen by UK listeners as their favourite invention of the last 150 years. It was invented in Paris by Pierre Lallement in 1866. Atomic and nuclear __2__ were voted the least favourite inventions.

Listeners were invited to nominate their favourite and least favourite inventions. Then a shortlist of ten 'best' and ten 'worst' inventions was drawn up for the poll. The computer, the __3__ and the World Wide Web were included in the list of ten 'best' inventions. Plastic __4__, mobile __5__ and car alarms were listed among the 'worst' inventions.

Interestingly, three inventions were selected for both lists: __6__, the telephone, and the internal combustion engine!

⊙ 2.35   Now listen and check.

5 VOCABULARY

Complete with *do* or *make*.

1 _____ an attempt
2 _____ damage
3 _____ a difference
4 _____ an exercise
5 _____ friends
6 _____ a list
7 _____ a mistake
8 _____ the shopping
9 _____ a sign
10 _____ sure
11 _____ the washing up
12 _____ some work

6 PRONUNCIATION

Write the words in the correct column.

> artist   attempt   believe   clockwork
> compose   create   damage
> display   engine   invent   machine
> practice   robot   surface

■■	■■
artist	*attempt*

⊙ 2.36   Now listen and check. Repeat the words.

7 SPEAKING

Which of the inventions mentioned in this lesson do you think is the best? And which is the worst? Tell another student, giving reasons for your choices.

8 WRITING

What do you think is the best invention of all time? And what is the worst? Write a paragraph about each invention.

● Who was it invented by?
● When was it invented?
● Why do you think it is the best/worst invention?

LANGUAGE WORKOUT

Complete.

Past simple passive
The first robot _____ created in 1865.
Several attempts _____ made in the last century.
The car _____ sketched **by** da Vinci in 1478.

We form the past simple passive with the past tense of _____ + past participle.

▶**Answers and Practice**
Language File page 119

4 Integrated Skills

Describing a process

1 OPENER

How much do you know about inventions?
Do the quiz: choose A, B or C.

1 Plastic surgery was first carried out in
   A the USA. **B** Italy. **C** India.

2 Cotton was first made in
   A England. **B** India. **C** Egypt.

3 Letters were used to count by the
   A Romans. **B** Arabs. **C** Indians.

4 Chocolate was first drunk in
   A France. **B** Spain. **C** Mexico.

5 Paper was invented in
   A China. **B** Greece. **C** Egypt.

6 Printing was invented in
   A Germany. **B** China. **C** England.

READING

2 Read *Ancient Inventions* and check your answers
to exercise 1.

3 Match five of these topics with paragraphs 1–5.

> Clothing Entertainment Food and drink
> Mathematics Medicine Travel
> Written communication

🔘 2.37 Now listen and check.

Ancient Inventions

1 People often think that plastic surgery is a modern American invention, somehow connected with Hollywood. However, thousands of years before America was discovered by Columbus, Indian doctors did complicated plastic surgery. A medical textbook called the *Sushruta Samhita*, which was written in approximately 600 BC, gives detailed instructions for doing 'nose jobs' – changing the shape of your nose.

2 Brightly coloured cotton clothes were made in India four and a half thousand years ago. This was at a time when Europeans wore animal skins. Until cotton factories were developed in England 200 years ago, India supplied the world with cotton clothes.

3 Although we call them Arabic numbers, the numbers that we use today came from India and it was there that 'zero' was invented in AD 499. The Romans had counted using letters (M=1000, D=500, C=100, L=50, X=10, V=5 and I=1) and this made mathematics very difficult. For example, four was written IV, forty XXXX, four hundred CCCC and four thousand MMMM. However, in the new Indian system, using zero, the same numbers were written 4, 40, 400, 4,000.

4 Chocolate was invented over 2,500 years ago! The Mayans and Aztecs lived in parts of Mexico and central America from 600 BC and grew cacao trees. They made a cold thick drink called *xocolatl* from the fruit of the tree. Although the Mayans and Aztecs loved chocolate, Europeans didn't discover it for another two thousand years. In 1519 the Spanish explorer Cortés visited Emperor Montezuma II of Mexico. To the explorer's great surprise, he found that Montezuma drank 50 cups of chocolate a day.

5 Paper was invented in China in AD 105 by Cai Lun, and the Chinese kept the process secret for more than 500 years. Although paper was introduced into Japan in AD 610, it didn't reach the West until much later. A hundred years after paper was first made, printing was invented in China – over a thousand years before it was invented in Europe. In China paper wasn't only used for books. Umbrellas, flags and toilet paper were made from it, as well as the world's first paper money.

4 LINKING WORD: *although*

Find examples of *although* in the text. Then rewrite these sentences using *although* instead of *but*.

1 Paper was made Japan in AD 610, but it wasn't made in Europe until 1151.
2 Printing was invented in the 3rd century, but it didn't reach Europe until 1455.
3 The Mayans and Aztecs loved *xocolatl*, but the Spanish thought it tasted awful until they added sugar.
4 Leonardo da Vinci lived 500 years ago, but he designed the first car.
5 Krysta Morlan was only 16, but she invented a waterbike.
6 Louis Braille couldn't see, but he developed a reading system for the blind.

5 LISTENING

🔘 2.38 Look at the pictures 1–6 showing how paper was made by the Chinese. Then listen to a description of the paper-making process and number sentences A–F to show the right order.

A The bark and leaves were boiled to make a pulp.
B This sheet was dried and the paper was ready.
C A thin sheet of pulp was left on the tray.
D The soft pulp was spread on a bamboo tray with small holes in it.
E Mulberry bark and leaves were collected and put in water.
F Water from the pulp ran away through the holes.

leaves
bark

6 SPEAKING

Use your answers to exercise 5 to tell each other how paper was made by the Chinese.

7 GUIDED WRITING

Write a process description of how paper was made by the Chinese, using this structure.

To make paper, … Then … When … After … Then … Finally, …

LEARNER INDEPENDENCE

8 Self assessment: Look back over this unit, think about what you've learnt, and complete.

About me
I've learnt …
I used to … but now I …
I can …
I haven't managed to … yet.
I have difficulty in …

About the lessons
What I like best is …
The most interesting thing is …
I'm not keen on …
I don't enjoy …

9 Word creation: Make 'people' nouns ending in *-er*, *-or* or *-ist* from these words.

act art design direct
engine invent journal novel
paint profess report run
science tour translate

-er	-or	-ist
designer	*actor*	*artist*

10 🔘 2.39 **Phrasebook**: Find these useful expressions in Unit 6. Then listen and repeat.

It's doing really well.
The idea was to …
in the first place
The possibilities are endless!
Believe it or not …
It's no secret.
It works!

Now think of other situations where you could use each of the expressions.

'It's doing really well.'
Talking about a band.

PROJECT *An extraordinary person*

1 Work in a group and make a list of extraordinary people who have done amazing or unusual things. They could be historical figures, famous inventors, explorers or adventurers, sports stars … or ordinary people with unusual skills or hobbies. They don't have to be well known – the important thing is that there is something extraordinary about them. Then choose one person to write about.

2 Research: Find out as much as you can about the person using the Internet or a library. If the person is still alive and lives close to you, why not make a list of questions and interview her/him? Or maybe you could do an email interview.

3 Work together and write about the extraordinary person. Read your work carefully and correct any mistakes. Illustrate it with drawings or photographs from magazines or the Internet. Show your work to the other groups.

Tanni Grey-Thompson: an extraordinary person

Tanni was born in Wales in 1969 with a condition called spina bifida and has used a wheelchair all her life. She is the UK's most successful disabled athlete ever. Her international sporting career began in 1988 and over the years she has won 16 Paralympic medals, including 11 gold medals. She has held numerous world records and won the London Wheelchair Marathon six times. Off the track, she is involved with a number of charities and is a member of the UK House of Lords.

Poem *Changes: The Things We Used To Do*

● Work in groups of three or four.

● Think about your own and your friends' lives a year ago. What changes have there been? For example, think about relationships, likes and dislikes, free time, family, holidays, music, sport and clothes.

● Now think of ways of completing these sentences:

I used to … but now I …
You used to … but now you …
We used to … but now we …

I used to like writing letters, but now I send text messages.
You used to play snakes and ladders, but now you play computer games.
We used to run to school, but now we walk slowly.

● Choose the best sets of three sentences and put them together to make a poem – it can be long or short.

● Give your poems to your teacher and listen. Can you guess which group wrote each poem?

REVISION

LESSON 1 Look at exercise 2 on page 74 and find examples of the past perfect. Write five questions and answer them.

Had Ryan been fascinated by electronics as a child?
Yes, he had.

LESSON 2 Write five sentences about what you used and didn't use to do at primary school. Think about lessons, teachers, clothes, sports, homework, holidays, etc.

We used to have English lessons.

LESSON 3 Complete with verbs in the past simple passive.

The first successful hot-air balloon __1__ (invent) in 1783. Air __2__ (heat) by a fire, the balloon __3__ (fill) with the hot air, and it took off. The passengers on the first hot-air balloon flight were three animals – a duck, a hen and a sheep __4__ (put) in the basket under the balloon. When the balloon __5__ (see) to be a success, the animals __6__ (follow) by people!

EXTENSION

LESSON 1 Complete these sentences using the past perfect.

1 The school bus was completely empty because …
2 The DJ couldn't play any music because …
3 The man at the door had only one shoe because …
4 She didn't buy her boyfriend a present because …
5 She didn't get the text message because …

LESSON 2 Imagine you are a newspaper reporter. Write an interview with someone who used to be a big pop star a few years ago. But now the star has no money and is no longer famous.

Reporter: Can you remember what it was like when
you were number one?
Star: Yes, it was great. Everyone used to like me
and want to be my friend. We used to have
all night parties, but now …

LESSON 3 Make your own general knowledge quiz and try it out on another student.

1 Who _____ (title of book) _____ by? (write)
2 When _____ (name of building) _____? (build)
3 Who _____ (title of song) _____ by? (sing)
4 When _____ (name of continent) _____? (discover)

YOUR CHOICE!

CONSTRUCTION Past simple active or passive?

Complete with the correct form of the verbs.

Although the ancient Greeks __1__ (know) about electrical forces, it wasn't until the 19th century that electricity __2__ (understand) properly. Then it __3__ (use) in practical ways and life __4__ (change) dramatically. Gas lamps and candles __5__ (replace) by electric light, electric trams __6__ (appear) on the streets, and lots of electrical appliances __7__ (invent). But one of the first electric irons, which __8__ (make) in 1889, __9__ (explode) and __10__ (kill) its inventor.

ACTION Game: *I used to be …*

● Work in a small group.

● In turn, imagine you are a famous person who is no longer alive. Don't say who you are, but tell the rest of the group one fact about yourself.

   I used to be a writer.

● The rest of the group asks *Yes/No* questions to find out who you used to be.

   A Did you use to live in the 19th century?

   B Did you use to live in England?

REFLECTION Past perfect

Match the examples a–f with language functions 1–3.

The past perfect is used …

1 to describe the earlier of two past events.
2 to talk about something that happened before a particular time in the past.
3 to explain why something happened.

a They got lost because they hadn't taken a map.
b The party had finished by midnight.
c After I'd been to the gym, I had a shower.
d She'd started working by the time she was 17.
e When we'd done our homework, we watched TV.
f He'd drunk lots of coffee, so he couldn't sleep.

INTERACTION *I'd never been so … before!*

● Work in a small group.

● Think of a dramatic event in your life, for example, when you were very excited, frightened, embarrassed or surprised.

● Make notes about what happened, when it happened, and why you felt the way you did.

● Tell each other about the event, ending:

   I'd never been so … before!

1 Read and complete. For each number 1–12, choose word or phrase A, B or C.

Teen sleepwalks to top of crane

A teenage sleepwalker ___1___ after she ___2___ asleep on the arm of a 40-metre-high crane, police have ___3___ reported.

Police and firefighters ___4___ to a building site in south-east London after a passer-by ___5___ the girl on the crane. A firefighter ___6___ up and discovered the 15-year-old girl was fast asleep. He didn't want to wake her in case she panicked and fell off the crane. Luckily he ___7___ the girl's mobile phone and called her parents. They then phoned their daughter to wake her up, and she ___8___ safely down to the ground. The rescue operation lasted ___9___ two hours.

Apparently the unnamed girl ___10___ her home in the middle of the night and climbed the crane while she was asleep. An expert at the London Sleep Centre said, 'I've treated people who ___11___ cars and ridden horses while asleep. One patient has even tried to fly a helicopter. But I've ___12___ heard of a more unusual case than this.'

1	**A** rescued	**B** is rescued	**C** was rescued
2	**A** found	**B** was found	**C** were found
3	**A** ever	**B** just	**C** yet
4	**A** called	**B** was called	**C** were called
5	**A** had noticed	**B** has noticed	**C** did notice
6	**A** has climbed	**B** climbed	**C** was climbed
7	**A** found	**B** was found	**C** has found
8	**A** brought	**B** had brought	**C** was brought
9	**A** for	**B** since	**C** during
10	**A** leaves	**B** has left	**C** had left
11	**A** drive	**B** has driven	**C** have driven
12	**A** ever	**B** never	**C** yet

2 Rewrite the sentences using the present perfect with *just*.

The match began a minute ago.
The match has just begun.

1 The plane landed five minutes ago.
2 We saw the film last night.
3 It started raining a few seconds ago.
4 The students left school last month.
5 I bought some new trainers yesterday.
6 We heard the news half an hour ago.

3 Two students are going backpacking in Asia. Write sentences using the present perfect with *yet* and *already*.

buy the plane tickets
They've already bought the plane tickets.

read all the guidebooks
They haven't read all the guidebooks yet.

1 book somewhere to stay the first night ✗
2 apply for visas ✓
3 plan their route ✓
4 buy a phrasebook ✗
5 have the necessary vaccinations ✓
6 save up enough money ✓
7 pack their rucksacks ✗
8 organise travel insurance ✗

4 Ask and answer questions using the present perfect with *ever*.

Rob/try snowboarding ✗
A Has Rob ever tried snowboarding?
B No, he hasn't.

1 Sophie/go on a roller coaster ✓
2 Steve/eat sushi ✗
3 Lisa/try bungee jumping ✓
4 Julie and Simon/visit Mexico ✗
5 Lisa/win a race ✓
6 Julie and Simon/be on TV ✗

Now write sentences.

Rob has never tried snowboarding.

5 Complete with the present perfect or past simple.

A ___1___ you ever ___2___ (make) a parachute jump?
B No, I ___3___ never ___4___ (want) to. What about you?
A I ___5___ (do) it last year.
B Really? ___6___ you ___7___ (enjoy) it?
A I ___8___ (be) terrified before I ___9___ (jump). But when my parachute ___10___ (open) I ___11___ (feel) great.
B Parachute jumping isn't for me – I ___12___ (be) afraid of heights all my life!

6 Write sentences using the present perfect with *for* and *since*.

they/live in this town/1980
They've lived in this town since 1980.

1 he/have guitar lessons/six months
2 she/not/contact us/last Friday
3 I/be awake/6am
4 you/know each other/two weeks
5 my parents/be married/25 years
6 we/live here/I was born
7 you/not/go on holiday/ages
8 I/have a headache/yesterday

7 Complete with the past perfect where possible. Otherwise use the past simple.

Chris Haas, 15, __1__ (invent) the Hands-On Basketball as a school project when he __2__ (be) nine. 'The idea __3__ (be) to make an invention to help people do something better,' he remembers. Chris's father __4__ (be) a basketball coach for many years before he __5__ (retire). 'I __6__ (know) how to shoot properly because my father __7__ (teach) me,' Chris says, 'so I __8__ (paint) hands on a basketball to show the other players how to hold it.' No one __9__ (think) of this before, and Chris __10__ (sell) his idea to a big company. He __11__ (not expect) to make a lot of money, but last year he __12__ (earn) $50,000 from his invention.

8 Think about life 300 years ago. Write sentences about what people used to do and didn't use to do.

travel by plane
They didn't use to travel by plane.

1 drive cars
2 travel by boat
3 cook food over a fire
4 buy frozen food
5 send emails
6 listen to the radio
7 read by candlelight
8 wash clothes by hand

9 Write sentences using the past simple passive.

the vacuum cleaner/invent/Herbert Booth/1901
The vacuum cleaner was invented by Herbert Booth in 1901.

1 radium/discover/Marie and Pierre Curie/1898
2 the first printed books/produce/China
3 the electric light bulb/invent/Swan and Edison/1879
4 Mount Everest/first climb/Tenzing and Hillary/1953
5 mobile phones/first use/1978
6 the London underground/open/1863
7 the first colour photos/take/James Maxwell/1861
8 potatoes/bring/to Europe/the 16th century

VOCABULARY

10 Complete with ten of these words.

accident award brick carpet cans
float habit headache inspiration
kite medal metal mend tyre

1 You can't fly a _____ if there's no wind.
2 A carpenter managed to _____ the broken chair.
3 A beautiful Indian _____ covered the floor.
4 Could I have two _____ of cola, please?
5 Smoking is a very dangerous _____.
6 It's easier to _____ in the sea than in a freshwater pool.
7 He had a motorbike _____ but luckily he wasn't hurt.
8 It must be wonderful to win an Olympic® gold _____.
9 They say genius is one per cent _____, and 99 per cent hard work.
10 She was delighted to win an _____ for her first novel.

11 Match these words with their definitions.

blind combine deaf entertain foreigner
recycle reduce simplify sphere vehicle

1 give a performance that people enjoy
2 bring or put together
3 something round, like a ball
4 unable to see
5 unable to hear
6 process waste so it can be used again
7 machine that travels on roads
8 opposite of *increase*
9 person from another country
10 make easier or less complicated

12 Match the words in list A with the words and phrases in list B.

A	B
1 become	a candle
2 do	by 50%
3 earn	damage
4 light	of an idea
5 perform	a language
6 reduce	money
7 think	in a play
8 translate	underwater
9 swim	well known

PREVIEW

COMMUNICATIVE AIMS
LEARNING HOW TO ...

1 Report requests and commands
2 Report what someone said
3 Report what someone asked
4 Criticise past actions
5 Talk about imaginary or unlikely situations
6 Give advice
7 Ask for agreement and check information

TOPICS AND VOCABULARY

Animals
Language
Phrasal verbs: opposites
Communication technology
Phrasal verbs with *go*
Water
Geographical features
Weather and climate
Illnesses and ailments
Survival kit
Buildings

A

They should have thought about the human cost.

B

You'd like to stay there, wouldn't you?

C

Ray said that inventing email had been a fun thing to do.

1 Match six of the communicative aims (1–7) with the pictures (A–F).

2 Complete the words and put them into categories.

> Animals

> Geographical features

> Weather and climate

b_ar cr_codile d_sert el_phant
for_st g_rilla k_ngaroo lak_
m_nsoon mo_ntain p_g r_in
r_ver s_nshine t_mperature
th_nderstorm w_terfall w_nd

3 🔘 3.01 Listen to extracts 1–3 from Units 7 and 8. Match them with A–C below.

A A description of a building
B A news report about an accident
C An interview about email

D

She asked him to get a ball.

E

They asked what he called his windmill.

F

What would you do if you were in a forest fire?

4 Do the news survey with three other students.

NEWS SURVEY

How do you usually get news about …?

➡ **School**
➡ **Family**
➡ **Local events**
➡ **Sport**
➡ **National events**
➡ **World events**

Which type of news is most important to you?

Tell another group about the results of your survey.

Believe it or not!

Oceans and seas cover 70% of the Earth's surface, with an average depth of about 3,700 metres, and they contain over 50% of all life on Earth!

1 OPENER

How much do you know about animal communication? Read these statements and decide: true or false?

1 Some dogs can understand over 100 words.
2 Dolphins, bats and many birds can copy sounds that they hear.
3 Some apes and monkeys can use and understand simple grammar.
4 Camels communicate across long distances by singing.

Now look at the photos. What kind of bird is it? What kind of animal is it? What do you think they can do?

2 READING

🔘 3.02 Read *Animal Talk*. What is the most surprising information in the text?

AFTER READING

3 Complete with Alex, Kanzi or Koko.

1 _____ uses sign language.
2 _____ could speak.
3 _____ uses a computer.
4 _____ could say about 150 words.
5 _____ understands about 2,000 words.
6 _____ watches films on TV.
7 _____ could count.
8 _____ invents words.
9 _____ has been on TV.

Animal Talk

'Calm down!' said Alex. 'Don't tell me to calm down!' replied Irene. Husband and wife? Brother and sister? No, Alex was an African grey parrot and Dr Irene Pepperberg trained him to talk – he had a vocabulary of about 150 words when he died in 2007. Alex could also count up to six, and identify shapes, colours and materials. And he had a close relationship with Dr Pepperberg. When she had to leave Alex with the vet for an operation, he asked her not to go. 'Stop!' he screamed. 'I love you! Come back!'

Apes are also famous for learning human language. Koko, a gorilla who was taught sign language, has learnt more than 1,000 signs and can understand about 2,000 English words. She also makes up words, for example, 'finger bracelet' (ring) and 'white tiger' (zebra). She has even done an Internet 'chat'! But one of the most famous animal 'language learners' is Kanzi, a bonobo chimpanzee, who communicates by touching symbols on a computer.

Kanzi has a vocabulary of over 3,000 words, and he responds to an enormous number of spoken commands and questions. In one test, the researcher, Dr Savage-Rumbaugh, asked him to wash a potato, and then she told him to turn off the water. She asked him to get a ball, and told him to take a red ball into the office. She told him to put a tomato in the fridge and to put a key in the fridge. Kanzi responded correctly to 74 per cent of 660 requests and instructions.

Kanzi is clearly a remarkable chimp. Once, Dr Savage-Rumbaugh's keys were stolen by another chimp at the research centre. She asked Kanzi to get them back for her. Kanzi went to talk to the guilty chimp, and brought back the stolen keys. And when he's relaxing, Kanzi likes watching TV – Tarzan is one of his favourite movies. Kanzi has also been on TV himself, on the Oprah Winfrey Show.

But can animals really learn and use language? If your parrot tells you not to be silly, it's probably because the parrot has often heard the phrase 'Don't be silly!' And critics believe that it's artificial to test apes on human language – they have their own natural way of communicating. Perhaps we should spend more time trying to understand how animals communicate with each other, instead of teaching them to communicate with us.

4 Which of these sentences are requests and which are commands? Match them with the reported requests and commands in the text.

1 'Put the tomato in the refrigerator.'
2 'Take the red ball into the office.'
3 'Can you get the ball?'
4 'Turn the water off.'
5 'Please would you get my keys back?'

Your response Do you think it's useful or ethical to try to teach animals human language? In what ways could it help/harm animals to teach them to communicate with humans?

5 PRONUNCIATION

🔘 3.03 Listen and repeat.

> **Linking**
> She had to leave Alex with the vet for an operation.
> She also makes up words, for example, 'white tiger'.
> She has even done an Internet chat!
> He responds to an enormous number …
> She asked him to get a ball.
> Can animals really learn and use language?

6 LISTENING

🔘 3.04 Listen to a researcher talking to a chimp called Charlie, and look at these sentences. Make a note of the mistake in each sentence.

1 'Charlie, can you pick up the red box?'
2 'No, don't eat the banana.'
3 'Take off my shoe, Charlie.'
4 'Charlie, would you put the ball on the desk?'
5 'Could you open the window, please, Charlie?'
6 'No, please don't stand on the table.'

Now ask and answer.

A Did she ask Charlie to pick up the red box?
B No, she asked him to …

7 VOCABULARY

Match the phrases 1–6 with their opposites a–f. How many of the phrasal verbs can you find in this lesson?

> **Word Bank** Phrasal verbs: opposites
>
> | | | | |
> |---|---|---|---|
> | 1 | Put it on. | a | Bring it back. |
> | 2 | Pick it up. | b | Come back. |
> | 3 | Go away. | c | Put it down. |
> | 4 | Stand up. | d | Turn it off. |
> | 5 | Take it away. | e | Take it off. |
> | 6 | Turn it on. | f | Sit down |

> **Extension** Look at the phrases with *it*. In each case, say what *it* could be.
>
>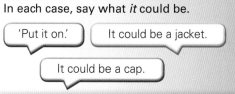
>
> 'Put it on.' It could be a jacket.
> It could be a cap.

8 SPEAKING

How often do your parents ask/tell you to do things? And how often do they ask/tell you not to do things? Tell another student, using the pictures for ideas.

They often tell me to be quiet.

9 WRITING

Write about things your parents asked/told you to do or not to do yesterday.

They asked me to turn down my music.

> ### LANGUAGE WORKOUT
>
> Complete.
>
> **Reported requests: *ask* + object + infinitive**
> 'Could you wash the potato?'
> → She _____ him _____ wash the potato.
> 'Please don't go!'
> → He asked her _____ _____ go.
>
> **Reported commands: *tell* + object + infinitive**
> 'Calm down!'
> → He _____ her _____ calm down.
> 'Don't be silly!'
> → The parrot told me _____ _____ be silly.
>
> The verb *tell* is always followed by an object.
>
> ▶**Answers and Practice**
> Language File page 119

Reporting what someone said
Reported statements: *say* and *tell*

Who put @ into email?

In English it is called simply 'at', but other languages have more interesting names. In South Africa it is 'monkey's tail'; in Denmark it is often 'pig's tail'; in France and Italy it is sometimes 'little snail'; in Greece it is 'little duck'; in Hungary it is 'worm'; in Poland it is sometimes 'little cat'; in Russia it is usually 'little dog'; in Sweden it is 'elephant's trunk' and Turkish emailers call it 'ear'.

The @ symbol is a prefix before usernames on social networking sites like Twitter, but its most common use is in email addresses. Today we talk to Ray Tomlinson, the man who put @ into email and so made it possible to send messages between computers all over the world.

Q: When and why did you invent email?

It was in 1971 and I'm not sure there was a real reason for inventing it. It was a fun thing to try out and probably took four to six hours to do. I can't remember exactly how long it took. Less than a day, spread over a week or two.

Q: How do you feel about spam and viruses?

I get annoyed when I get spam. It's a tough problem but we're going to solve it. So far the solutions aren't working – they either filter too much or not enough. We must find a better way to stop spam. Viruses are another problem and you usually get them from an email attachment. An ISP could throw away all emails with attachments, but then email wouldn't be any use. We'll have to find a solution.

Q: A lot of people say email has changed society – do you agree?

There isn't an easy answer to that. Email has had an effect, but I don't think people are really different now – they simply communicate more. Friendly people can still be friendly by email. And now it's easier to communicate with more people than before.

1 OPENER

How often do you ...

make phone calls?   write letters?
send emails?   send text messages?
use social networking sites?

Which do you do most/least often?

2 READING

What do you call the symbol @ and what is it used for?

🔘 3.05 Now read *Who put @ into email?*
What advantages and disadvantages of email does the text mention?

AFTER READING

3 True, false, or no information? Correct the false sentences.

1 Ray Tomlinson said he had invented the computer in 1971.
2 He said it was easy to invent email.
3 He told the interviewer that email was a tough problem.
4 He said that they were going to solve the problem of spam.
5 He said that solutions to spam were working.
6 He told the interviewer that email had had an effect on society.
7 He said that people didn't write so many letters now.
8 He said it was harder to communicate with more people than before.

4 Match these reported statements with Ray's words in the text.

1 Ray said that inventing email had been a fun thing to do.
2 He said he couldn't remember exactly how long it took to invent email.
3 He told the interviewer that he got annoyed when he got spam.
4 He said that they were going to find a way to solve the problem of spam.
5 He told the interviewer that they had to find a better way to stop spam.
6 He said he didn't think people were really different now.

Your response What are other advantages and disadvantages of email as a means of communication? What about text messages, instant messaging, and social networking sites? Have friendships changed because of these technologies?

5 VOCABULARY

Match these words with their definitions.

> **Word Bank** Email
>
> attachment Internet
> ISP spam virus

1 computer system which lets people worldwide exchange information
2 program which damages or destroys information on computers
3 Internet Service Provider
4 computer file sent with an email
5 'junk' emails sent to people who don't want them

6 PRONUNCIATION

🔘 3.06 Listen and repeat.

/g/ dog	/k/ dock
pig	pick
dug	duck
bag	back
game	came
good	could

Now listen and write the words you hear.

7 LISTENING

🔘 3.07 Peter is having problems with his girlfriend Natasha. Look at what Natasha said. Then listen and find out what actually happened.

What Natasha said	What happened
'I'll meet you at 8.'	She didn't turn up until …
'The film begins at 8.30.'	It started at …
'You can borrow my MP3 player.'	She lent it to …
'I've left your birthday present at home.'	She hadn't …
'I must get home early.'	She went out …
'You didn't phone me.'	Her phone was …

Now tell each other what Natasha said, and what actually happened.

> She said she would meet him at 8, but she didn't turn up until …

8 WRITING

When did you last hear good news about these topics?

> Sport Family Education Friends Music

How did you hear the news? Did someone tell you face to face, on the phone, in a letter, a text message or an email? Did you hear the news on the radio or on TV? Did you read it in the newspaper? Report what the person, programme or newspaper said.

Last night it said on TV that my team had won the match.

> **Extension** What is the most important news you have had recently? Tell another student what happened and how you heard about it.

LANGUAGE WORKOUT

Complete.

Reported statements

Direct speech	Reported speech
'I'm not sure.'	→ He said (that) he **wasn't** sure.
'I don't think people are different.'	→ He said (that) he **didn't** think people **were** different.
'The solutions aren't working.'	→ He said (that) the solutions **weren't** working.
'It took four to six hours.'	→ He said (that) it **had taken** four to six hours.
'Email has had an effect.'	→ He said (that) email **had had** an effect.
'We're going to solve it.'	→ He said (that) they **were going** to solve it.
'We must find a better way.'	→ He told her (that) they **had to** find a better way.
'I can't remember.'	→ He said (that) he **couldn't** remember.
'We'll have to find a solution.'	→ He said (that) they **would** have to find a solution.

Direct speech	Reported speech	Direct speech	Reported speech
Present simple	→ _____	am/is/are going to	→ _____
Present continuous	→ _____	must	→ _____
Past simple	→ _____	can	→ _____
Present perfect	→ _____	will	→ _____

▶**Answers and Practice**
Language File pages 119–120

They asked how he had got the idea

Reporting what someone asked
Reported questions

1 OPENER

Look at the photo. What is the boy standing in front of? What is it used for?

2 READING

3.08 Read the text. Why did William build a windmill?

3 AFTER READING

Find reported questions in the text to match these questions. Then match them with the answers.

Questions

1 Have you gone back to school?
2 How did you get the idea?
3 What do you call your windmill?
4 What else is your windmill used for?
5 Are other villages building windmills?

Answers

a He said it was called *magetsi a mphepo*, which means 'electric wind' in Chichewa, his language.
b He said that he was a student at the African Leadership Academy (ALA) in South Africa.
c He replied that it came from books he borrowed from his primary school library.
d He answered that it was early days and he wasn't sure if they were.
e He said that the people in the village used it to charge their mobile phones.

Your response Imagine you were in a village in Malawi, with no electricity or water, little food, and no money to pay for school. How would you feel? What would you do?

William Kamkwamba: *the boy who harnessed the wind*

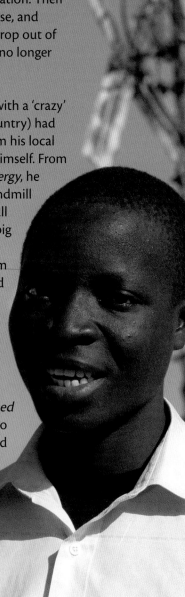

There had been no rain for months in the village of Masitala in central Malawi in southern Africa. Fourteen-year-old William Kamkwamba's family were farmers, but their crops failed because there was no water. Their small stock of food went down and down, and they had no money. Soon the family were hungry all the time, and William's dog died of starvation. Then the rain came and with it cholera and disease, and some of the villagers died. William had to drop out of secondary school because his family could no longer afford the £50 a year school fees.

But William was a remarkable young man with a 'crazy' idea. His village (like many others in the country) had no electricity. William borrowed books from his local primary school library to try and educate himself. From two books, *Exploring Physics* and *Using Energy*, he worked out how to build a home-made windmill which generated electricity. He made a small test windmill and then went ahead with a big one. He built his five-metre-high windmill from bits of his father's old bicycle, and from wood and old car parts. Soon his family had electric light and could pump water.

An interview with William in the Malawian *Daily Times* was picked up by bloggers worldwide. Since then, the media interest has been phenomenal. William has co-authored a book, *The Boy Who Harnessed The Wind*, and given dozens of TV and radio interviews. In the interviews, reporters asked the teenage inventor how he had got the idea and what else his windmill was used for. They asked what he called his windmill and if other villages were building windmills. They also wanted to know if he had gone back to school.

4 ROLE PLAY

Role play an interview between a reporter and William Kamkwamba.

The reporter asked
– how long he had worked on the windmill.
– what the villagers had thought of his 'electric wind'.
– if they had changed their minds.
– what the best thing was about his windmill.
– how he had got a place at ALA.
– if he liked being at ALA.
– if he had visited other countries.
– if he had enjoyed the conference.
– what he wanted to do next?

William said
– he had built it in three months.
– at first they had said it was magic.
– they had. Because now they could charge their mobile phones.
– it was free. All the parts were free and the wind was free.
– he had won a scholarship.
– it was great. There were students there from 53 countries.
– he had been to the USA, and to a conference in Tanzania.
– he had. He had been very scared but it had gone all right.
– he wanted to go on with his studies and get a place at a college in the USA.

> How long did you work on the windmill?

> I built it in *three* months.

🔘 3.09 Now listen and check.

5 VOCABULARY

Which of the phrasal verbs can you find in this lesson? Match the verbs with their meanings.

Word Bank Phrasal verbs with *go*

go ahead with   go away   go back
go down   go on   go up

1 rise/increase
2 start
3 fall/become less
4 leave
5 continue
6 return

Extension Write sentences using the six phrasal verbs.

6 PRONUNCIATION

Write the words in the correct column.

educate   electric   inventor   leadership
library   reporter   secondary   starvation

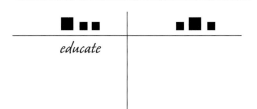

educate

🔘 3.10 Now listen and check.
Repeat the words.

7 WRITING

Ask another student about what they did last night, and note down the answers. Ask about:

Times	When did you …?
Homework	Did you …? What …?
People	Who did you …?
Food	What did you have …?
TV	Did you watch …?

Now write sentences reporting the questions and answers.

I asked Luca when he had gone to bed. He said he had gone to bed at eleven o'clock.

Extension Write sentences reporting the questions you were asked and your answers.
Luca asked me when I had gone to bed. I said I had gone to bed at half past ten.

LANGUAGE WORKOUT

Complete.

Reported questions

Direct speech		Reported speech
'Are other villages building windmills?'	→	They asked **if** other villages **were building** windmills.
'Have you gone back to school?'	→	They wanted to know ＿＿ he ＿＿ ＿＿ back to school.
'What else is your windmill used for?'	→	They asked ＿＿ else his windmill ＿＿ ＿＿ for.
'How did you get the idea?'	→	They asked ＿＿ he ＿＿ ＿＿ the idea.

In reported *Yes/No* questions, we use ＿＿ before the reported question. We don't use the auxiliary verb *do* in reported questions.

▶**Answers and Practice**
Language File pages 119–120

Telling a story

1 OPENER

Look at the newspaper headline and the photos. What do you think the newspaper story is about? Which of these words do you expect to find in it?

coastguard dinghy emergency
helicopter illness keyboard
success vet wave watertight

AMAZING RESCUE
–THANKS TO MOBILE PHONE

Two teenagers capsized in the sea off the south coast of England and called Japan on a mobile phone to ask for help.

Brother and sister Ken and Emily Booth were on a sailing holiday near Southampton. But because of huge waves, their dinghy capsized and they were thrown into the sea.

Ken, 17, and Emily, 16, spent 30 minutes trying to right the capsized dinghy, but without success. They couldn't get back into the dinghy, and they couldn't attract the attention of passing ships. After they'd been in the water for about 40 minutes, the situation was getting serious, and they felt very cold. Then Emily remembered her mobile phone in its watertight container in her pocket and reached for it.

But she didn't think of dialling 999, the emergency number. Instead she phoned their father, who was 6,000 miles away in Tokyo on a business trip. Emily explained: 'I thought it would be quicker to phone someone I knew and tell them our position. I dialled Dad's number and he contacted the coastguard.'

About ten minutes later, after they had held on to the dinghy for nearly an hour, they heard a helicopter. Next, everything happened very quickly, and Ken and Emily were picked up and carried to safety.

Afterwards, the coastguard said that the teenagers were lucky to be alive and very, very lucky that the mobile had worked. 'Anyone in trouble should contact the coastguard direct on 999,' he added.

READING

2 Read the newspaper story and answer the questions.

1 Where did Ken and Emily Booth capsize?
2 Why did their dinghy capsize?
3 How long did they spend trying to right the dinghy?
4 When did Emily remember her mobile?
5 How did they feel by then?
6 How far is Tokyo from Southampton?
7 How were the teenagers rescued?
8 What did the coastguard say anyone in trouble should do?

3 Find words in the story which mean:

1 small sailing boat *n*
2 turned over in the water *v*
3 closed so that water can't get in *adj*
4 opposite of failure *n*
5 something you can put things in *n*
6 person who helps people or ships in trouble *n*
7 opposite of danger *n*
8 get in touch with *v*
9 turn over a boat which has capsized *v*

4 **Linking words**: sequencing adverbs.
Look at the text and find these words. Notice how they are used.

> after then later next afterwards

Sequencing adverbs are like signposts. They help us to find our way through a story.

5 LISTENING

You are going to hear a radio news report which covers the same story as the newspaper. First, look at the questions in exercise 2 again.

🔘 3.11 Now listen and note down the answers from the radio news.

SPEAKING

6 Look at your answers to exercise 2 and exercise 4, and compare the newspaper and radio reports. Tell each other about the differences.

A In the newspaper, it said that Ken and Emily had capsized off the south coast of England.

B It said on the radio that they'd capsized off the south coast of Britain.

7 Look at the newspaper story again and role play the conversation between a journalist and Emily.

Journalist **Emily**

> Ask Emily where she was when they capsized.

> Reply.

> Ask why the dinghy capsized.

> Explain why.

> Ask what they did when they fell into the sea.

> Reply.

> Ask why she didn't dial 999.

> Explain why not.

> Ask how they were rescued.

> Describe what happened.

> Ask how she felt after the rescue.

> Reply.

8 GUIDED WRITING

Write your own news story about two people in an amazing rescue. Use sequencing adverbs to help readers find their way through the story. Use the newspaper story and these questions to help you.

- Who are the people and how old are they? Where are they from?
- Where were they and what were they doing when they got into trouble?
- What happened to them? Did they get lost or have an accident? Was someone injured?
- Who did they contact to ask for help? How did they make contact?
- What happened when help arrived? How were the people rescued?
- What did they say after the rescue?

Choose a headline for your story and read or show it to other students in the class. Which rescue story is the most amazing?

LEARNER INDEPENDENCE

9 You can practise reading and listening to news stories in English on the Internet. You can also learn lots of new vocabulary! The BBC has an excellent site with news stories in simple English for young people at: http://news.bbc.co.uk/cbbcnews/hi/world/

10 Word creation: Make nouns ending in *-tion* from these verbs, and complete the sentences.

> attend communicate describe inform invent invite operate situate

1 Thanks to the _____ of mobile phones, it's easier to contact people.
2 People go to hospital if they need an _____.
3 Email and text messaging are useful means of _____.
4 I waved to attract her _____, but she didn't see me.
5 What's your address? I'll send you an _____ to my party.
6 You can find out lots of _____ on the World Wide Web.
7 It's important to keep calm in a dangerous _____.
8 Did you see the robbers? Can you give me a _____ of them?

11 🔘 3.12 **Phrasebook**: Find these useful expressions in Unit 7. Then listen and repeat.

> Calm down!
> I can't remember exactly.
> I get annoyed when …
> It's a tough problem.
> There isn't an easy answer.
> How did you get the idea?
> … but without success
> It said on the radio that …

Now write a five-line dialogue using at least three of the expressions.

LANGUAGE LINKS

This leaflet tells you how to dispose of an electrical household appliance. Do you recognise some words in the different languages? What are the languages?

Which words are similar in the different languages?

Which language has the longest words? Which uses the most capital letters?

FR Participons à la protection de l'environnement!
Votre appareil contient de nombreux matériaux valorisables ou recyclables. Confiez celui-ci dans un point de collecte ou à défaut dans un centre service agréé pour que son traitement soit effectué.

GB Protect the environment!
Your appliance contains valuable materials which can be recovered or recycled. Leave it at a local civic waste collection point.

DE Schützen Sie die Umwelt!
Ihr Gerät enthalt mehrere unterschiedliche, wiederverwertbare Wertstoffe. Bitte geben Sie Ihr Gerät zum Entsorgen nicht in den Hausmüll, sondern bringen Sie es zu einer speziellen Entsorgungsstelle für Elektrokleingeräte (Wertstoffhof).

IT Partecipiamo alla protezione dell'ambiente!
Il vostro apparecchio è composto da diversi materiali che possono essere riciclati. Lasciatelo in un punto di raccolta o presso un Centro Assistenza Autorizzato.

ES ¡Participe en la conservación del medio ambiente!
Su electrodoméstico contiene materiales recuperables y/o reciclables. Entréguelo al final de su vida útil en un Centro de Recogida Específico o en uno de nuestros Servicios Oficiales Post Venta donde será tratado de forma adecuada.

TR Çevremizi koruyalım!
Kullandığınız elektronik aletler tamir edilebilinir yada geri dönüşümü olan değerli materyaller ihtiva eder. Lütfen bu tip aletleri bulunduğunuz bölgedeki atık toplama noktasına bırakın.

Look at leaflets for electrical appliances in your home. Find more words that you recognise in other languages.

SKETCH *Hotel Reception*

🔘 3.13 Read and listen.

MANAGER Good evening, sir, can I help you?
GUEST   Yes, I've booked a room for tonight.
MANAGER What's your surname?
GUEST   Watt.
MANAGER I asked what your surname was.
GUEST   My surname is Watt.
MANAGER Oh, right.
GUEST   No, my surname isn't Wright – it's Watt. W-A-T-T.
MANAGER Yes, sir. And what's your first name?
GUEST   No, I said Watt was my surname.
MANAGER Could you please tell me your first name?
GUEST   Oh, I see! It's Richard.
MANAGER Thank you, Mr Watt. Address?
GUEST   No, I don't want a dress. I want a room.
MANAGER Sir, I need to know where you live.
GUEST   I live in the USA.
MANAGER Can you be more specific?
GUEST   I live in a large apartment in Los Angeles.
MANAGER Mr Watt, please tell me your address.
GUEST   Apartment 34, 281 West 47th Street, Los Angeles.
MANAGER Thank you, sir. Here's your key. You're in room 420.
GUEST   For 20? But I booked a room for one!
MANAGER That's right, sir. Room 420 is a single room.
GUEST   A single room for 20 people – this is a very strange hotel!
MANAGER Well, Mr Watt, we have some very strange guests!

Now act out the sketch in pairs.

Game *Guess what they said*

- Work in groups of four: A, B, C and D.

- Choose a topic from this list:

  TV Sport Weather Holidays
  Music Animals People

- A writes a question about the topic for B. B writes a reply.

- C and D ask A and B up to five questions to find out what A's question was and what B's answer was. Then a new topic is chosen and A and B, C and D change roles.

  C Did you ask if he had watched the news on TV last night?
  A Yes, I did.
  D Did you say that you had?
  B Yes, I did.

REVISION

LESSON 1 Write sentences about things your teacher asked/told you to do or not to do:

- in today's lesson.
- for homework.

She asked me to hand out the photocopies.

LESSON 2 Look at exercise 7 on page 91. Write sentences about what Natasha said, and what actually happened.

She said she would meet him at 8, but she didn't turn up until 8.30.

LESSON 3 Write sentences reporting Peter's questions to Natasha.

Peter's questions
Why didn't you phone me?
What are you doing this evening?
Will you have dinner with me?
Do you like Japanese food?
Have you ever tried sushi?
How often do you eat fish?

He asked why ...

EXTENSION

LESSON 1 Write five requests beginning *Can/Could/Will/Would you ...?* Then exchange your requests with another student, and write sentences reporting your partner's requests.

Could you lend me your mobile phone?
Petra asked me to lend her my mobile phone.

LESSON 2 Complete these questions. Then ask two or three other students the questions and write sentences reporting their answers.

What's your favourite ...?   What happened ...?

Do you like ...?   Have you ever ...?

Where are you going ...?

Adam said his favourite sport was basketball.

LESSON 3 Look at exercise 7 on page 93. Ask three students similar questions about last weekend and write sentences reporting the questions and answers.

I asked Barbara when she had gone to bed on Saturday. She said she had gone to bed at midnight.

YOUR CHOICE!

CONSTRUCTION Reported speech

Put the words in the right order.

1 window to the he her close asked
2 not I shout him to asked
3 told be teacher the to them quiet
4 mind she rain she didn't said the that
5 was I that taxi told waiting the them
6 to us told we hurry you that had
7 time asked was she the what him
8 right wanted he the was answer know if to

REFLECTION Reported speech

Match the examples a–j with the language functions 1–4.

Reported speech is used to report:

1 Requests   2 Commands   3 Statements   4 Questions

a His father told him not to be late.
b She said he couldn't remember anything.
c He asked what her mobile number was.
d He said that there would be another bus soon.
e She asked me to buy some bread.
f He told the class to stop talking.
g I asked him not to forget.
h She said that she had won the competition.
i She told them it was going to be a great party.
j They wanted to know if he needed some help.

ACTION Game: *Blind walking*

- Work in pairs A and B. A closes his/her eyes or puts on a blindfold.

- B asks A to stand up, move around the room and sit down somewhere else, using *Can/Could/Will/Would you ...?*

  Can you take three steps forward?
  Would you turn left?

- A must keep his/her eyes closed, but can ask questions.

  A Sorry, what did you say?
  B I asked you to turn left.

- B mustn't touch A or let A bump into objects or other students.

INTERACTION Be your parent!

- Work in a small group. Choose to role play being your father or mother.

- Ask two or three 'parents' in your group about their son/daughter. Ask what he/she is like at home and what they hope he/she will do in the future.

- In your role as your mother/father, report to the group what you learnt from the other 'parents'.

  You said your son was always polite and helpful!

GLOBAL ENGLISH

1 _____

There's a cheer in the busy elementary school classroom in Sapporo, Japan. Junko, the teacher, has just said 'Right, class, it's DEAR time!'. Twenty-eight eight-to-nine-year-olds smile and chatter as they stop what they're doing and take out their English storybooks. DEAR stands for 'Drop Everything And Read' and Junko's class do this for five minutes every day. 'The kids love it,' she comments, 'and they take the books home to finish them. It makes English seem real – not just another school subject.' As in many other countries, English has recently become a compulsory part of the Japanese elementary school curriculum.

2 _____

With the spread of English around the world, new varieties of the language have developed. Take Singapore, for example, where the local variety of English is called 'Singlish'. The population of Singapore comes from a number of different ethnic groups – 76.8% Chinese, 13.9% Malay, 7.9% Indian and 1.4% others. English is used for communication between the different ethnic groups and for international business and tourism. Singlish includes words from the local languages, but also gives new meanings to existing English words. For example, in English the adjective 'solid' means 'hard or firm', but in Singlish it means 'great', as in 'Did you see that goal! Really solid!' And the Singlish word for 'fantastic' comes from the Malay language, _shiok_, as in 'That soup was shiok!'

3 _____

Hani is Swedish and works for an international pharmaceutical company in the German-speaking part of Switzerland. 'Our parent company is in France,' she says, 'but the official company language is English. Almost all written communication is in English and so are our meetings. When the only people present are Swiss, they naturally speak Swiss-German, but if I join them, they switch to English. They say it's to show that they're not talking about me behind my back! Most of the people I work with here speak at least three languages well.'

Martin from the UK teaches at a university in Antwerp in Belgium. 'The main language here is Flemish,' he explains, 'which is very close to Dutch. I'm trying to learn it, but all my classes are in English.' Martin's students come from all over the world. 'And most of them don't speak much Flemish either,' Martin adds.

4 ___

India is a multi-lingual country with 6,661 mother tongues, 25 different writing systems, and 22 main languages, with English as an 'additional' language. The Indian education system is the largest in the world – India has 50% more children than China – and there are 1.2 million schools, 6 million teachers and 250 million students. Many states in India have started teaching English in the first class of primary school, and others have schools where subjects are studied in English. Why? 'Because the parents demand it,' an official said. 'And if we don't provide it, parents who can afford the fees will send their children to private schools.'

Two leading Indian businessmen explain why English is so important. Manish Sabharwal, the chairman of a recruitment agency, puts it like this: 'English is like Microsoft® Windows®. It's an operating system.' And Nandan Nilekani, co-founder of Infosys Technologies, says 'I believe that English is about access. I have always argued for the teaching of English to everybody so they get access to modern society.'

1 READING

Read the text and match four of these headings with paragraphs 1–4.

> Working in English   Young readers of English
> Computers   Reasons for teaching English
> Number of learners of English
> New kinds of English   Teacher training

○ 3.14 Now listen and check.

2

Answer the questions with information from the box.

> *How many?* 1.2 million 76.8 6,661 *Where?*
> Belgium India Japan Singapore Switzerland

1 What percentage of the population of Singapore is Chinese?
2 Where do people with different first languages use English as a working language?
3 In which country do international students study in English?
4 How many different languages are spoken in India?
5 How many schools are there in India?
6 Which two countries have recently started teaching English to young learners?

3 VOCABULARY

Match these words with their definitions.

1 global *adj*
2 compulsory *adj*
3 curriculum *n*
4 ethnic group *n*
5 switch *v*
6 demand *v*
7 operating system *n*
8 founder *n*

a subjects studied at school
b worldwide
c software that tells a computer what to do
d someone who starts an organisation or business
e people who have the same culture, language and traditions
f something that has to be done because of a rule or law
g say firmly that you want something
h change

4 MINI-PROJECT
Learning languages

Work with another student and make notes about language learning in your country. Check your facts in the library or on the Internet.

● What languages do students learn at school?
● Do you have to learn particular languages, or can you choose?
● At what age do students start language learning?
● For how many years do students study languages?
● What language examinations can they take?
● How could the teaching of languages be improved?

Work together and use your notes to write a report about language learning in your country. Read your work carefully and correct any mistakes. Then compare your report with other students.

They should have thought ...

Criticising past actions
should(n't) have/ought to have

1 OPENER

Do the *Water Facts Quiz*: choose A, B or C.

⊙ 3.15 Now listen and check.

2 READING

⊙ 3.16 Read *Water is Life.* What two problems is Kate Ellis concerned about?

Water Facts Quiz

1 How much of the water on Earth is salt water, which humans can't drink?
   A 97.5%   **B** 95%   **C** 92.5%
2 Most fresh water can't be used because it's frozen in the polar ice caps. So how much of the world's fresh water is available for use?
   A 10%   **B** 5%   **C** 1%
3 For how many days can humans live without water?
   A 3   **B** 5   **C** 7
4 The average amount of water needed to produce a kilo of potatoes is 1,000 litres. How many litres of water does it take to produce a kilo of beef?
   A 17,500   **B** 29,500   **C** 42,500
5 What is the recommended minimum amount of water per person per day for cooking, drinking and personal hygiene?
   A 30 litres   **B** 50 litres   **C** 70 litres
6 The average US citizen uses 500 litres of water a day, and the average UK citizen uses 200 litres a day. How many litres of water a day does the average citizen of the Gambia in West Africa use?
   A 2.5   **B** 4.5   **C** 10.5

Water is Life

We interviewed environmental campaigner Kate Ellis about lessons we can learn from the past.

Q Why are you so concerned about water?
A Because it's essential to life. Water will be as important in the twenty-first century as oil was in the twentieth. By 2025 two-thirds of the world's population may face a shortage of water.

Q So what are governments doing about it?
A They've known about the problem for a long time. They started building more large dams to store water in the 1990s. But there have been many mistakes.

Q What kind of mistakes?
A By the end of the twentieth century there were more than 50,000 large dams on more than half the world's major rivers. These dams have wiped out species, flooded huge areas of land and displaced tens of millions of people.

Q In other words, you think governments shouldn't have built so many dams.
A That's right. They should have thought about the human cost and they ought to have considered the environmental consequences. Dams can be used to generate electricity as well as to store water, and they're positive aspects. But I'm worried that more dam building projects are underway now, for example in Africa, when people should have learnt lessons from the mistakes of the past.

3 AFTER READING

Match the questions with the answers. There are three wrong answers.

1 How many people may not have enough water by 2025?
2 What did governments do in the 1990s about the future water shortage?
3 What are two of the good things about large dams?
4 How many people have lost their homes because of dam building?
5 Why does Kate think governments shouldn't have built so many dams?

a They take a long time to build and a lot of people are needed to work on them.
b Because of their effect on the people and the countryside around them.
c They started building more large dams.
d Half of the people in the world.
e They store water and can generate electricity.
f Tens of millions.
g Because they are very expensive.
h 66% of the people on Earth.

Your response Was there anything in the quiz or interview which surprised you? How much water do you think you have used today? What is your government doing about water shortage?

4 SPEAKING

Say what these people should and/or shouldn't have done to save water this week, using these phrases.

use a hosepipe   go to a public swimming pool
save the rainwater   turn off the tap
wash the car every day   have a shower
have a bath   use a watering can

5 PRONUNCIATION

3.17 Listen and repeat.

/dʒ/   /ʃ/   /tʃ/
George shouldn't have watched the shark chew the ship – he should have jumped in shouting 'Jaws!' and punched it.

6 SPEAKING

Think about situations in your life when you did or didn't do things which you are not happy about now. Make notes under these headings and then tell another student about them.

Age *12*
Situation *Shop*
What I did/didn't do
Saw friend steal a CD but didn't tell anyone.
What I should/shouldn't have done
Told him to put the CD back.

One day, when I was 12, I was in a record shop. I saw one of my friends steal a CD, but I didn't say anything. I should have told him to put the CD back.

Extension Think about situations where things went wrong and mistakes were made. Tell another student what the people involved should have done.

7 WRITING

Write two paragraphs about the situations in exercise 6, one paragraph about yourself and one about the student you talked to.

LANGUAGE WORKOUT

Complete.

should(n't) have/ought to have
They should _____ thought about the human cost.
Governments _____ _____ built so many dams.
They _____ _____ _____ considered the environmental consequences.

We can use *should have* or *ought to have* with the same meaning. The negative forms are *shouldn't have* and *oughtn't to have* (not *ought to haven't*).

▶**Answers and Practice**
Language File page 120

What would you do?

Talking about imaginary or unlikely situations
Giving advice
Second conditional

SURVIVAL QUESTIONNAIRE
What would you do to survive in these situations?

1 What would you do in the desert if you didn't have enough water?
A I'd eat a lot because there's water in food.
B I wouldn't eat and I'd breathe through my nose.
C I'd walk as fast as possible and look for an oasis.

2 What if you were in an area where there were lots of snakes?
A I'd walk as quietly as possible.
B I'd wait until it was dark before moving.
C I'd make as much noise as I could with my feet.

3 What if you were outside in a thunderstorm and lightning was near?
A If I were near a big tree, I'd stand under it for shelter.
B I'd join other people and ask everyone to hold hands.
C I'd take off all metal objects and crouch on the ground.

4 If you were lost in a forest without a phone, how would you let your friends know where you were?
A I'd shout 'Help!' as loudly as I could in a deep voice.
B I'd scream really loudly.
C I'd whistle loudly and as high as possible.

5 What would you do if you were out walking and met a bear?
A I'd run away as fast as I could.
B I wouldn't run, I'd back away slowly.
C I'd climb up the nearest tree.

6 If you had to cross a fast river with waist-high water, which way would you face?
A I'd face upstream.
B I'd face the opposite bank.
C I'd face downstream.

7 What would you do if you were in a forest fire?
A I'd run uphill to get as high as I could.
B I'd work out which way the wind was blowing, and run in the same direction.
C I'd run away from the fire towards a wide road or a river.

1 OPENER

Look at the pictures in the *Survival Questionnaire*. Which of these words do you expect to find in the questionnaire?

bear desert fire forest ice jungle
lightning mountain oasis river
snow thunderstorm waterfall wind

2 READING

Read and answer the questionnaire. Compare your answers with other students.

3 AFTER READING

Turn to page 121 and find out your score. Compare your scores with other students

Your response Would you enjoy the challenge of these survival situations, or would you be frightened?

4 LISTENING

🔘 3.18 Julie gave Simon the questionnaire. Listen and write down his answers. What's his score?

5 SPEAKING

Ask and answer questions about these imaginary situations. What would you say and do? How would you feel?

1 You meet an alien.
2 You're stuck in a lift.
3 You win a million dollars.
4 You lose your bag.
5 You see a ghost.
6 You meet your favourite star.

If I met an alien, I'd invite it home for tea.

Extension Think of three more imaginary situations and ask a student what they would say, do and feel.

8 **If you were on a steep hill covered in large slippery rocks, what would be the safest way to climb it?**
A I'd take off my boots and socks, and climb barefoot.
B I'd keep my socks and boots on.
C I'd take off my boots but keep my socks on.

9 **If you were lost in a forest and very hungry, how would you decide which plants were safe to eat?**
A I'd take a small leaf or berry and put it on my lip for five minutes.
B I'd look and see what the birds were eating and do the same.
C I'd eat all the plants except those with red or purple berries.

10 **What would you do if you were in a boat on the edge of a waterfall?**
A I'd jump out of the boat and go over the waterfall feet first.
B I'd jump out of the boat and dive over the waterfall.
C I wouldn't jump. I'd stay in the boat and hold on tight.

6 LISTENING

🔘 3.19 Look at these phrases, and listen to the advice given to people with problems 1–6. Match the phrases with the problems.

lie down   take more exercise   see a dentist
take an aspirin   stop talking   count sheep
take a deep breath and count to 100
go to bed later   drink a glass of water
eat lots of oranges   drink hot lemon and honey
read a boring book

1   I've got hiccoughs.
2   I've got toothache.
3   I think I'm getting a cold.
4   I can't get to sleep at night.
5   I've got a headache.
6   I've got a cough and a sore throat.

Extension Do you agree with the advice you heard? Give your advice in response to the problems using *If I were you, I'd/I wouldn't …* You can add your own ideas.

7 PRONUNCIATION

Which of these words contain the sound /f/?

cough   enough   ghost   hiccough   high   laugh
lightning   night   thought   through   tight   weight

🔘 3.20 Listen and check. Repeat the words.

8 SPEAKING

Imagine you were going backpacking with another student, and you could only take *ten* of these items with you. Which items would you take and why?

Word Bank Survival kit

a box of matches   candles   a compass   a camera
a first aid kit   insect spray   a magnifying glass   a map
a mobile   a needle and thread   a pencil and paper
a penknife   plastic bags   a radio   safety pins
a small mirror   a spoon   sun cream   sunglasses
a torch   an umbrella   a water bottle   a whistle

> If we took a box of matches, we could light a fire.

Now tell other students which items you would take.

> We'd take a box of matches so we could light a fire.

9 WRITING

A British friend of yours is going on a camping holiday in your country next week and asks your advice about what to take. Write some helpful advice – and think about the weather!

If I were you, I'd take some insect spray. There are lots of mosquitoes at this time of the year.

LANGUAGE WORKOUT

Complete.

Second conditional
If + past simple, would(n't) …

If I **met** a bear, I **would run away** as fast as I could.
If I **were** near a big tree, I _____ _____ under it for shelter.
If I _____ on the edge of a waterfall, I _____n't _____ out of the boat.
What _____ you _____ if you _____n't _____ enough water?
What _____ you _____ outside in a thunderstorm?

We use the second conditional to talk about imaginary present or unlikely future situations.

▶**Answers and Practice**
Language File page 120

You'd like to stay there, wouldn't you?

Asking for agreement and checking information
Question tags

1 OPENER

Match these buildings with the photos.

> exhibition pavilion   hotel
> igloo   museum   skyscraper

LISTENING

2 🔘 3.21 Sophie is looking at a website about unusual buildings with her boyfriend Zak. Listen and number the photos in the order you hear about them.

A

B

C

D

E

3 ⊙ 3.22 Listen to five extracts from the recording in exercise 2 and choose the correct answer.

1 The modern art museum is in Athens/Vienna.
2 The skyscraper is in Dubai/Shanghai and is 828/1,828 metres high.
3 The exhibition pavilion changed colour/shape when people moved around in it.
4 The hotel suite is in Greece/Italy. It's called the Governor Villa and costs £4,500/£5,400 a night.
5 The world's biggest igloo is 14/40 metres round, 12 metres across and 5 metres high. It's in Puvirnituq in northern/southern Canada.

Your response Which of the places in the photos would you like to visit and why? What's your favourite building in your town/country?

4 PRONUNCIATION

⊙ 3.23 Complete with these question tags, and then listen and check your answers. Repeat the sentences.

> can it   did she   didn't he
> do you   doesn't he   isn't it
> weren't they   would he

1 The hotel room is in Athens, _____?
2 You don't know what that is, _____?
3 The photos were of special places, _____?
4 Zak asked Sophie about the photos, _____?
5 Sophie didn't expect Zak to know about the tallest skyscraper, _____?
6 Zak wouldn't like to stay in the Governor Villa, _____?
7 Zak likes the modern art museum, _____?
8 The igloo can't hold 500 people, _____?

We use question tags with falling intonation to ask for agreement, and with rising intonation to check information. Which of the sentences have falling intonation and which have rising intonation?

5 SPEAKING

Do the *Inspiration Quiz* without looking back in the book. Discuss your answers with another student using question tags. Then look back and check your answers.

INSPIRATION QUIZ

1 Where was Bethany Hamilton bitten by a shark?
2 How many languages does Ziad Youssef Fazah claim to speak?
3 Who invented BookCrossing?
4 Which planet is closest to the Sun?
5 What will the population of the world be in 2050?
6 What was the big house in *Rebecca* called?
7 Who rode round the world on motorbikes?
8 How many gold medals did Usain Bolt win in Beijing?
9 What things did Leonardo da Vinci invent?
10 How many words could Alex the parrot say?
11 Who invented email?
12 What did William Kamkwamba call his invention?

A It was on an island, wasn't it?
B It begins with H, doesn't it?

> **Extension** Make your own five-question *Inspiration Quiz* and ask another student to do it.

6 WRITING

Write two paragraphs describing other people, places or things in *New Inspiration 3* without giving their names. Then read out your paragraphs. Can the other students guess who or what they are about?

It's a beautiful old town in the Andes mountains. You walk along the Inca trail until you find the city high up on the edge of a mountain.

LANGUAGE WORKOUT

Complete.

Question tags
You can see that, _____ you?
You'd like to stay there, _____ you?
It's been in the news, _____ it?
You didn't expect me to know that, _____ you?
Zak thinks the modern art museum is cool, **doesn't** he?
They looked at the website, **didn't** they?

Affirmative statement → negative tag
Negative statement → affirmative tag

▶**Answers and Practice**
Language File page 120

AUSTRALIA

1 Australia is the largest island, the smallest continent, and the sixth largest country in the world – its area is 7,686,900 square km. It lies to the south of Asia between the Indian and Pacific Oceans. The population of Australia is 22 million and the capital city is Canberra. The official language is English and the currency is the Australian dollar.

2 The Aborigines have lived in Australia for about 50,000 years. There are now only around 250,000 Aboriginal Australians and the government is making major efforts to preserve their culture. Over 70% of Australians live in cities or towns, mostly on the south-east and south-west coasts. The largest (and oldest) city is Sydney, with a population of 4.5 million.

3 Australia is famous for its 'outback', the hot dry land of the interior – about two-thirds of the country is rocky desert or semi-desert. On the eastern coastal plains there are grasslands, largely watered by Australia's longest river, the Murray-Darling (3,696km). Australia also has mountain ranges; its highest mountain is Mount Kosciuszko (2,228m) in the south-east. The island of Tasmania lies off the south-east coast, and off the north-east coast is the Great Barrier Reef. This coral reef is over 2,000km long, and it's the largest living structure in the world!

4 Well-known Australian animals include the kangaroo, koala and platypus, and birds such as the emu and the 'laughing' kookaburra. The tropical rainforests in the north have a huge variety of birds, crocodiles, poisonous spiders and snakes. And the Great Barrier Reef is home to hundreds of sharks and thousands of tropical fish.

5 The typical climate is warm, with lots of sunshine and little rain. Average temperatures in Sydney are 8–16°C in July and 18–26°C in January. Much of the Australian interior has a continental climate, with high temperatures during the day which drop considerably at night. There are often monsoons in the tropical north, and hurricanes and cyclones on the north-east and north-west coasts. But droughts are also common – a third of the country has under 26mm of rain a year!

1 OPENER

Which of these words do you associate with Australia? Which do you associate with Canada? Which words refer to weather?

| coral reef   cyclone   desert   drought |
| forest   grasslands   ice   monsoon |
| outback   prairie   rainforest   tundra |

READING

2 Read the description of Australia and match five of these headings with paragraphs 1–5.

| Geography   Industry and agriculture |
| Key facts   The people   Weather   Wildlife |

3.24 Now listen and check.

3 Student A   Ask Student B questions 1–7 about Australia.
Student B   Find the answers as quickly as possible!

1 How big is Australia?
2 What's its capital city?
3 How many Aborigines live there today?
4 What's the population of Sydney?
5 What's the highest mountain?
6 What's special about the Great Barrier Reef?
7 What's Australia's typical climate like?

Now change roles. Ask and answer questions 8–14.

8 What's the population of Australia?
9 How long have the Aborigines lived there?
10 How many Australians live in cities and towns?
11 What's the longest river?
12 Where is Tasmania?
13 Name two Australian animals and two birds.
14 Where are monsoons common?

4 LISTENING

🔘 3.25   Look at the factfile and listen to a description of Canada.

Student A Complete the notes in the yellow sections.
Student B Complete the notes in the blue sections.

CANADA FACTFILE

Area: _____ million square km   **Population:** _____
Capital: Ottawa   **Official languages:** English, _____
Currency: Canadian _____

Number of Native Canadians: _____
_____% of Canadians live in cities/towns.
_____% live within 200km of US border.
Largest city: Toronto (_____ million)

_____ **Canada:** mainly forest, tundra, ice and snow
_____ **Canada:** Rocky Mountains
Highest mountain: Mount Logan (_____m)
West-central Canada: prairie grassland
_____-**central plains:** major industrial areas
Most _____ river: St Lawrence.
_____ **river:** Mackenzie (4,241km)
Niagara Falls: _____ falls in the world
Also _____ lakes, over 60% of the world's lakes

Canadian wildlife: polar _____, moose, caribou, elk, brown bear, grizzly bear, wild cats, _____ off east/west coasts
Over _____ different kinds of birds

_____ **Canada:** short hot summers, long cold winters
East and _____ coasts: warmer winters, cooler summers
Ottawa temperatures: January –6 to –15°C; July 15 to _____°C
_____ **Canada:** extremely cold all year
West and south-east Canada: a lot of _____; other areas much drier

5 SPEAKING

Students A and B work together. Use your notes from exercise 4 to tell each other about Canada. If you could visit either Australia or Canada, which would you choose? Tell each other why.

6 GUIDED WRITING

Write a description of your country or a country which you are interested in. Use the headings and the text about Australia to help you.

LEARNER INDEPENDENCE

7 Where can you read or hear English outside school? Tick the chart and add more ideas if possible.

	Read	Hear
in shops		
in restaurants/cafés		
in hotels		
at the travel agent's		
in museums		
at the cinema		
on TV/on the radio		
on the Internet		
at the railway station		

Now compare your chart with another student. Give examples of things you can you see/hear in English, for example:

notices and signs   brochures
announcements
news programmes

8 Word creation: Complete the chart with adjectives ending in -al.

Noun	Adjective
centre	
coast	
continent	
electric	
environment	
globe	
music	
nature	
office	
tropics	

9 🔘 3.26   Phrasebook:
Listen and repeat these useful expressions.

What would you do?
What if ...?
If I were you, I'd ...
I've got hiccoughs.
I've got toothache.
I've got a headache.
I get it.
You must be joking.

Now think of three different ways to complete the two incomplete expressions.

Inspiration EXTRA!

PROJECT *Extreme places*

1 Work in a group and make a list of extreme places – parts of the world which are difficult to live in. They can be difficult because they are very hot, cold, wet or dry, or because they are very high, or very remote. Then choose two to write about.

2 Research: Find out information about each place and make notes.

- Where is it? Who lives there?
  What language(s) do they speak?
- What is the landscape like? (Jungle, desert, or ice and snow? Are there hills, rivers, lakes, trees?)
  What kind of wildlife is there?
- What is the weather like? Maximum and minimum temperatures?
- How do you get there?
- What's good about the place?
  What problems are there?

3 Work together and use your notes to write about the extreme places. Read your work carefully and correct any mistakes. Find photographs from magazines or online for your project. Show your work to the other groups.

Tristan da Cunha is the most remote inhabited group of islands in the world. It is in the middle of the South Atlantic Ocean, about halfway between South Africa and Argentina, and under 300 people live on the largest of the six islands. They speak a dialect of English.

The islands are volcanic with rocky coastlines and steep cliffs. There are few trees but there is plenty of wildlife, including many species of birds and sea creatures. The weather is often very wet with up to 200cm of rain a year, but it is never extremely hot or cold.

Tristan da Cunha has no airport, so the only way to get there is by boat – the trip takes about a week from South Africa. The islands are very beautiful and life is very quiet – some of the young people who live there think it is much too quiet!

Game *Word Race*

- Work in small groups.
- Choose a topic from this list. Then each write down as many words as you can about that topic in one minute.

  Buildings Communication Illness
  School Water Weather

- Compare your results and make sure all the words are to do with the topic. Then check the meanings of the words other students have which you don't. The student with the most words wins.

Limerick

🔘 3.27 Read and listen.

There was a young woman called Mabel

Who wanted to dance on the table.

'Don't know if I should

I would if I could

But I'm not sure if I'm able.'

REVISION

LESSON 1 Your friend Max is always in trouble. This is what happened yesterday morning. Write sentences telling him what he should and shouldn't have done.

He was late for school because he missed the bus.
He missed the bus because he got up late.
He got up late because he didn't wake up on time.
He didn't wake up on time because he forgot to set his alarm clock.
He didn't remember to set it because he went to bed very late.

You shouldn't have been late for school. You ...

LESSON 2 Write sentences saying what you would feel and what you would do in these imaginary situations.

You're lost in a strange town.
You're on a train and you've lost your ticket.
You've revised for the wrong questions in an exam.
You've chosen clothes in a shop but then find you don't have any money on you.

If I were lost in a strange town, I would ...

LESSON 3 Write a paragraph describing a person or place in your country. Read out your paragraph but don't say the name for the person or place. Can the other students guess who or what it is?

EXTENSION

LESSON 1 Think about situations where a friend or member of your family forgot something, made a mistake or did something wrong. Write sentences about what they should or shouldn't have done.

My friend Tim should have said sorry when he forgot to meet me.

LESSON 2 Imagine that you were head or director of your school for a day. Write sentences saying what things you would change and why.

First of all, I would pay the teachers a lot more because teaching us is hard work.

LESSON 3 Look back through *New Inspiration 3*. Which lessons did you enjoy most and why? Which lessons were more difficult and why? Then work with another student and guess which lessons they enjoyed most or found more difficult, and why.

> You really enjoyed the lesson about describing pictures, didn't you? I think it's because you like art.

YOUR CHOICE!

CONSTRUCTION Question tags

Complete with the correct question tag.

1 The teenagers were lucky to be alive, _____?
2 She'd been a surfer for a long time, _____?
3 You'd like to go up the skyscraper, _____?
4 He's been a runner for years, _____?
5 It's the best lesson in the book, _____?
6 She understands 2,000 words, _____?
7 She asked Kanzi to get the keys, _____?
8 He would run away, _____?

REFLECTION Question tags

Match the beginnings of the rules with the endings.

1 In the present simple we make the tag
2 In the past simple we make the tag
3 When the main verb is *be* in the present and past simple, we make the tag
4 In the present perfect and past perfect we make the tag

a with *is/isn't, are/aren't, was/wasn't* and *were/weren't*.
b with *do/does* or *don't/doesn't*.
c with *has/hasn't, have/haven't* and *had/hadn't*.
d with *did/didn't*.

ACTION Game: *Back to the board*

• Work in a small group.
• Student A stands with his/her back to the board. Student B chooses a word from this unit, writes it on the board so that the other students can see it, and tells student A the first letter of the word.
• Student A asks the other students up to ten *Yes/No* questions to find the word.

Is it a noun?
Is it an animal?

• If A guesses the word, he/she chooses the next word.

INTERACTION *If you were a ..., what ... would you be?*

Ask each other questions using these words.

colour animal kind of food car
sport kind of music TV programme
sound country month

A If you were a colour, what colour would you be?
B If I were a colour, I'd be green because ...

1 Read and complete. For each number 1–12, choose word or phrase A, B or C.

TEENAGER SAVES TOURIST IN RAINFOREST

How __1__ you survive if you were lost in the rainforest? A tourist who was lost for a week in the rainforest of Queensland, north-eastern Australia, said he __2__ on bananas and chewing gum.

Stuart Ridley was rescued __3__ a teenager on a helicopter tour saw him flashing sunlight off a mirror from his camera. Ridley, 27, explained that he __4__ his car because he wanted a closer look at wildlife in the rainforest. But it was dark when he turned back, __5__ he couldn't find his car.

Reporters asked Ridley how he __6__ during his week in the rainforest. He __7__ them he had found plenty of water to drink – he was in the wettest part of Australia – but he had got very hungry. 'I only had six bananas and a packet of chewing gum in my rucksack.' And he was also concerned __8__ snakes – the Queensland rainforest is home to the taipan, one of the most dangerous snakes in the world.

Ridley saw helicopters flying overhead during the week but he couldn't __9__ their attention. Finally, a teenage helicopter passenger, Susie Ward, 15, saw the light from the mirror and asked the pilot __10__ back round the area.

When Ridley was picked up and flown to safety, he apologised for causing trouble. 'I __11__ have left my car', he said. He was very grateful to the teenager who spotted him from the helicopter. 'She probably saved my life, __12__ she?'

1	**A** will	**B** would	**C** did
2	**A** live	**B** did live	**C** lived
3	**A** after	**B** by	**C** while
4	**A** would leave	**B** had left	**C** did leave
5	**A** so	**B** then	**C** because
6	**A** did survive	**B** survive	**C** had survived
7	**A** said	**B** told	**C** replied
8	**A** about	**B** because	**C** of
9	**A** pull	**B** make	**C** attract
10	**A** to fly	**B** flying	**C** fly
11	**A** should	**B** shouldn't	**C** oughtn't
12	**A** did	**B** had	**C** didn't

2 Write sentences reporting the requests with *asked* and the commands with *told*.

1 Mrs Flynn said, 'Rob, will you tidy your room, please.'
2 The teacher said, 'Students, don't make so much noise.'
3 Julie said, 'Simon, you must take it easy.'
4 The researcher said, 'Kanzi, would you get my keys back?'
5 'Bethany, try it one more time,' said her father.
6 'Natasha, please don't be late,' said Peter.
7 The police officer shouted 'Stop!' at the thief.
8 'Try out new dance routines,' said Adam to the contestants.

3 Report these statements.

'I'm going for a swim,' said Shane.
Shane said he was going for a swim.

1 'I'm not looking for a girlfriend,' said Rob.
2 'I want to be a doctor,' said Sophie.
3 'I danced for five hours,' said Joni.
4 'I can't concentrate for long,' said Lara.
5 'We'll try to solve the mystery,' said Sherlock Holmes.
6 'I've never ridden a horse,' said Steve.
7 'We must find a way to stop spam,' said Ray.
8 'I won't come back,' said Bill Hobbs.

4 Zak looked worried, so Sophie asked him questions. Report her questions using *asked*.

'Are you all right?'
She asked if he was all right.

1 'What's the matter?'
2 'Where did you lose it?'
3 'How much money was in it?'
4 'Do you know the number of the bus?'
5 'Have you told the police?'
6 'Are you going to phone them?'
7 'Why aren't you more careful?'

5 Rewrite these sentences using *should/shouldn't have*.

He was wrong to drive so fast.
He shouldn't have driven so fast.

1 Why didn't you ask me to help you?
2 I was silly to stay out so late last night.
3 Why didn't the students work harder?
4 It was a bad idea for us to sail the dinghy in the storm.
5 You were wrong to read my diary.
6 Why didn't you phone the police?
7 The team ought to have won the match.
8 Why did I listen to you?

6 Write sentences using the correct form of the verbs: past simple or *would*.

1 If I (have) toothache, I (go) to the dentist.
2 You (not get) hiccoughs if you (not eat) so quickly.
3 Where (you/live) if you (can) live anywhere?
4 If you (be) on a roller coaster, how (you/feel)?
5 If I (know) the answer, I (tell) you.
6 The singer (not perform) well if she (have) a sore throat.
7 If we (not have) water, we (die).
8 What (you/say) if your country (win) the World Cup?

7 Give advice to someone who can't sleep at night, using *If I were you, I'd/I wouldn't ...* and these phrases.

1 drink coffee in the evening
2 buy a new bed
3 try to relax
4 eat cheese for dinner
5 read ghost stories in bed
6 stop worrying about it

8 Complete with question tags.

1 Ray Tomlinson invented email, _____?
2 It didn't take him long, _____?
3 You'd like to go to the party, _____?
4 You don't want to be late, _____?
5 It hasn't rained for ages, _____?
6 We waste a lot of water, _____?
7 Emus can't fly, _____?
8 Chimpanzees have got tails, _____?

VOCABULARY

9 Complete with twelve of these words.

annoyed attachment beef crops currency desert
electricity emergency guilty honey monsoon
shelter shortage snail solution tropical

1 I've done nothing wrong, so I don't feel _____.
2 You can't use a hosepipe because there's a _____ of water.
3 Do you get _____ when people don't listen to you?
4 Don't worry – I have the _____ to your problem!
5 I received the email, but I couldn't open the _____.
6 Please hurry up, you're as slow as a _____.
7 If you have a sore throat, try drinking hot lemon and _____.
8 Many dams are used to generate _____.
9 It was raining hard, so we stood in a shop doorway for _____.
10 When you go abroad, you often need to buy foreign _____.
11 In the UK, you dial 999 to contact the _____ services.
12 Roast _____ is a traditional English meal.

10 Match these words with their definitions.

bracelet consequence cool a dozen
firm igloo peak plain *n* safety trunk

1 opposite of *danger*
2 large flat area of land
3 living space made of ice
4 piece of jewellery worn on the arm
5 highest point
6 elephant's nose
7 opposite of *warm*
8 hard or solid
9 twelve
10 result

11 Match the verbs in list A with the words and phrases in list B.

	A	B
1	attract	a deep breath
2	take off	a problem
3	hold	the tap
4	keep	attention
5	solve	your mind
6	take	calm
7	change	on tight
8	turn off	your shoes

LEARNER INDEPENDENCE
SELF ASSESSMENT

Look back at Lessons 1–3 in Units 7 and 8.

How good are you at ...?	✓ Fine	? Not sure
1 Reporting requests and commands Workbook pp74–75 exercise 2	☐	☐
2 Reporting what someone said Workbook pp76–77 exercises 2–4	☐	☐
3 Reporting what someone asked Workbook pp78–79 exercises 2 and 3	☐	☐
4 Criticising past actions Workbook pp86–87 exercises 1–3	☐	☐
5 Talking about imaginary or unlikely situations Workbook pp88–89 exercises 1–3	☐	☐
6 Giving advice Workbook p89 exercise 4	☐	☐
7 Asking for agreement and checking information Workbook pp90–91 exercises 1–4	☐	☐

Not sure? Have a look at Language File pages 119–120 and do the Workbook exercise(s) again.

Now write an example for 1–7

1 My mother told me to wash my hands.

LANGUAGE FILE

Present simple and present continuous

UNIT 1 LESSON 1

- We use the present simple to talk about states, routines, timetables and regular actions:

    She lives in Liverpool.
    I work in a shop every Saturday.
    We often go to clubs.
    He doesn't have a girlfriend.
    What do you care about?

- We also use the present simple to talk about what people do in their jobs and occupations:

    What do you do? (= What's your job?)
    I'm a teacher.
    She's a doctor.

- We use the present continuous to talk about temporary events and what is happening now.

    She's learning Spanish.
    He isn't looking for a girlfriend.
    What are you reading at the moment?

- We can also use the present continuous to talk about future arrangements, and we often say the time and/or place:

    What are you doing at half term?
    I'm spending a week in Spain.

- See also Unit 4 Lesson 2.
- We form the present continuous with *am/is/are* + present participle (-*ing* form).
- **Spelling:** verb + *ing*

    Most verbs add *ing*:

    learn – learning   read – reading

    Verbs ending in *e* drop the *e* and add *ing*:

    write – writing   make – making

    But we don't make a change after *be* or *ee*:

    be – being   see – seeing

    Other verbs:

    get – getting   swim – swimming   run – running
    put – putting   sit – sitting   travel – travelling

PRACTICE: Present simple and present continuous

1 Complete with the correct form of the verbs.

1 What _____ Rob usually _____ (do) after school?
2 He _____ (go) to the park with his friends and they _____ (play) football.
3 What _____ Sophie _____ (do) at the moment?
4 She _____ (listen) to music.
5 _____ she _____ (work) every Saturday?
6 Where _____ she _____ (spend) half term?
7 _____ you _____ (worry) about street crime?
8 I _____ (think) some city streets _____ (get) quite dangerous.

Adverbial phrases of frequency

UNIT 1 LESSON 1

How often?

every	day
	night
once a	week
twice a	month
three times a	year

We use adverbial phrases of frequency to answer the question:
How often . . . ? They usually go at the end of the sentence:

He goes swimming every Sunday morning.
I go to the cinema once or twice a month.

Past simple

UNIT 1 LESSONS 2 AND 3

- There are two past simple forms of *be: was* and *were*:

    The surfing was fantastic.
    We were really excited.
    I wasn't good enough.
    Was she also on the phone home?

- **Regular verbs**

    Spelling: affirmative forms of regular verbs

    Most verbs add *ed*:

    last – lasted   want – wanted

    Verbs ending in *e* add *d*:

    like – liked   phone – phoned

    Verbs ending in a consonant + *y* change the *y* to *i* and add *ed*:

    try – tried   worry – worried

    But verbs ending in a vowel + *y* just add *ed*:

    play – played   enjoy – enjoyed

- **Irregular verbs**

    There is a complete list of all the irregular verbs in *New Inspiration 3* on page 127.

- **Regular** and **irregular** verbs both form the negative and questions in the same way.

    I didn't care.
    It didn't mean anything to me.
    Why didn't I enjoy it more?
    Did she feel the same as me?

PRACTICE: Past simple

2 Complete with the past simple of the verbs.

1 Where _____ Sara and Joni _____ for their holiday? (go)
2 _____ Sara and Joni on holiday with their parents? (be)
3 How long _____ the party _____ ? (last)
4 _____ Joni good enough for Sara's friends? (be)
5 _____ Joni _____ Sara's friends? (like)
6 How _____ Joni _____ when her mum phoned? (feel)
7 When _____ Joni nearly _____ ? (cry)
8 Why _____ Joni _____ round? (turn)

Now find the past tense of the verbs in Joni's blog on page 12 and answer the questions with full sentences.

Past simple and past continuous

UNIT 1 LESSON 3

- We use the past simple to describe a completed event or a short action at a particular time in the past:

  The attack happened so fast.

  I didn't scream.

- We use the past continuous to describe a longer activity, to give the background to an event in the past simple. The event in the past simple often 'interrupts' the past continuous activity.

  She was waiting for the next big wave when she saw the shark.

  She asked everyone 'When can I surf again?' while she was recovering in hospital.

  What was she thinking when the shark attacked?

- We often use *when* and *while* to link actions or events that happen at the same time:

  When he kicked the crocodile, it let him go.

  While/When he was swimming, he heard a splash.

  We have to use *when* for short actions; *while* suggests longer background events.

- We form the past continuous with *was/were* + present participle (-*ing* form).

PRACTICE: Past simple and past continuous

3 Complete with correct form of the verbs.

Tourists in shark attack

Simon Donnell, 17, from Belfast, __1__ (escape) from a shark attack yesterday. Simon was on holiday in Florida with a group of friends. One day they all got together and __2__ (go) out in a small boat to see sharks.

  'The sea was quite calm,' Simon said, 'and for the first two hours we __3__ (not see) any sharks at all. The boat __4__ (pull) bags of dead fish behind it to attract sharks but none __5__ (come). We __6__ (laugh) about our bad luck when suddenly everything __7__ (change). I __8__ (notice) that four or five small sharks __9__ (swim) around us. I __10__ (get) up and __11__ (go) over to the side of the boat. The boat __12__ (move) quite slowly and the water was clear. I __13__ (look) into the water when suddenly a huge white shark __14__ (appear). The shark __15__ (swim) fast and it __16__ (crash) into the boat. It was like Jaws! I __17__ (look) around. Most of my friends __18__ (scream) or __19__ (cry). But suddenly the shark __20__ (disappear) into the blue water.

  It was a small boat and we were really lucky to get away from such a big shark.'

Verb + gerund

UNIT 2 LESSON 1

- A gerund (-*ing* form) is a noun formed from a verb. We can use a gerund after these verbs:

  avoid   enjoy   go (+ activity)   *hate   can't help   keep   like   love   mind   risk   can't stand   start   stop*

  He avoids seeing Bella.

  You can't help laughing.

  Things keep going wrong.

  She risks losing her life.

  Jake starts fighting to protect Pandora.

- We can also use a gerund after prepositions:

  *Edward is afraid **of** losing Bella.*

  *He's fed up **with** looking for work.*

  *Can they succeed **in** rescuing her?*

  *They are both good **at** singing.*

  *I feel **like** going to the cinema.*

  *I'm not keen **on** seeing musicals.*

PRACTICE: Verb/Preposition and gerund

4 Complete with the correct form of the verbs.

1 I feel like _____ a DVD. (buy)
2 Let's go _____. (shop)
3 I'm interested in _____ *Tron: Legacy*. (see)
4 I'm not keen on _____ science fiction films. (watch)
5 How about _____ *1408*? (get)
6 I don't like _____ scared! (be)
7 Let's stop _____ and get an action movie. (talk)
8 Steven Spielberg is famous for _____ action films. (make)
9 I dream of _____ Johnny Depp. (meet)

so/nor + auxiliary verbs

UNIT 2 LESSON 1

Agreeing

I love …	So do I.
I'm scared of …	So am I.
I don't mind …	Nor do I.
I can't stand …	Nor can I.

- We use *so* + auxiliary verb to agree with affirmative statements.
- We use *nor* + auxiliary verb to agree with negative statements.

Verb + infinitive

UNIT 2 LESSON 2

- We can use *to* + infinitive after these verbs:
  agree   ask   decide   expect   help   hope   know how   learn   manage   mean   need   offer   pretend   promise   refuse   seem   teach   tell   want   would like

- These verbs **always** take an object before the infinitive:
  teach   tell
  > I can teach **you** to dance.
  > He told **us** to try out new dance routines.

- These verbs **never** take an object before the infinitive:
  agree   decide   hope   know how   learn   manage   offer   pretend   refuse   seem
  > I hope to help you.
  > They learn to sing.
  > What can you just manage to do?
  > Don't pretend to be a poet.
  > Don't refuse to experiment.

- These verbs **often** take an object before the infinitive:
  ask   expect   help   mean   need   promise   want   would like
  > We expect **you** to obey the rules.
  > I expect to be on time.
  > They can help **you** to develop your talents.
  > They can help to cook supper.
  > I promised **her** to work hard.
  > I want **you** to practise your songs.
  > I want to go home.
  > I'd like **you** to visit me.
  > I'd like to welcome you.

- See also Unit 7 Lesson 1.

PRACTICE: Verb (+ object) + infinitive

5 Complete with the infinitive of the verbs. Include the object pronouns *her, us* or *you* where necessary.

Frank, one of the Star School contestants, writes an email home.
We had a great first day. Tony, the director, welcomed us and said he expected __1__ (obey) the rules. I like Jess, the voice coach, very much and I want __2__ (help) me with my singing. She said: 'I will help __3__ (find) your special voice.' I also hope __4__ (learn) jazz dance with Adam. He wanted __5__ (promise) __6__ (work) together and try out new ideas. We all want __7__ (be) songwriters and Rachel is going to teach __8__ (write) songs. I hope I manage __9__ (do) it. I promise __10__ (try) hard.

Present simple passive

UNIT 2 LESSON 3

- We use the passive to focus on the action rather than the agent (the person or thing that performs the action):
  > The book is registered at www.bookcrossing.com
  > You are invited to pick it up.
  > Each book is labelled.

- When we want to refer to the agent, we use *by* + noun:
  > The books are found by other people.
  > The website is visited by around one million members.

- We form the present simple passive with the present tense of *be* + past participle. There is a complete list of all the irregular past participles in *New Inspiration 3* on page 127.

- See also Unit 6 Lesson 3.

PRACTICE: Present simple passive

6 Write sentences using the present simple passive.

1. sushi/eat/in Japan
2. saris/wear/by women in India
3. Portuguese/speak/in Brazil
4. kangaroos/find/in Australia
5. over 250 kinds of olives/grow/in Spain
6. a lot of cotton/produce/Egypt
7. Ferrari sports cars/make/in Italy
8. the sitar/play/in India

---

must and *can't*

UNIT 3 LESSON 1

- We use *must* and *can't* to make logical deductions.

- We use *must* to show that we are sure that something is true:
  > Scientists are sure there must be others.
  > You must be joking!

- We use *can't* to show that we are sure that something is untrue:
  > We can't be the only planet where there is life.
  > You can't be serious.

- We don't use *mustn't* to make deductions.

- See also Unit 3 Lesson 2.

PRACTICE: *must* and *can't*

7 Complete with *must* or *can't*.

1. 'Where's she going?'
   'It _____ be somewhere special because she's wearing her best clothes.'
2. He had two pizzas for lunch, so he _____ be hungry now.
3. Can you see Sue? There _____ be many people with red hair and a green coat!
4. Everyone loves her new song – it _____ be number one next week.
5. Lost your keys? You _____ be serious! They _____ be somewhere in your room.
6. 'He failed his exams!'
   'But that _____ be true – there _____ be some mistake.'

---

could, may and might

UNIT 3 LESSON 1

- We use *could, may* and *might* to show we think something is possibly true:
  > Jack could be at home. He may be at the gym.
  > He might be away. (Less likely)

must and *mustn't/can't* *have to/has to* and *don't/doesn't have to*
UNIT 3 LESSON 2

- We can use both *must* and *have to* to express present and future obligation, often when talking about rules:
  You must/You have to = It's obligatory.
  You must stay awake in a cheese factory.
  They have to avoid the police.
  Everyone has to obey the law.
- We often use *must* instead of *have to* to show we feel strongly about something:
  You must stop smoking.
- We can use *mustn't* and *can't* to express present and future prohibition:
  You mustn't/You can't = It's not allowed.
  You mustn't fall asleep.
  You can't take a lion to the cinema.
- *You can = It's allowed.*
- We use *don't have to* to express lack of obligation:
  You don't have to = It's not necessary.
  Americans don't have to worry.
- The past tense of both *must* and *have to* is *had to*:
  The men had to plan their journey carefully.
- See also Unit 3 Lesson 1.

> **PRACTICE: *must, mustn't/can't* and *have/has to***
>
> **8** Here are some more strange US laws. Rewrite them using the correct form of the verbs in brackets.
>
> 1 You aren't allowed to whistle underwater in Vermont. (can)
> 2 You can't sing in the bath in Pennsylvania. (must)
> 3 It's against the law to keep a donkey in the bath in Georgia. (can)
> 4 You must wear shoes when driving in Alabama. (have to)
> 5 It's forbidden to eat ice cream on Sundays in Oregon. (can)
> 6 In Elko, Nevada everyone walking in the street must wear a mask. (have to)
> 7 In North Dakota it's illegal to lie down and fall asleep with your shoes on. (can)
> 8 In Oklahoma City you can't walk backwards while you're eating a hamburger. (must)
> 9 All cats have to wear three bells in Cresskill, New Jersey. (must)

Reflexive pronouns
UNIT 3 LESSON 2

myself	ourselves
yourself	yourselves
himself/herself/itself	themselves

- We use a reflexive pronoun when the subject and the object are the same:
  He enjoys himself. (NOT *He enjoys him.*)
- We often use reflexive pronouns after these verbs and phrases:
  behave   enjoy   express   find   help   hurt   look after   take care of
- Reflexive pronouns aren't usually used after:
  feel   get up   hurry   remember   wake up   worry
- We also use reflexive pronouns for emphasis:
  Do it yourself!

> **PRACTICE: Reflexive pronouns**
>
> **9** Complete with reflexive pronouns.
>
> 1 We all enjoyed _____ at the party.
> 2 She's looking forward to living by _____.
> 3 He fell off his bike, but he didn't hurt _____.
> 4 Please everyone, help _____ to more food.
> 5 I sometimes talk to _____ when I'm thinking.
> 6 Have fun, Richard, and take care of _____.

should/ought to and *shouldn't* *had better (not)*
UNIT 3 LESSON 3

- We can use *should/ought to* and *shouldn't* to give advice and warnings:
  You should try to ignore them.
  You ought to have a word with her parents.
  They shouldn't copy your work.
  What should I do?
- *should* and *ought to* have the same meaning. They are not as strong as *must* and *have to*.
- There is no *to* between *should* and the main verb; *ought* is followed by *to* + infinitive.
- The negative form *oughtn't to* is less common than *shouldn't*:
  They oughtn't to copy your work.
- We can use *had better* instead of *should* when something is important **now**:
  You'd better tell a teacher or your parents.
  They'd better not do it any more.

> **PRACTICE: *should/ought to, shouldn't* and *had better (not)***
>
> **10** Rewrite the sentences using the correct form of the verb or phrase in brackets.
>
> 1 It's important to do revision for your exams. (should)
> 2 He was rude to his parents and he should say sorry. (ought)
> 3 It's nearly midnight – you ought to go to bed. (had better)
> 4 It's silly to wear uncomfortable shoes. (should).
> 5 You shouldn't be late for school tomorrow. (had better)
> 6 You should listen to your teacher. (ought)

Adjective + infinitive
UNIT 3 LESSON 3

- We can use *to* + infinitive after these adjectives:
  difficult   easy   good   hard   helpful   illegal   important (im)possible   lucky   normal   nice   pleased   rude   sensible silly   wrong
  I think it's difficult to keep a secret.
  It's normal to feel nervous about exams.
  We were lucky to get away from the shark.
  Pleased to meet you!

Verbs of perception + present participle
can/could + verbs of perception
UNIT 4 LESSON 1

- We use the present participle after *see*, *watch*, *notice*, *hear*, *listen to*, *smell* and *feel* to talk about a continuous activity:

    She saw furniture moving.
    A police officer watched a chair flying through the air.
    Janet heard someone walking around in her bedroom.

- We often use *can/could* before *see*, *hear*, *smell*, *taste*, and *feel*:

    I can hear Janet talking.
    I could see things happening.
    Cats can't taste sugar.

PRACTICE: Verbs of perception + present participle

11 Complete with the present participle of these verbs.

| cook   dance   leave   play   sing   sit   touch   walk |

1 She listened to the rock star _____ her favourite song.
2 Shh – can you hear someone _____ up the stairs?
3 Let's watch the contestants _____ the salsa.
4 I could see people _____ tennis from my window.
5 Mmm – I can smell dinner _____.
6 When we saw the bus _____, we knew we were late.
7 She felt a snake _____ her foot and screamed.
8 He noticed a new student _____ at the back and asked her name.

---

will/won't, shall and going to
UNIT 4 LESSON 2

- We can use *will* and *won't* (*will not*) to say what we hope or predict for the future:

    I hope it won't rain tomorrow.
    I'll have seven years' bad luck.

- We also use *will* and *won't* for offers, promises, and decisions made at the time of speaking:

    I'll lend you my lucky charm.
    I'll read out your horoscope.
    I'll keep my fingers crossed!
    Never mind – I'll buy another one.

- We can also use *Shall I ...?* to make offers:

    Shall I read out your horoscope?
    Shall I role play the interview with you?

- We use *going to* + infinitive to talk about future plans and intentions:

    I'm going to stay in bed all day.
    Are you going to go out?
    I'm not going to worry about it.

- We also use *going to* + infinitive to predict the future from present evidence which suggests that something is very likely to happen:

    The weather is going to be great tomorrow!

- There is sometimes very little difference in meaning between *going to* + infinitive (plans and intentions) and the present continuous (future arrangements):

    He's going to see the dentist tomorrow.
    (Plan: He probably has an appointment.)
    He's seeing the dentist tomorrow.
    (Arrangement: He has an appointment.)

- We often use the present continuous to avoid the phrase *going to go*:

    Are you going (to go) out later?

PRACTICE: *will/won't* and *going to*

12 Complete with *'ll/won't* or (*be*) *going to*.

WOMAN   Look at the time – it's really late. I __1__ miss the train.
MAN   I __2__ drive into town. I __3__ give you a lift to the station.
WOMAN   Oh, thank you. Wait a second – I __4__ get my jacket.
MAN   And you'd better take an umbrella. Look at the sky.
WOMAN   Yes, it __5__ start raining soon.
MAN   I'm sure you __6__ be late. We __7__ be there in five minutes.
WOMAN   You're driving too fast – look out!
MAN   Sorry, I __8__ slow down.

First conditional
UNIT 4 LESSON 3

- We use the first conditional to talk about the possible future when discussing the consequences of actions or events. First conditional sentences have this structure:

    If + present simple, future simple
    If you follow this advice, your memory will improve!
    If you write things down, you won't forget them so easily,

- The *if* clause can follow the main clause:

    Future simple, *if* + present simple
    You will remember things if you concentrate.

- We often leave out the conditional verb when the meaning is clear:

    What (will you do) if you can't sleep tonight?

PRACTICE: First conditional

13   Write sentences using the first conditional.

you/catch the train/hurry
    You'll catch the train if you hurry.

1 you/feel better/take more exercise
2 he/have an accident/drive so fast
3 they/pass the exam/work hard
4 I/not spend any money/stay at home
5 you/get a prize/win the competition
6 we/not go to the gig/not get free tickets
7 she/find her keys/tidy her room
8 I/not get lost/take a map

Present perfect

UNIT 5 LESSONS 1, 2 AND 3

- We can use the present perfect to talk about recent completed actions or events:

  I've done my homework.

  She has passed her exams.

  We don't say the exact time of the action or event, but we can refer to an unfinished period of time, for example *all day, today, this week/month/year.*

  I haven't seen her today.

  Have you had fun this week?

- We can use the present perfect with *just* to talk about very recent events:

  They have just arrived in Kazakhstan.

- We use the present perfect with *already* to emphasise that something has happened:

  They have already travelled across Europe.

- We use the present perfect with *yet* to show that we expect something to happen; *yet* goes at the end of negative statements and questions:

  They haven't completed a quarter of their journey yet.

  Have they crossed Asia yet?

- We can also use the present perfect, often with *ever/never*, to talk about experiences in the time up to now.

  ever = at any time. It is used mainly in questions:

  Have you ever wondered what it's like?

  Have you ever wanted to ski off a mountain?

  ever is also used in affirmative statements after superlatives:

  It's the most exciting thing I've ever done.

  never = at no time. It is used mainly in statements:

  I've never had so much fun.

  I've never done anything like it before.

- We also use the present perfect with *for* and *since* to talk about the unfinished past.

- We use *for* + a period of time to say how long something has lasted:

  I've had to do drug tests for years.

  Simon has had a bad headache for a couple of days.

- We use *since* + a specific point in time to say when something started:

  I've won hundreds of medals since I was at school.

  We've been friends ever since we met.

  We've been here since 9am.

- We form the present perfect with *have/has* + past participle.

- For regular verbs the past participle is the same as the past tense: *work, worked, worked.*

- For some irregular verbs the past participle is the same as the past tense, but for many it is different: *be, was/were, been.* There is a complete list of all the irregular verbs in *New Inspiration 3* on page 127.

- The past participle of *go* can be *gone* or *been* (= *gone and returned*):

  He's gone to Rio. = He's in Rio now.

  He's been to Rio. = He's visited Rio but he's not there now.

PRACTICE: Present perfect

14 Put the verbs in the present perfect and complete with *just, already* or *yet.*

1 It _____ _____ _____ (start) to rain – we're going to get wet.

2 I _____ _____ _____ (see) *Shrek* twice. Can't we watch another DVD?

3 _____ you _____ (read) the new JK Rowling book _____ ?

4 I _____ _____ _____ (watch) the news. What a terrible accident!

5 She _____ _____ (not reply) to my email _____.

6 He's a brilliant footballer – he _____ _____ _____ (score) 100 goals!

7 The song only came out yesterday and there _____ _____ _____ (be) thousands of downloads.

8 Great! Sue _____ _____ _____ (send) me a text – she's passed her driving test.

15 Complete with the present perfect of the verbs and *ever* or *never.*

1 She _____ _____ _____ (see) anything like it.

2 _____ you _____ _____ (think) about going on holiday on your own?

3 I _____ always _____ (want) to, but I _____ _____ _____ (have) enough money.

4 Why _____n't you _____ _____ (learn) to swim?

5 Because I _____ _____ _____ (live) near the sea, and I hate swimming pools.

6 _____ your parents _____ _____ (leave) you at home when they _____ _____ (go) on holiday?

16 Complete the phrases with *for* or *since.*

1 _____ a couple of minutes		9 _____ a while
2 _____ I got up		10 _____ 13 June
3 _____ last Wednesday		11 _____ ages
4 _____ four days		12 _____ 2005
5 _____ a week		13 _____ I was born
6 _____ Christmas		14 _____ the lesson began
7 _____ last summer		15 _____ three years
8 _____ two months		

17 Complete with the present perfect of the verbs and *for* or *since.*

1 People _____ (ask) Usain Bolt lots of questions _____ the Beijing Olympics.

2 He _____ (be) a runner _____ he was seven.

3 He _____ (live) in Jamaica _____ he was born.

4 He _____ (be) a full-time athlete _____ years now.

5 He _____ (won) lots of races _____ his first one at the age of seven.

6 He _____ (know) his friend NJ _____ over 20 years.

Present perfect and past simple

UNIT 5 LESSONS 2 AND 3

- We can use the present perfect to talk about an indefinite time in the past:

    Kite surfing has recently become very popular worldwide.
- We use the past simple to talk about a specific time in the past:

    Kite surfing started in France in the 1980s.
- We use the present perfect with *for* and *since* to talk about the unfinished past:

    I've been at home for three hours.
    I've been at home since 4pm.
- We can express the same ideas using the past simple:

    I came home three hours ago.
    I came home at 4pm.

PRACTICE: Present perfect and past simple

18   Complete with the correct form of the verbs.

1 _____ you ever _____ (try) snowboarding?
2 Yes, I _____ (have) a go last winter. It _____ (be) great fun.
3 _____ your parents ever _____ (let) you drive their car?
4 No, because we haven't got one! My dad _____ (have) a motorbike for a while but he _____n't _____ (let) me ride it.
5 _____ you ever _____ (do) something that you regretted?
6 You mean something I _____ (feel) bad about afterwards? Yes, once I _____ (steal) some chocolate from a shop. It _____ (be) a long time ago, but I _____ never _____ (forget) it.

Past perfect

UNIT 6 LESSON 1

Past perfect	Past simple	NOW

- We use the past perfect to describe the earlier of two past events, to make the order of events clear. We use the past simple for the more recent event:

    She had spent a lot of time in hospital and needed to do exercises.
    Ruth had planned to go to university, but instead she left school.
- If the order of events is clear, we don't need to use the past perfect for the earlier event:

    After I (had) finished my homework, I watched TV.
    But compare these sentences:
    The train left when I reached the station.
    (I saw the train)
    The train had left when I reached the station.
    (I didn't see the train.)

- We often use the past perfect with *because* to explain why something happened:

    The players were delighted because they had won the match.
- We often use the past perfect with time phrases beginning by *(the time)*, *since*:

    Ryan had won awards by the time he was 16.
    Louis Braille had been blind since the age of three.
- We form the past perfect with *had* + past participle.
- Contractions of *had*: I'd/you'd/he'd/she'd/we'd/they'd

PRACTICE: Past perfect

19   Complete with the past simple or past perfect of the verbs. Use the text on page 74 to help you.

1 At first Ruth _____ (not think) that she _____ (invent) something special.
2 Ruth _____ (not leave) school when she _____ (create) the StairSteady.
3 By the time Ryan _____ (be) 16, he _____ (design) award-winning robots.
4 Krysta _____ (love) cycling but she _____ (not ride) a bike for a long time.
5 Charles Barbier _____ (visit) the school for the blind after Louis _____ (be) there for two years.
6 Louis _____ (develop) Braille from the system that Barbier _____ (tell) him about three years before.

---

used to + infinitive

UNIT 6 LESSON 2

- We can use *used to* when we talk about past habits and states:

    It used to be a car tyre.
    We used to mend our clothes.
    We didn't use to buy so much.
    Why did we use to buy fewer shoes?
- For present habits and states, we use the present simple:

    He walks to school every day. (NOT He uses to walk …)

PRACTICE: *used to*

20   Complete with the correct form of *used to*.

1 ✗ People _____ spend so much time shopping.
2 ✓ We _____ produce less rubbish.
3 ✗ We _____ consume so much.
4 ? _____ you _____ make your own clothes?
5 ✗ I _____ recycle bottles and paper.
6 ? _____ you _____ throw old clothes away?

Past simple passive

UNIT 6 LESSON 3

- We use the past simple passive to focus on a past action rather than the agent:

  The first robot was created in 1865.

  Several attempts were made in the last century.

- When we want to refer to the agent, we use *by* + noun:

  *The car was sketched **by** da Vinci in 1478.*

- We form the past simple passive with *was/were* + past participle.

- See also Unit 2 Lesson 3.

PRACTICE: Past simple passive

21   Write sentences using the past simple passive.

the microphone/invent/1877

The microphone was invented in 1877.

1 the first petrol-driven car/build/1885
2 the first newspapers/publish/1609
3 the Eiffel Tower/complete/1889
4 modern safety matches/invent/1855
5 the tomb of Tutankhamun/discover/1923
6 the Channel Tunnel/open/1994
7 the first postage stamps/use/1840
8 Barack Obama/elect/US President/2008

---

ask/tell + object + infinitive

UNIT 7 LESSON 1

- We can use *ask* + object + infinitive to report requests:

  'Could you wash the potato?'

  → *She asked him to wash the potato.*

  'Please don't go!'

  → *He asked her not to go.*

- We can use *tell* + object + infinitive to report commands and instructions:

  'Calm down!'

  → *He told her to calm down.*

  'Don't be silly!'

  → *The parrot told me not to be silly.*

- See also Unit 2 Lesson 2.

PRACTICE: *ask/tell* + object + infinitive

22   Write sentences reporting the requests with *asked* and the commands with *told*.

Doctor: 'You should stop smoking, Mr Davies.'

The doctor told Mr Davies to stop smoking.

1 Teacher: 'Anya, could you clean the board, please?'
2 Mother: 'Children, go to bed!'
3 Rob: 'Mum, can you give me some money?'
4 Coach: 'Right, team, you must win the match.'
5 Firefighter: 'Please keep calm, everyone, and leave the building'.
6 Julie: 'Simon, would you carry my rucksack?'
7 Pilot: 'Passengers, fasten your seatbelts.'
8 Teacher: 'Sit down, everyone.'

Reported statements and questions

UNIT 7 LESSONS 2 AND 3

- Tenses, pronouns and possessive adjectives usually change in reported speech.

- **Reported statements: *say* and *tell***

  'I'm not sure.'

  → *He said (that) he wasn't sure.*

  'I don't think people are different.'

  → *He said (that) he didn't think people were different.*

  'The solutions aren't working.'

  → *He said (that) the solutions weren't working.*

  'It took four to six hours.'

  → *He said (that) it had taken four to six hours.*

  'Email has had an effect.'

  → *He said (that) email had had an effect.*

  'We're going to solve it.'

  → *He said (that) they were going to solve it.*

  'We must find a better way.'

  → *He told her (that) they had to find a better way.*

  'I can't remember.'

  → *He said (that) he couldn't remember.*

  'We'll have to find a solution.'

  → *He said (that) they would have to find a solution.*

- **Reported questions**

  Reported *Yes/No* questions: we use *if* before the reported question.

  Reported *Wh-* questions: we use the question word before the reported question.

  'Are other villages building windmills?'

  → *They asked if other villages were building windmills.*

  'Have you gone back to school?'

  → *They wanted to know if he had gone back to school.*

  'What else is your windmill used for?'

  → *They asked what else his windmill was used for.*

  'How did you get the idea?'

  → *They asked how he (had) got the idea.*

  The subject–verb order in reported questions is the same as in statements.

- In reported speech, verbs in the present usually change into the past, and verbs in the past usually change into the past perfect:

Direct speech		Reported speech
Present simple	→	Past simple
Present continuous	→	Past continuous
Past simple	→	Past perfect
Present perfect	→	Past perfect
am/is/are going to	→	was/were going to
must	→	had to
can	→	could
will	→	would

- Time phrases and other reference words also usually change in reported speech:

today	→	that day
tonight	→	that night
tomorrow	→	the next/following day
yesterday	→	the day before
now	→	then
here	→	there
this	→	that/the

PRACTICE: Reported statements and questions

23 Write Ray Tomlinson's comments about email and the Internet in reported speech.

1 'I'm not a household name for inventing email.'
2 'It doesn't bother me – it's not the centre of my life.'
3 'Computer experts know what I've done.'
4 'We must look at how people communicate.'
5 'People can communicate more easily by email.'
6 'In the past people went to libraries.'
7 'In the future they will use the Internet.'
8 'Internet use is going to increase enormously.'
9 'It's exciting because so much is happening.'

24 Anna asked Will questions about his mobile phone. Report her questions using *asked*.

1 What is your mobile phone number?
2 Do you use your phone mainly to send texts or to make calls?
3 Are you thinking of changing your mobile phone?
4 When did you first get a mobile phone?
5 Have you ever forgotten to charge your mobile phone?

should(n't) have/ought to have
UNIT 8 LESSON 1

- We can use *should(n't) have* and *ought to have* to criticise past actions, and to express regret about things people have or haven't done:
  They should have thought about the human cost.
  Governments shouldn't have built so many dams.
  They ought to have considered the environmental consequences.
- *should have* and *ought to have* have the same meaning. The negative form *oughtn't to have* (NOT *ought to haven't*) is less common than *shouldn't have*.

PRACTICE: *should have* and *shouldn't have*

25 Write sentences using *should have* or *shouldn't have*.

You forgot your father's birthday.
I shouldn't have forgotten my father's birthday.

1 You didn't make your bed this morning.
2 You didn't finish your homework before you went out.
3 You left your sports bag at school.
4 You were rude to the bus driver on the way home.
5 You didn't remember to bring your dictionary home.
6 You forgot to phone your teacher back.
7 You didn't help clear the table after dinner.
8 You came home after midnight.

Second conditional
UNIT 8 LESSON 2

- We use the second conditional to talk about imaginary present or unlikely future situations:
  If I met a bear, I would run away as fast as I could.
  If I were near a big tree, I would stand under it for shelter.
  If I were on the edge of a waterfall, I wouldn't jump out of the boat.
  What would you do if you didn't have enough water?
  Note the use of *were* instead of *was* in second conditional sentences.
- We often leave out the conditional verb when the meaning is clear:
  What (would you do) if you were outside in a thunderstorm?
- We use *If I were you, I'd/I wouldn't …* to give advice:
  If I were you, I'd take some insect spray.
- Second conditional sentences have this structure:
  If + past simple, would(n't) …
- The *if* clause can follow the main clause:
  would(n't) … if + past simple
  I'd take some insect spray if I were you.
- Contractions of *would*: *I'd/you'd/he'd/she'd/we'd/they'd*

PRACTICE: Second conditional

26 Write sentences using the correct form of the verbs: past simple or *would …*

1 How (you/survive) if you (get) lost in the mountains?
2 If my mobile (work), I (dial) the emergency number.
3 What (you/do) if the battery (be) flat?
4 If I (have) a mirror, I (try) to send signals.
5 (you/feel) scared if you (be) alone?
6 I (sing) rap songs if I (feel) scared.
7 What if you (have) to spend the night in the mountains?
8 If I (be) cold, I (make) a fire.

Question tags
UNIT 8 LESSON 3

- We can use question tags with **falling** intonation to ask for agreement when we are sure about something:
  You'd like to stay there, wouldn't you?
  You didn't expect me to know that, did you?
  Zak thinks the modern art museum is cool, doesn't he?
  They looked at the website, didn't they?
- We can use question tags with **rising** intonation to check if something is true:
  You can see that, can't you?
  It's been in the news, hasn't it?
- When the statement in the first part of the sentence is affirmative, the question tag is negative.
- When the statement in the first part of the sentence is negative, the question tag is affirmative.

PRACTICE: Question tags

27 Complete with question tags.

1 It was your birthday yesterday, _____?
2 You didn't have a party, _____?
3 He can't play the trumpet, _____?
4 You like reggae, _____?
5 She wants to go to university, _____?
6 She's passed all her exams, _____?
7 We aren't late, _____?
8 They'd like to win the match, _____?

UNIT 4   **LESSON 2**

How superstitious are you?

Questionnaire scores

Mostly As

You're quite superstitious, aren't you! You aren't alone. But try not to let superstitions worry you, because things can go wrong if you are too anxious.

Mostly Bs

You aren't very superstitious and you don't expect bad luck. But you do give in to superstition sometimes, just for fun.

Mostly Cs

You are very rational and down-to-earth. You don't take any notice of superstitions and you don't believe in the supernatural.

UNIT 8   **LESSON 2**

Survival Questionnaire

Questionnaire answers

1   A ✗   If you ate a lot, you'd use up the water in your body.
    B ✓   This would be the best way to avoid losing water.
    C ✗   If you walked as fast as possible, you'd lose water through sweating.

2   A ✗   This would be a bad idea as snakes are frightened by noise, not silence.
    B ✗   This would also be a mistake as some snakes hunt at night and you wouldn't be able to see them.
    C ✓   Good thinking! Snakes are frightened by noise and would get out of your way.

3   A ✗   If lightning hit the tree, you'd be in trouble.
    B ✗   Very bad idea. You should keep away from other people.
    C ✓   This would be the safest thing to do.

4   A ✓   Correct! You can hear a deep voice from further away and shouting 'Help!' would make it clear what you want!
    B ✗   If you screamed, your friends might think it was a bird or an animal.
    C ✗   Same problem. People could think a whistle was a bird or an animal.

5   A ✗   If you ran away, the bear would probably run after you, and bears can run faster than people.
    B ✓   This would be the best way to escape the bear.
    C ✗   Bears can climb trees too.

6   A ✗   This would be the most dangerous thing to do, because the strength of the water could push you over.
    B ✓   This would be the best way to cross the river.
    C ✗   This would be almost as dangerous as facing upstream!

7   A ✗   If you ran uphill, you'd be in more danger because fire travels faster uphill.
    B ✗   This wouldn't be a good idea if the wind was blowing towards the fire.
    C ✓   This would be the best way to escape the fire.

8   A ✗   Climbing barefoot would be dangerous, because your feet could slip and you could hurt yourself.
    B ✗   The same problem – the boots would slip on the rocks.
    C ✓   This would be best, because you wouldn't slip and you would be able to feel the rocks under your feet.

9   A ✓   Obviously it would be best only to eat plants you recognised. But if the unknown plant was poisonous, you'd feel an unpleasant sensation on your lip.
    B ✗   Eating the same as the birds wouldn't be a good idea. What was safe for them wouldn't necessarily be safe for you.
    C ✗   The colour of the berries wouldn't tell you if they were poisonous or not.

10   A ✓   If you went over the waterfall feet first, you'd be more likely to survive
    B ✗   If you dived over the waterfall, you could hit your head at the bottom.
    C ✗   If you stayed in the boat, you could be trapped or injured by it.

Score one point for each correct answer.

Questionnaire scores

1–3   If I were you, I wouldn't leave home!
4–6   I wouldn't feel safe travelling with you!
7–8   You should survive most dangerous situations.
9–10   Who are you – James Bond?!

WORD LIST

★ = fairly common words   ★★ = very common words   ★★★ = the most common and basic words

WELCOME! & UNIT 1

achievement (n) ★★★	/ə'tʃiːvmənt/
action (n) ★★★	/'ækʃ(ə)n/
although (conj) ★★★	/ɔːl'ðəʊ/
amazingly (adv)	/ə'meɪzɪŋli/
ambition (n) ★★	/æm'bɪʃ(ə)n/
arrest (v) ★★	/ə'rest/
astronaut (n) ★	/'æstrə,nɔːt/
attack (n) ★★★	/ə'tæk/
autobiography (n)	/,ɔːtəʊbaɪ'ɒgrəfi/
bite (off) (v) ★★	/baɪt/
boots (n pl) ★★★	/buːts/
bright (colour) (adj) ★★★	/braɪt/
calm (adj) ★★	/kɑːm/
care (about) (v) ★★★	/keə(r)/
carriage (n) ★	/'kærɪdʒ/
championship (n) ★★★	/'tʃæmpiənʃɪp/
cheer (v) ★★	/tʃɪə(r)/
clear (adj) ★★★	/klɪə(r)/
college (n) ★★★	/'kɒlɪdʒ/
compete (v) ★★★	/kəm'piːt/
cool (adj) ★★★	/kuːl/
crime (n) ★★★	/kraɪm/
cry (v) ★★★	/kraɪ/
denim (adj)	/'denɪm/
department store (n) ★★	/dɪ'pɑːtmənt ,stɔː/
disabled (adj) ★★	/dɪs'eɪb(ə)ld/
environment (n) ★★★	/ɪn'vaɪrənmənt/
exam(ination) (n) ★★	/ɪg'zæm/
experience (n) ★★★	/ɪk'spɪəriəns/
fare (n) ★★	/feə(r)/
female (adj) ★★★	/'fiːmeɪl/
fine (n) ★★	/faɪn/
fortune teller (n)	/'fɔːtʃən ,telə/
frequently (adv)	/'friːkwəntli/
give in (v)	/,gɪv 'ɪn/
half term (n)	/,hɑːf 'tɜːm/
home game (n)	/'həʊm ,geɪm/
hoodie (n)	/'hʊdi/
illegal (adj) ★★	/ɪ'liːg(ə)l/
illiterate (adj)	/ɪ'lɪtərət/
income (n) ★★★	/'ɪnkʌm/
jaw (n) ★★	/dʒɔː/
kick (v) ★★★	/kɪk/
law (n) ★★★	/lɔː/
minister (n) ★★★	/'mɪnɪstə(r)/
non-violent (adj)	/,nɒn'vaɪələnt/
organise (v) ★★★	/'ɔː(r)gənaɪz/
own (v) ★★★	/əʊn/
owner (n) ★★★	/'əʊnə(r)/
pain (n) ★★★	/peɪn/
part-time (adj) ★★	/'pɑːt,taɪm/
physically (adv) ★★	/'fɪzɪkli/
poor (adj) ★★★	/pɔː(r), pʊə(r)/
posh (adj)	/pɒʃ/
professional (adj) ★★★	/prə'feʃ(ə)nəl/
property (n) ★★★	/'prɒpə(r)ti/
punch (v) ★	/pʌntʃ/
realise (v) ★★★	/'rɪəlaɪz/
recover (v)	/,riː'kʌvə(r)/
law (n) ★★★	/lɔː/
minister (n) ★★★	/'mɪnɪstə(r)/
non-violent (adj)	/,nɒn'vaɪələnt/
organise (v) ★★★	/'ɔː(r)gənaɪz/
own (v) ★★★	/əʊn/
owner (n) ★★★	/'əʊnə(r)/
pain (n) ★★★	/peɪn/
part-time (adj) ★★	/'pɑːt,taɪm/
physically (adv) ★★	/'fɪzɪkli/
poor (adj) ★★★	/pɔː(r), pʊə(r)/
posh (adj)	/pɒʃ/
professional (adj) ★★★	/prə'feʃ(ə)nəl/
property (n) ★★★	/'prɒpə(r)ti/

punch (v) ★	/pʌntʃ/
realise (v) ★★★	/'rɪəlaɪz/
recover (v)	/,riː'kʌvə(r)/
result (n) ★★★	/rɪ'zʌlt/
row (n) ★	/raʊ/
score (v) ★★★	/skɔː(r)/
scream (v) ★★	/skriːm/
seat (n) ★★★	/siːt/
separate (adj) ★★★	/'sep(ə)rət/
separate (v) ★★★	/'sepəreɪt/
shape (n) ★★★	/ʃeɪp/
shock (n) ★★★	/ʃɒk/
significant (adj) ★★★	/sɪg'nɪfɪkənt/
sixth form (n)	/'sɪksθ ,fɔːm/
skates (n pl) ★	/skeɪts/
solo (adv)	/'səʊləʊ/
struggle (n) ★★	/'strʌg(ə)l/
successfully (adv)	/sək'sesf(ə)li/
turn (= become) (v) ★★★	/tɜː(r)n/
violin (n) ★	/,vaɪə'lɪn/
voice (n) ★★★	/vɔɪs/
volunteer (n) ★★	/,vɒlən'tɪə(r)/
warning (n) ★★★	/'wɔː(r)nɪŋ/
wolf (n) ★	/wʊlf/

FEELINGS

angry (adj) ★★★	/'æŋgri/
bored (adj) ★★	/bɔː(r)d/
cheerful (adj) ★	/'tʃɪə(r)f(ə)l/
depressed (adj) ★★	/dɪ'prest/
embarrassed (adj) ★	/ɪm'bærəst/
excited (adj) ★★	/ɪk'saɪtɪd/
fed up (adj) ★	/,fed 'ʌp/
frightened (adj) ★	/'fraɪt(ə)nd/
happy (adj) ★★★	/'hæpi/
lonely (adj) ★★	/'ləʊnli/
miserable (adj) ★	/'mɪz(ə)rəb(ə)l/
nervous (adj) ★★	/'nɜː(r)vəs/
pleased (adj) ★★	/pliːzd/
sad (adj) ★★★	/sæd/
scared (adj) ★★	/skeə(r)d/
terrified (adj)	/'terəfaɪd/
tired (adj) ★★★	/'taɪə(r)d/
worried (adj) ★★★	/'wʌrid/

PHRASAL VERBS WITH *GET*

get away (v)	/,get ə'weɪ/
get back (v)	/,get 'bæk/
get on (well) (v)	/,get 'ɒn (wel)/
get out (of) (v)	/,get 'aʊt (əv)/
get over (v)	/,get 'əʊvə/

POLITICS

boycott (n)	/'bɔɪkɒt/
civil rights (n pl)	/,sɪv(ə)l 'raɪts/
democracy (n) ★★★	/dɪ'mɒkrəsi/
elect (v) ★★★	/ɪ'lekt/
election (n) ★★★	/ɪ'lekʃ(ə)n/
head of state (n)	/,hed əv 'steɪt/
human rights (n pl) ★	/,hjuːmən 'raɪts/
leader (n) ★★★	/'liːdə(r)/
movement (n) ★★★	/'muːvmənt/
parliament (n) ★★★	/'pɑː(r)ləmənt/
politician (n) ★★★	/,pɒlə'tɪʃ(ə)n/
politics (n) ★★★	/'pɒlətɪks/
power (n) ★★★	/'paʊə(r)/
right (n) ★★★	/raɪt/
vote (n & v) ★★★	/vəʊt/

PREFIXES *DIS-* AND *UN-*

(dis)agree (v) ★★★	/ə'griː/
(dis)appear (v) ★★★	/ə'pɪə(r)/
(un)comfortable (adj) ★★★	/'kʌmftəb(ə)l/
(un)friendly (adj) ★★★	/'fren(d)li/
(un)happy (adj) ★★★	/'hæpi/
(un)lucky (adj) ★★★	/'lʌki/
(un)popular (adj) ★★★	/'pɒpjʊlə(r)/
(un)usual (adj) ★★★	/'juːʒʊəl/

WATER

lake (n) ★★	/leɪk/
splash (n)	/splæʃ/
surf (n & v)	/sɜː(r)f/
surfboard (n)	/'sɜː(r)f,bɔː(r)d/
surfer (n)	/'sɜːfə/
wave (n) ★★★	/weɪv/

EXPRESSIONS

fail/pass an exam	/,feɪl/,pɑːs ən ɪg'zæm/
fall asleep	/,fɔːl ə'sliːp/
go wrong	/,gəʊ 'rɒŋ/
in the open	/,ɪn ði: 'əʊpən/
take part (in)	/,teɪk 'pɑːt (ɪn)/
tell the truth	/,tel ðə 'truːθ/

UNIT 2

attend (v) ★★★	/ə'tend/
attractive (adj) ★★★	/ə'træktɪv/
avoid (v) ★★★	/ə'vɔɪd/
background (n) ★★★	/'bæk,graʊnd/
being (n) ★★	/'biːɪŋ/
bench (n) ★★	/bentʃ/
boatman (n)	/'bəʊtmən/
captain (n) ★★★	/'kæptɪn/
coach (person) (n) ★★	/kəʊtʃ/
comic book (n)	/'kɒmɪk ,bʊk/
comment (n) ★★★	/'kɒment/
cover (n) ★★★	/'kʌvə(r)/
curse (n)	/kɜː(r)s/
depend (on) (v) ★★★	/dɪ'pend/
divorced (adj) ★★	/dɪ'vɔː(r)st/
dream (of) (v) ★★	/driːm/
employer (n) ★★★	/ɪm'plɔɪə(r)/
enthusiastic (adj) ★★	/ɪn,θjuːzi'æstɪk/
expect (v) ★★★	/ɪk'spekt/
expedition (n) ★★	/,ekspə'dɪʃ(ə)n/
experiment (v) ★	/ɪk'speri,ment/
expression (n) ★★★	/ɪk'spreʃ(ə)n/
finder (n)	/'faɪndə(r)/
foreground (n)	/'fɔː(r),graʊnd/
genius (n) ★	/'dʒiːniəs/
globe (n)	/gləʊb/
goal (= aim) (n) ★★★	/gəʊl/
good-looking (adj) ★★	/,gʊd 'lʊkɪŋ/
guard (n) ★★★	/gɑː(r)d/
handkerchief (n) ★	/'hæŋkə(r),tʃɪf/
horror (n) ★★	/'hɒrə(r)/
human (adj & n) ★★★	/'hjuːmən/
increasing (adj)	/ɪn'kriːsɪŋ/
incredibly (adv) ★	/ɪn'kredəbli/
inhabit (v) ★	/ɪn'hæbɪt/
intelligent (adj) ★★	/ɪn'telɪdʒ(ə)nt/
keen (on) (adj) ★★★	/kiːn/
keep (...ing) (v) ★★★	/kiːp/
kidnap (v) ★	/'kɪdnæp/
label (v) ★★	/'leɪb(ə)l/
library (n) ★★★	/'laɪbrəri/
lie (on) (v) ★★★	/laɪ/
low (adj) ★★★	/ləʊ/
manage (v) ★★★	/'mænɪdʒ/
mining (n) ★	/'maɪnɪŋ/
note (n) ★★★	/nəʊt/
obey (v) ★★	/ə'beɪ/
painting (n) ★★★	/'peɪntɪŋ/
pine tree (n)	/'paɪn ,triː/
poet (n) ★★	/'pəʊɪt/
pretend (v) ★★	/prɪ'tend/
range (n) ★★★	/reɪndʒ/
realistic (adj) ★★	/,rɪə'lɪstɪk/

register (v) ★★★ /'redʒɪstə(r)/
relaxed (adj) ★ /rɪ'lækst/
remind (v) ★★★ /rɪ'maɪnd/
remove (v) ★★★ /rɪ'muːv/
report (back) (v) ★★★ /rɪ'pɔː(r)t/
response (n) ★★★ /rɪ'spɒns/
risk (v) ★★ /rɪsk/
rule (n) ★★★ /ruːl/
straw (adj) ★★ /strɔː/
style (n) ★★★ /staɪl/
succeed (in) (v) ★★★ /sək'siːd/
sunset (n) ★ /'sʌnˌset/
take out (v) /ˌteɪk 'aʊt/
talent (n) ★★ /'tælənt/
trainer (person) (n) ★ /'treɪnə(r)/
try out (v) /ˌtraɪ 'aʊt/
unique (adj) ★★★ /ju'niːk/
upset (adj) ★★ /ʌp'set/
vest (n) /vest/
virtual (adj) ★★ /'vɜː(r)tʃʊəl/
war (n) ★★★ /wɔː(r)/
wonder (v) ★★★ /'wʌndə(r)/

ADJECTIVE SUFFIXES -FUL AND -LESS
careful (adj) ★★★ /'keə(r)f(ə)l/
careless (adj) ★ /'keə(r)ləs/
colourful (adj) ★ /'kʌlə(r)f(ə)l/
colourless (adj) /'kʌlə(r)ləs/
hopeful (adj) ★ /'həʊpf(ə)l/
hopeless (adj) /'həʊpləs/
painful (adj) ★★ /'peɪnf(ə)l/
painless (adj) /'peɪnləs/
successful (adj) ★★★ /sək'sesf(ə)l/
truthful (adj) /'truːθf(ə)l/

ART STYLES
expressionism (n) /ɪk'spreʃ(ə)nˌɪz(ə)m/
impressionism (n) /ɪm'preʃ(ə)nɪz(ə)m/
pop art (n) /'pɒp ˌɑːt/
realism (n) ★ /'rɪəˌlɪz(ə)m/
surrealism (n) /sə'rɪəˌlɪz(ə)m/

FILMS
action film (n) /'ækʃ(ə)n ˌfɪlm/
animation (n) /ˌænɪ'meɪʃ(ə)n/
comedy (n) ★★ /'kɒmədi/
documentary (n) ★ /ˌdɒkjʊ'ment(ə)ri/
drama (n) ★★★ /'drɑːmə/
horror film (n) /'hɒrə ˌfɪlm/
musical (n) /'mjuːzɪk(ə)l/
romantic film (n) /rəʊ'mæntɪk ˌfɪlm/
science fiction film (n) /saɪəns 'fɪkʃ(ə)n ˌfɪlm/

OPINIONS
amazing (adj) ★★ /ə'meɪzɪŋ/
awful (adj) ★★ /'ɔːf(ə)l/
boring (adj) ★★ /'bɔːrɪŋ/
brilliant (adj) ★★★ /'brɪljənt/
disappointing (adj) ★ /ˌdɪsə'pɔɪntɪŋ/
excellent (adj) ★★★ /'eksələnt/
exciting (adj) ★★ /ɪk'saɪtɪŋ/
funny (adj) ★★★ /'fʌni/
interesting (adj) ★★★ /'ɪntrəstɪŋ/
scary (adj) ★ /'skeəri/
silly (adj) ★★ /'sɪli/
terrible (adj) ★★★ /'terəb(ə)l/
thrilling (adj) /'θrɪlɪŋ/

PERFORMANCE AND DANCE
audition (v) /ɔː'dɪʃ(ə)n/
ballet (n) ★ /'bæleɪ/
breakdancing (n) /'breɪkˌdɑːnsɪŋ/
partner (n) ★★★ /'pɑː(r)tnə(r)/
salsa (n) /'sælsə/
dance routine (n) /'dɑːns ruːˌtiːn/
ballroom (n) /'bɔːlruːm/

PHRASAL VERBS WITH UP
come up with (v) /ˌkʌm 'ʌp wɪð/

give up (v) /ˌgɪv 'ʌp/
grow up (v) /ˌgrəʊ 'ʌp/
look up (v) /ˌlʊk 'ʌp/
pick up (v) /ˌpɪk 'ʌp/
set up (v) /ˌset 'ʌp/
stand up (v) /ˌstænd 'ʌp/
turn up (v) /ˌtɜːn 'ʌp/

EXPRESSIONS
a great deal /ə ˌgreɪt 'diːl/
Best of luck! /ˌbest əv 'lʌk/
come to life /ˌkʌm tə 'laɪf/
fall in love /ˌfɔːl ɪn 'lʌv/
in particular /ˌɪn pə'tɪkjʊlə/

UNIT 3
according to (prep) ★★★ /ə'kɔː(r)dɪŋ ˌtuː/
aim (v) ★★★ /eɪm/
army (n) ★★★ /'ɑː(r)mi/
as long as (conj) /əz 'lɒŋ əz/
balanced diet (n) /'bælənst ˌdaɪət/
boil (v) ★ /bɔɪl/
breath (n) ★★★ /breθ/
breathe (v) ★★ /briːð/
bully (n & v) ★ /'bʊli/
cause (v) ★★★ /kɔːz/
cheat (v) ★ /tʃiːt/
claim (v) ★★★ /kleɪm/
cloud (n) ★★★ /klaʊd/
community worker (n) /kə'mjuːnəti ˌwɜːkə/
concentrate (v) ★★★ /'kɒns(ə)nˌtreɪt/
confused (adj) ★★ /kən'fjuːzd/
control (n) ★★★ /kən'trəʊl/
cyber bullying (n) /'saɪbə ˌbʊliɪŋ/
determined (adj) ★★ /dɪ'tɜː(r)mɪnd/
dignity (n) ★★ /'dɪgnəti/
dirty (adj) ★★ /'dɜː(r)ti/
distance (n) ★★★ /'dɪstəns/
dress (v) ★★★ /dres/
drinking water (n) /'drɪŋkɪŋ ˌwɔːtə/
electricity (n) ★★★ /ɪˌlek'trɪsəti/
excitedly (adv) /ɪk'saɪtɪdli/
explosion (n) ★★ /ɪk'spləʊʒ(ə)n/
export (n) ★★★ /'ekspɔː(r)t/
factory (n) ★★★ /'fæktri/
fair (adj) ★★★ /feə(r)/
figure (= number) (n) ★★★ /'fɪgə(r)/
firmly (adv) /'fɜːmli/
full-time (adj) ★★ /'fʊlˌtaɪm/
greenhouse gas (n) /ˌgriːnhaʊs 'gæs/
gun (n) ★★★ /gʌn/
handsome (adj) ★★ /'hæns(ə)m/
heartbroken (adj) /'hɑː(r)tˌbrəʊkən/
heating (n) ★★ /'hiːtɪŋ/
helpful (adj) ★★ /'helpf(ə)l/
however (conj) ★★★ /haʊ'evə(r)/
identify (v) ★★★ /aɪ'dentɪfaɪ/
ignore (v) ★★ /ɪg'nɔː(r)/
inauguration (n) /ɪˌnɔːgjʊ'reɪʃ(ə)n/
influence (v) ★★★ /'ɪnfluəns/
intend (v) ★★★ /ɪn'tend/
investigate (v) ★★★ /ɪn'vestɪgeɪt/
knock (v) ★★ /nɒk/
limit (v) ★★★ /'lɪmɪt/
liquid (n) ★★ /'lɪkwɪd/
lottery ticket (n) /'lɒtəri ˌtɪkɪt/
marks (n pl) ★★★ /mɑː(r)ks/
mixture (n) ★★★ /'mɪkstʃə(r)/
mood (n) ★★★ /muːd/
motorbike (n) ★ /'məʊtə(r)ˌbaɪk/
mysterious (adj) ★★ /mɪ'stɪəriəs/
mystery (n) ★★ /'mɪst(ə)ri/
neither … nor (conj) /ˌnaɪðə 'nɔː/
nicely (adv) /'naɪsli/
on standby (adv) /ˌɒn 'stændbaɪ/
overcoat (n) /'əʊvə(r)ˌkəʊt/
panic (v) ★ /'pænɪk/
pearl (n) ★ /pɜː(r)l/

possibility (n) ★★★ /ˌpɒsə'bɪləti/
price (n) ★★★ /praɪs/
promise (n) ★★★ /'prɒmɪs/
proper (adj) ★★★ /'prɒpə(r)/
proverb (n) /'prɒvɜː(r)b/
purpose (n) ★★★ /'pɜː(r)pəs/
pyjamas (n pl) ★ /pə'dʒɑːməz/
rapidly (adv) /'ræpɪdli/
refrigerator (n) /rɪ'frɪdʒəˌreɪtə(r)/
remote (adj) ★★ /rɪ'məʊt/
respect (n & v) ★★★ /rɪ'spekt/
revision (n) ★★ /rɪ'vɪʒ(ə)n/
robot (n) ★ /'rəʊbɒt/
rocky (adj) ★ /'rɒki/
scene (n) ★★★ /siːn/
sensible (adj) ★★ /'sensəb(ə)l/
similar (adj) ★★★ /'sɪmɪlə(r)/
situation (n) ★★★ /ˌsɪtʃu'eɪʃ(ə)n/
skill (n) ★★★ /skɪl/
slim (adj) ★★ /slɪm/
solar power (n) /'səʊlə ˌpaʊə/
solve (v) ★★★ /sɒlv/
speed (v) ★★ /spiːd/
stressed (adj) /strest/
support (v) ★★★ /sə'pɔː(r)t/
surface (n) ★★★ /'sɜː(r)fɪs/
switch off (v) /ˌswɪtʃ 'ɒf/
telescope (n) ★ /'telɪˌskəʊp/
treat (v) ★★★ /triːt/
trillion (n) /'trɪljən/
unknown (adj) ★★ /ʌn'nəʊn/
vacation (n) /və'keɪʃ(ə)n/
whale-hunting (n) /'weɪlˌhʌntɪŋ/

ADJECTIVE PREFIXES IL-, IN- AND IM
(il)legal (adj) ★★★ /'liːg(ə)l/
(il)logical (adj) /'lɒdʒɪk(ə)l/
(im)perfect (adj) ★★★ /'pɜː(r)fɪkt/
(im)polite (adj) ★ /pə'laɪt/
(im)possible (adj) ★★★ /'pɒsəb(ə)l/
(in)correct (adj) ★★★ /kə'rekt/
(in)credible (adj) ★ /'kredəb(ə)l/
(in)visible (adj) ★★ /'vɪzəb(ə)l/

BOOKS
romantic novel (n) /rəʊˌmæntɪk 'nɒv(ə)l/
non-fiction (n) /ˌnɒn'fɪkʃ(ə)n/
detective story (n) /dɪ'tektɪv ˌstɔːri/
biography (n) ★ /baɪ'ɒgrəfi/
author (n) ★★★ /'ɔːθə(r)/

THE LAW
against the law /əˌgenst ðə 'lɔː/
break a law /ˌbreɪk ə 'lɔː/
criminal (n) ★ /'krɪmɪn(ə)l/
forbidden (adj) ★ /fə(r)'bɪd(ə)n/
law-breaking (adj) /'lɔːˌbreɪkɪŋ/
licence (n) ★★★ /'laɪs(ə)ns/
underworld (n) /'ʌndə(r)ˌwɜː(r)ld/

PHRASAL VERBS WITH DOWN
calm down (v) /ˌkɑːm 'daʊn/
lie down (v) /ˌlaɪ 'daʊn/
sit down (v) /ˌsɪt 'daʊn/
slow down (v) /ˌsləʊ 'daʊn/
turn down (v) /ˌtɜːn 'daʊn/
write down (v) /ˌraɪt 'daʊn/

POLITICS
aid (n) ★★ /eɪd/
developing world (n) /dɪˌveləpɪŋ 'wɜːld/
government (n) ★★★ /'gʌvə(r)nmənt/
poverty (n) ★★ /'pɒvə(r)ti/
fair trade (n) /ˌfeə 'treɪd/
policy (n) ★★★ /'pɒləsi/

SPACE
astronomer (n) /ə'strɒnəmə(r)/
atmosphere (n) /'ætməsfɪə/
galaxy (n) /'gæləksi/

WORD LIST

gravity (n) /'grævəti/
light year (n) /'laɪt ˌjɪə/
orbit (n) /'ɔːbɪt/
planet (n) ★★ /'plænɪt/
solar system (n) /'səʊlə ˌsɪstəm/
star (n) ★★★ /staː(r)/
UFO (Unidentified Flying Object) (n) /ˌjuː ef 'əʊ/
universe (n) /'juːnɪvɜːs/

EXPRESSIONS

break a promise /ˌbreɪk ə 'prɒmɪs/
get married /ˌget 'mærɪd/
keep a secret /ˌkiːp ə 'siːkrət/
make a difference /ˌmeɪk ə 'dɪfrəns/
put on weight /ˌpʊt ɒn 'weɪt/
stay awake /ˌsteɪ ə'weɪk/
tell lies /ˌtel 'laɪz/
work for a living /'wɜːk fər ə ˌlɪvɪŋ/

UNIT 4

accidentally (adv) ★ /ˌæksɪ'dent(ə)li/
adore (v) /ə'dɔː(r)/
anger (n) ★★ /'æŋgə(r)/
annual (adj) ★★★ /'ænjuəl/
anxious (adj) ★★ /'æŋkʃəs/
associate (n) ★ /ə'səʊsiət/
brain (n) ★★★ /breɪn/
bruise (n) /bruːz/
calendar (n) ★★ /'kælɪndə(r)/
category (n) /'kætəg(ə)ri/
clap (v) ★ /klæp/
code (n) ★★★ /kəʊd/
coin (n) ★★ /kɔɪn/
communicate (v) ★★ /kə'mjuːnɪkeɪt/
conclusion (n) ★★★ /kən'kluːʒ(ə)n/
confess (v) ★★ /kən'fes/
connection (n) ★★★ /kə'nekʃ(ə)n/
consolidation (n) /kən,sɒlɪ'deɪʃ(ə)n/
crash (computer) (v) ★★ /kræʃ/
dare (v) ★★ /deə(r)/
differently (adv) /'dɪfrəntli/
diver (n) /'daɪvə(r)/
drown (v) ★★ /draʊn/
fancy dress ball (n) /ˌfænsi 'dres bɔːl/
fix (v) ★★★ /fɪks/
floor (n) ★★★ /flɔː(r)/
forecast (n) ★★ /'fɔː(r)kɑːst/
fright (n) /fraɪt/
hairbrush (n) /'heə(r)ˌbrʌʃ/
happening (n) /'hæp(ə)nɪŋ/
honeymoon (n) ★ /'hʌniˌmuːn/
housekeeper (n) /'haʊsˌkiːpə(r)/
impatiently (adv) /ɪm'peɪʃ(ə)ntli/
improve (v) ★★★ /ɪm'pruːv/
increase (v) ★★★ /ɪn'kriːs/
inquest (n) /'ɪŋkwest/
juggle (v) /'dʒʌg(ə)l/
kite (n) ★ /kaɪt/
knock (n) ★ /nɒk/
ladder (n) ★★ /'lædə(r)/
landmark (n) /'læn(d)ˌmɑː(r)k/
leaf (pl leaves) (n) ★★★ /liːf/
lip (n) ★★★ /lɪp/
memorable (adj) /'mem(ə)rəb(ə)l/
memory (n) ★★★ /'mem(ə)ri/
nasty (adj) /'nɑːsti/
notice (v) ★★★ /'nəʊtɪs/
painter (n) ★★ /'peɪntə(r)/
personalise (v) /'pɜː(r)s(ə)nəlaɪz/
play back (v) /ˌpleɪ 'bæk/
presence (n) ★★★ /'prez(ə)ns/
process (v) /prə'ses/
prove (v) ★★★ /pruːv/
psychic investigator (n) /ˌsaɪkɪk ɪn'vestɪgeɪtə/
rational (adj) ★★ /'ræʃ(ə)nəl/
recall (v) ★★★ /rɪ'kɔːl/
reply (v) ★★★ /rɪ'plaɪ/

research (n) ★★★ /rɪ'sɜː(r)tʃ, 'riːsɜː(r)tʃ/
rise (v) ★★★ /raɪz/
role (n) ★★★ /rəʊl/
servant (n) ★★★ /'sɜː(r)v(ə)nt/
shelf (pl shelves) (n) ★★ /ʃelf/
sideways (adv) ★ /'saɪdweɪz/
suicide (n) /'suːɪsaɪd/
terror (n) ★★ /'terə(r)/
verdict (n) ★★ /'vɜː(r)dɪkt/
wig (n) /wɪg/

PHRASAL VERBS WITH OUT

find out (v) /ˌfaɪnd 'aʊt/
go out (v) /ˌgəʊ 'aʊt/
look out (v) /ˌlʊk 'aʊt/
read out (v) /ˌriːd 'aʊt/
take out (v) /ˌteɪk 'aʊt/
try out (v) /ˌtraɪ 'aʊt/

SUPERSTITION

haunted (adj) /'hɔːntɪd/
haunting (n) /'hɔːntɪŋ/
horoscope (n) /'hɒrəˌskəʊp/
lucky charm (n) /ˌlʌki 'tʃɑːm/
prediction (n) ★★ /prɪ'dɪkʃ(ə)n/
supernatural (n) /ˌsuːpə(r)'nætʃərəl/
superstition (n) /ˌsuːpə(r)'stɪʃ(ə)n/
superstitious (adj) /ˌsuːpə(r)'stɪʃəs/

EXPRESSIONS

a memory like a sieve /ə ˌmemri laɪk ə 'sɪv/
down-to-earth /ˌdaʊn tuː 'ɜːθ/
follow advice /ˌfɒləʊ əd'vaɪs/
give someone a lift /ˌgɪv sʌmwʌn ə 'lɪft/
It makes no difference. /ɪt ˌmeɪks nəʊ 'dɪfrəns/
It's on the tip of my tongue. /ɪts ɒn ðə ˌtɪp əv maɪ 'tʌŋ/
pay attention /ˌpeɪ ə'tenʃ(ə)n/
put on clothes /ˌpʊt ɒn 'kləʊðz/
take no notice /ˌteɪk nəʊ 'nəʊtɪs/
Touch wood. /ˌtʌtʃ 'wʊd/
turn off the lights /ˌtɜːn ɒf ðə 'laɪts/

UNIT 5

agency (n) ★★★ /'eɪdʒ(ə)nsi/
airline (n) ★★ /'eə(r)ˌlaɪn/
altitude sickness (n) /'æltɪtjuːd ˌsɪknəs/
assist (v) ★★★ /ə'sɪst/
attitude (n) ★★★ /'ætɪˌtjuːd/
authorities (n pl) ★★★ /ɔː'θɒrətiz/
beef (n) ★★ /biːf/
benefit (v) ★★★ /'benɪfɪt/
border (n) ★★★ /'bɔː(r)də(r)/
bouncy (adj) /'baʊnsi/
business (n) ★★★ /'bɪznəs/
call in (at) /ˌkɔːl 'ɪn (æt)/
challenging (adj) /'tʃælɪndʒɪŋ/
charitable (adj) ★ /'tʃærɪtəb(ə)l/
cigarette (n) ★★★ /ˌsɪgə'ret/
coach (vehicle) (n) ★★ /kəʊtʃ/
combine (v) ★★★ /kəm'baɪn/
community (n) ★★★ /kə'mjuːnəti/
company (n) ★★★ /'kʌmp(ə)ni/
cook (n) ★★ /kʊk/
cost (n) ★★★ /kɒst/
cut out (v) /ˌkʌt 'aʊt/
drug (n) ★★★ /drʌg/
economy (n) ★★★ /ɪ'kɒnəmi/
efficient (adj) ★★★ /ɪ'fɪʃ(ə)nt/
entertain (v) ★★ /ˌentə(r)'teɪn/
exhausting (adj) /ɪg'zɔːstɪŋ/
face (v) ★★★ /feɪs/
fame (n) ★★ /feɪm/
first aid (n) /ˌfɜːst 'eɪd/
fortunate (adj) ★★ /'fɔː(r)tʃənət/
freshwater (adj) /'freʃˌwɔːtə(r)/
guinea pig (n) /'gɪni ˌpɪg/
habit (n) ★★★ /'hæbɪt/
headache (n) /'hedˌeɪk/

highlight (v) ★★ /'haɪˌlaɪt/
hostel (n) /'hɒst(ə)l/
import (v) ★★ /ɪm'pɔː(r)t/
involve (n) ★★★ /ɪn'vɒlv/
line (n) ★★★ /laɪn/
litre (n) ★ /'liːtə(r)/
llama (n) /'lɑːmə/
local (adj) ★★ /'ləʊk(ə)l/
magic (adj) ★★ /'mædʒɪk/
medal (n) ★★ /'med(ə)l/
metal (n) ★★★ /'met(ə)l/
mile (n) ★★★ /maɪl/
motorcycle (n) /'məʊtə(r)ˌsaɪk(ə)l/
novelty (n) ★ /'nɒv(ə)lti/
opportunity (n) ★★★ /ˌɒpə(r)'tjuːnəti/
piece (n) ★★★ /piːs/
plant (v) ★★ /plɑːnt/
point (n) ★★★ /pɔɪnt/
preach (v) ★ /priːtʃ/
public transport (n) ★ /ˌpʌblɪk 'trænspɔːt/
push (v) ★★★ /pʊʃ/
resort (n) ★ /rɪ'zɔː(r)t/
responsible (adj) ★★★ /rɪ'spɒnsəb(ə)l/
roast (adj) /rəʊst/
roll (v) ★★★ /rəʊl/
rollercoaster (n) /'rəʊləˌkəʊstə/
salary (n) ★★ /'sæləri/
sector (n) ★★★ /'sektə(r)/
souvenir (n) ★ /ˌsuːvə'nɪə(r)/
sphere (n) ★ /sfɪə(r)/
staff (n) ★★★ /stɑːf/
steep (adj) ★★ /stiːp/
steer (v) ★ /stɪə(r)/
strap (v) /stræp/
test (n & v) ★★★ /test/
tidy (adj) ★ /'taɪdi/
trail (n) /treɪl/
trek (n) /trek/
uncontrollably (adv) /ˌʌnkən'trəʊləbli/
valuable (adj) ★★★ /'væljʊb(ə)l/
vital (adj) ★★★ /'vaɪt(ə)l/
wear off (v) /ˌweər 'ɒf/
whizz (v) /wɪz/
worth (adj) ★★★ /wɜː(r)θ/
youth centre (n) /'juːθ ˌsentə/

NOUN SUFFIX -ITY

activity (n) ★★★ /æk'tɪvəti/
electricity (n) ★★★ /ɪˌlek'trɪsəti/
nationality (n) ★ /ˌnæʃə'næləti/
popularity (n) ★★ /ˌpɒpjʊ'lærəti/
possibility (n) ★★★ /ˌpɒsə'bɪləti/
reality (n) ★★★ /ri'æləti/
responsibility (n) ★★★ /rɪˌspɒnsə'bɪləti/
speciality (n) ★ /ˌspeʃi'æləti/

SPORT

bungee jumping (n) /'bʌndʒiː ˌdʒʌmpɪŋ/
free running (n) /ˌfriː 'rʌnɪŋ/
ice hockey (n) /'aɪs ˌhɒki/
kite surfing (n) /'kaɪt ˌsɜːfɪŋ/
paragliding (n) /'pærəˌglaɪdɪŋ/
para-skiing (n) /'pærəˌskiːɪŋ/
relay (n) /'riːleɪ/
sailing (n) /'seɪlɪŋ/
skiing (n) /'skiːɪŋ/
snowboarding (n) /'snəʊˌbɔː(r)dɪŋ/
sphereing (n) /'sfɪərɪŋ/
water-skiing (n) /'wɔːtə ˌskiːɪŋ/
zorbing (n) /'zɔːbɪŋ/

EXPRESSIONS

as a rule /ˌæz ə 'ruːl/
fall out (with) /ˌfɔːl 'aʊt (wɪð)/
get rid of /ˌget 'rɪd əv/
hit it off /ˌhɪt ɪt 'ɒf/
in case /ˌɪn 'keɪs/
set a record /ˌset ə 'rekɔːd/
straight away /ˌstreɪt ə'weɪ/

UNIT 6

ad (= advertisement) (n)	/æd/
advantage (n) ★★★	/əd'vɑːntɪdʒ/
approximately (adv) ★★	/ə'prɒksɪmətli/
attempt (n) ★★★	/ə'tempt/
balance (v) ★★	/'bæləns/
bamboo (n)	/ˌbæm'buː/
bar (n) ★★★	/bɑː(r)/
bark (of tree) (n) ★	/bɑː(r)k/
blind (adj) ★★	/blaɪnd/
bottle top (n)	/'bɒt(ə)l ˌtɒp/
brick (n) ★★	/brɪk/
brush (n) ★★	/brʌʃ/
campaign (n) ★★★	/kæm'peɪn/
can (n) ★★	/kæn/
carpenter (n)	/'kɑː(r)pɪntə(r)/
carpet (n) ★★	/'kɑː(r)pɪt/
carton (n)	/'kɑː(r)t(ə)n/
chamber (n) ★★	/'tʃeɪmbə(r)/
clockwork (n)	/'klɒkˌwɜː(r)k/
complicated (adj) ★★	/'kɒmplɪˌkeɪtɪd/
compose (v) ★★	/kəm'pəʊz/
connect (v) ★★★	/kə'nekt/
construct (v) ★★★	/kən'strʌkt/
consume (v) ★★	/kən'sjuːm/
cupboard (n) ★★	/'kʌbə(r)d/
deaf (adj) ★★	/def/
design (n) ★★★	/dɪ'zaɪn/
detailed (adj) ★★★	/'diːteɪld/
dot (n) ★	/dɒt/
electronics (n) ★★	/ˌelek'trɒnɪks/
endless (adj) ★★	/'endləs/
enemy (n) ★★★	/'enəmi/
entirely (adv) ★★★	/ɪn'taɪə(r)li/
full-scale (adj)	/ˈfʊlˌskeɪl/
glove (n) ★★	/glʌv/
handrail (n)	/'hændˌreɪl/
highly (adv) ★★★	/'haɪli/
hot water bottle (n)	/hɒt 'wɔːtə bɒt(ə)l/
imaginative (adj) ★	/ɪ'mædʒɪnətɪv/
inspiration (n) ★★	/ˌɪnspə'reɪʃ(ə)n/
interestingly (adv)	/'ɪntrəstɪŋli/
jumbo jet (n)	/ˌdʒʌmbəʊ 'dʒet/
list (v) ★★★	/lɪst/
material (n) ★★★	/mə'tɪəriəl/
mobility (n) ★	/məʊ'bɪləti/
mulberry (n)	/'mʌlb(ə)ri/
nominate (v) ★	/'nɒmɪneɪt/
pencil case (n)	/'pens(ə)l ˌkeɪs/
plant (n) ★★★	/plɑːnt/
plastic surgery (n)	/ˌplæstɪk 'sɜːdʒəri/
poll (n) ★★	/pəʊl/
pot (n) ★★	/pɒt/
powered (adj)	/'paʊəd/
printing (n) ★★	/'prɪntɪŋ/
process (n) ★★★	/'prəʊses/
product (n) ★★★	/'prɒdʌkt/
pulp (n)	/pʌlp/
pyramid (n) ★	/'pɪrəmɪd/
rail (n) ★★★	/reɪl/
raised (adj) ★	/reɪzd/
recycle (v) ★	/riː'saɪk(ə)l/
recycled (adj)	/riː'saɪk(ə)ld/
reduce (v) ★★★	/rɪ'djuːs/
resource (n) ★★★	/rɪ'zɔː(r)s/
run into (v)	/'rʌn ˌɪntuː/
saucepan (n) ★	/'sɔːspən/
self-propelled (adj)	/ˌselfprə'peld/
sell out (v)	/ˌsel 'aʊt/
sheet (n) ★★★	/ʃiːt/
shortlist (n)	/'ʃɔːtˌlɪst/
shut (v) ★★★	/ʃʌt/
sign language (n)	/'saɪn ˌlæŋgwɪdʒ/
simplify (v) ★	/'sɪmplɪfaɪ/
sketch (v) ★	/sketʃ/
skins (n pl) ★★★	/skɪnz/
slide (v) ★★	/slaɪd/
soft (adj) ★★★	/sɒft/
soldier (n) ★★★	/'səʊldʒə(r)/
sophisticated (adj) ★★	/sə'fɪstɪˌkeɪtɪd/
spread (v) ★★★	/spred/
stairs (n pl) ★★★	/steə(r)z/
strength (n) ★★★	/streŋθ/
stylish (adj) ★	/'staɪlɪʃ/
supply (v) ★★★	/sə'plaɪ/
system (n) ★★★	/'sɪstəm/
throw away (v)	/ˌθrəʊ ə'weɪ/
tray (n) ★★	/treɪ/
turn into (v)	/ˌtɜːn 'ɪntuː/
tyre (n) ★★	/'taɪə(r)/
vehicle (n) ★★★	/'viːɪk(ə)l/
waste (n) ★★★	/weɪst/
wear out (v)	/ˌweə(r) 'aʊt/
workout (n)	/'wɜː(r)kaʊt/
yoghurt (n)	/'jɒgə(r)t/

INVENTIONS AND DISCOVERIES

aqualung (n)	/'ækwəˌlʌŋ/
atomic bomb (n)	/əˌtɒmɪk 'bɒm/
bicycle (n) ★★	/'baɪsɪk(ə)l/
car alarm (n)	/'kɑːr əˌlɑːm/
computer (n) ★★★	/kəm'pjuːtə(r)/
helicopter (n) ★★	/'helɪˌkɒptə(r)/
internal combustion engine (n)	/ɪnˌtɜːn(ə)l kəm'bʌstʃ(ə)n ˌendʒɪn/
light bulb (n)	/'laɪt ˌbʌlb/
mobile phone (n) ★★	/ˌməʊbaɪl 'fəʊn/
nuclear bomb (n)	/ˌnjuːkliə 'bɒm/
parachute (n)	/'pærəˌʃuːt/
telephone (n) ★★★	/'telɪˌfəʊn/
television (n) ★★★	/'telɪˌvɪʒ(ə)n/
vacuum cleaner (n)	/'vækjuːəm ˌkliːnə/
World Wide Web (n)	/ˌwɜːld waɪd 'web/
X-ray (n) ★	/'eks ˌreɪ/
zip (n) ★	/zɪp/

MATERIALS

cotton (n & adj) ★★	/'kɒt(ə)n/
glass (n & adj) ★★★	/glɑːs/
metal (n & adj) ★★★	/'met(ə)l/
paper (n & adj) ★★★	/'peɪpə(r)/
plastic (n & adj) ★★★	/'plæstɪk/
rubber (n & adj) ★★	/'rʌbə(r)/
wood (n & adj) ★★★	/wʊd/
wool (n & adj) ★★	/wʊl/

NOUN SUFFIX -OR

actor (n) ★★★	/'æktə(r)/
director (n) ★★★	/də'rektə(r), daɪ'rektə(r)/
emperor (n) ★	/'emp(ə)rə(r)/
inventor (n) ★	/ɪn'ventə(r)/
professor (n) ★★	/prə'fesə(r)/
translator (n)	/træns'leɪtə(r)/

NOUN SUFFIX -ER

designer (n) ★★	/dɪ'zaɪnə(r)/
engineer (n) ★★★	/ˌendʒɪ'nɪə(r)/
explorer (n)	/ɪk'splɔːrə(r)/
listener (n) ★	/'lɪs(ə)nə(r)/
painter (n) ★★	/'peɪntə(r)/
printer (n) ★★	/'prɪntə(r)/
recycler (n)	/riː'saɪklə/
reporter (n) ★	/rɪ'pɔːtə(r)/
runner (n) ★★	/'rʌnə(r)/
supporter (n) ★★★	/sə'pɔː(r)tə(r)/

NOUN SUFFIX -IST

artist (n) ★★★	/'ɑː(r)tɪst/
journalist (n) ★★	/'dʒɜː(r)nəlɪst/
novelist (n) ★	/'nɒvəlɪst/
scientist (n) ★★★	/'saɪəntɪst/
tourist (n) ★★★	/'tʊərɪst/

PHRASES WITH DO

do damage	/ˌduː 'dæmɪdʒ/
do an exercise	/ˌduː ən 'eksəsaɪz/
do the shopping	/ˌduː ðə 'ʃɒpɪŋ/
do the washing up	/ˌduː ðə wɒʃɪŋ 'ʌp/
do some work	/ˌduː səm 'wɜːk/

PHRASES WITH MAKE

make an attempt	/ˌmeɪk ən ə'tempt/
make a difference	/ˌmeɪk ə 'dɪfrəns/
make friends	/ˌmeɪk 'frendz/
make a list	/ˌmeɪk ə 'lɪst/
make a mistake	/ˌmeɪk ə mɪ'steɪk/
make a sign	/ˌmeɪk ə 'saɪn/
make sure	/ˌmeɪk 'ʃɔː/

OTHER EXPRESSIONS

in the first place	/ˌɪn ðə 'fɜːst pleɪs/
on display	/ˌɒn dɪ'spleɪ/
put into practice	/ˌpʊt ɪntə 'præktɪs/

UNIT 7

annoyed (n) ★★	/ə'nɔɪd/
artificial (adj) ★★	/ˌɑː(r)tɪ'fɪʃ(ə)l/
bit (n) ★★	/bɪt/
bracelet (n)	/'breɪslət/
bring back (v)	/ˌbrɪŋ 'bæk/
call centre (n)	/'kɔːl sentə/
capsize (v)	/kæp'saɪz/
cholera (n)	/'kɒlərə/
co-author (v)	/ˌkəʊ'ɔːθə/
coastguard (n)	/'kəʊs(t)ˌgɑː(r)d/
command (n) ★★★	/kə'mɑːnd/
container (n) ★★	/kən'teɪnə(r)/
correctly (adv)	/kə'rek(t)li/
crazy (adj) ★★	/'kreɪzi/
critic (n) ★★★	/'krɪtɪk/
crops (n pl) ★★	/krɒps/
dinghy (n)	/'dɪŋi, 'dɪŋgi/
direct (adv) ★	/dɪ'rekt, daɪ'rekt/
dozen (n) ★	/'dʌz(ə)n/
dumb (adj)	/dʌm/
educate (v) ★★	/'edjʊkeɪt/
effect (n) ★★★	/ɪ'fekt/
either … or (conj)	/ˌaɪðə(r) … 'ɔː/
electronically (adv)	/ˌelek'trɒnɪkli/
farmer (n) ★★★	/'fɑː(r)mə(r)/
fees (n pl) ★★★	/fiːz/
generate (v) ★★★	/'dʒenəreɪt/
giggle (v) ★	/'gɪg(ə)l/
global (adj) ★★★	/'gləʊb(ə)l/
growing (adj) ★★★	/'grəʊɪŋ/
guilty (adj) ★★★	/'gɪlti/
hold on (v)	/ˌhəʊld 'ɒn/
home-made (adj)	/'həʊmˌmeɪd/
importance (n) ★★★	/ɪm'pɔː(r)t(ə)ns/
injure (v) ★★	/'ɪndʒə(r)/
instruction (n) ★★★	/ɪn'strʌkʃ(ə)n/
interviewer (n) ★	/'ɪntə(r)ˌvjuːə(r)/
leadership (n) ★★★	/'liːdə(r)ʃɪp/
make up (= invent)	/ˌmeɪk 'ʌp/
media (n)	/'miːdiə/
mother-to-be (n)	/ˌmʌðətə'biː/
natural (adj) ★★★	/'nætʃ(ə)rəl/
nearby (adj) ★★	/ˌnɪə(r)'baɪ/
next door (adv) ★	/ˌneks 'dɔː/
phenomenal (adj)	/fə'nɒmɪn(ə)l/
pregnant (adj) ★★	/'pregnənt/
pump (v) ★	/pʌmp/
relationship (n) ★★★	/rɪ'leɪʃ(ə)nʃɪp/
remarkable (adj) ★★★	/rɪ'mɑː(r)kəb(ə)l/
report (n) ★★★	/rɪ'pɔː(r)t/
request (n) ★★★	/rɪ'kwest/
right (v)	/raɪt/
secondary school (n)	/'sekənd(ə)ri ˌskuːl/
shyly (adv)	/'ʃaɪli/
solution (n) ★★★	/sə'luːʃ(ə)n/
starvation (n)	/stɑː(r)'veɪʃ(ə)n/
stock (n) ★★★	/stɒk/
store (v) ★★	/stɔː(r)/
suburb (n) ★	/'sʌbɜː(r)b/
symbol (n) ★★	/'sɪmb(ə)l/
tail (n) ★★	/teɪl/
technology (n) ★★★	/tek'nɒlədʒi/

tough (adj) ★★★ /tʌf/
trunk (animal) (n) ★ /trʌŋk/
unborn (adj) /ʌn'bɔː(r)n/
villager (n) ★ /'vɪlɪdʒə(r)/
watertight (adj) /'wɔːtə(r)ˌtaɪt/
windmill (n) /'wɪn(d)ˌmɪl/

ANIMALS

ape (n) /eɪp/
cat (n) ★★★ /kæt/
chimpanzee (n) /ˌtʃɪmpæn'ziː/
dog (n) ★★★ /dɒg/
duck (n) ★★ /dʌk/
elephant (n) ★ /'elɪfənt/
gorilla (n) /gə'rɪlə/
monkey (n) ★ /'mʌŋki/
pig (n) ★★ /pɪg/
snail (n) /sneɪl/
tiger (n) ★ /'taɪgə(r)/
worm (n) ★ /wɜː(r)m/
zebra (n) /'zebrə/

EMAIL

attachment (n) ★★ /ə'tætʃmənt/
filter (v) ★ /'fɪltə(r)/
Internet (n) ★★★ /'ɪntə(r)ˌnet/
ISP (Internet Service Provider) (n) /ˌaɪ es 'piː/
junk (n) ★ /dʒʌŋk/
spam (n) /spæm/
virus (n) ★★★ /'vaɪrəs/

NOUN SUFFIX -TION

attention (n) ★★★ /ə'tenʃ(ə)n/
communication (n) ★★★ /kəˌmjuːnɪ'keɪʃ(ə)n/
description (n) ★★★ /dɪ'skrɪpʃ(ə)n/
information (n) ★★★ /ˌɪnfə(r)'meɪʃ(ə)n/
invention (n) ★★ /ɪn'venʃ(ə)n/
invitation (n) ★★ /ˌɪnvɪ'teɪʃ(ə)n/
operation (n) ★★★ /ˌɒpə'reɪʃ(ə)n/
situation (n) ★★★ /ˌsɪtʃu'eɪʃ(ə)n/

PHRASAL VERBS WITH GO

go ahead with (v) /ˌgəʊ ə'hed wɪð/
go away (v) /ˌgəʊ ə'weɪ/
go back (v) /ˌgəʊ 'bæk/
go down (v) /ˌgəʊ 'daʊn/
go on (v) /ˌgəʊ 'ɒn/
go up (v) /ˌgəʊ 'ʌp/

EXPRESSIONS

attract attention /əˌtrækt ə'tenʃ(ə)n/
charge a mobile /ˌtʃɑː(r)dʒ ə 'məʊbaɪl/
in broken English /ɪn ˌbrəʊkən 'ɪŋglɪʃ/
in trouble /ˌɪn 'trʌb(ə)l/
It's early days. /ɪts ˌɜːli 'deɪz/
take off clothes /ˌteɪk ɒf 'kləʊðz/
turn off the water /ˌtɜːn ɒf ðə 'wɔːtə/

UNIT 8

Aboriginal (adj) /ˌæbə'rɪdʒ(ə)n(ə)l/
Aborigine (n) /ˌæbə'rɪdʒəni/
agriculture (n) ★★ /'ægrɪˌkʌltʃə(r)/
announcement (n) ★★★ /ə'naʊnsmənt/
aspect (n) ★★★ /'æspekt/
aspirin (n) ★ /'æsprɪn/
back away (v) /ˌbæk ə'weɪ/
barefoot (adv) /'beə(r)ˌfʊt/
berry (n) ★ /'beri/
brochure (n) ★ /'brəʊʃə(r)/
citizen (n) ★★★ /'sɪtɪz(ə)n/
concerned (adj) ★★★ /kən'sɜː(r)nd/
consequence (n) ★★★ /'kɒnsɪkwəns/
consider (v) ★★★ /kən'sɪdə(r)/
considerably (adv) ★★ /kən'sɪd(ə)rəbli/
crouch (v) ★ /kraʊtʃ/
cubic metre (n) /ˌkjuːbɪk 'miːtə/
currency (n) ★★★ /'kʌrənsi/
dentist (n) ★ /'dentɪst/
displace (v) /dɪs'pleɪs/

dollar ($) (n) ★★ /'dɒlə(r)/
effort (n) ★★★ /'efə(r)t/
essential (adj) ★★★ /ɪ'senʃ(ə)l/
honey (n) ★ /'hʌni/
hygiene (n) ★ /'haɪdʒiːn/
igloo (n) /'ɪgluː/
industry (n) ★★★ /'ɪndəstri/
lemon (n) ★★ /'lemən/
minimum (adj) ★★ /'mɪnɪməm/
native (adj) ★★ /'neɪtɪv/
notice (n) ★★★ /'nəʊtɪs/
pavilion (n) /pə'vɪliən/
positive (adj) ★★★ /'pɒzətɪv/
preserve (v) ★★★ /prɪ'zɜː(r)v/
recommended (adj) /ˌrekə'mendɪd/
shelter (n) ★★ /'ʃeltə(r)/
shortage (n) ★★ /'ʃɔː(r)tɪdʒ/
skyscraper (n) /'skaɪˌskreɪpə(r)/
slippery (adj) /'slɪpəri/
species (n pl) ★★★ /'spiːʃiːz/
structure (n) ★★★ /'strʌktʃə(r)/
survive (v) ★★★ /sə(r)'vaɪv/
tight (adv) ★ /taɪt/
underway (adj) /ˌʌndə(r)'weɪ/
use (n) ★★★ /juːs/
variety (n) ★★★ /və'raɪəti/
waist (n) ★★ /weɪst/
wipe out (v)

ADJECTIVE SUFFIX -AL

central (adj) ★★★ /'sentrəl/
coastal (adj) ★★ /'kəʊst(ə)l/
continental (adj) ★★ /ˌkɒntɪ'nent(ə)l/
electrical (adj) ★★ /ɪ'lektrɪk(ə)l/
environmental (adj) ★★★ /ɪnˌvaɪrən'ment(ə)l/
global (adj) ★★★ /'gləʊb(ə)l/
musical (adj) ★★ /'mjuːzɪk(ə)l/
natural (adj) ★★★ /'nætʃ(ə)rəl/
official (adj) ★★★ /ə'fɪʃ(ə)l/
tropical (adj) ★★ /'trɒpɪk(ə)l/

ANIMALS

brown bear (n) /ˌbraʊn 'beə/
caribou (n) /'kærəbuː/
crocodile (n) /'krɒkədaɪl/
elk (n) /elk/
emu (n) /'iːmjuː/
grizzly bear (n) /ˌgrɪzli 'beə(r)/
kangaroo (n) /ˌkæŋgə'ruː/
koala (n) /kəʊ'ɑːlə/
kookaburra (n) /'kʊkəˌbʌrə/
moose (n) /muːs/
platypus (n) /'plætɪpəs/
polar bear (n) /'pəʊlə ˌbeə/
shark (n) ★ /ʃɑː(r)k/
snake (n) ★ /sneɪk/
spider (n) ★ /'spaɪdə(r)/
whale (n) ★★ /weɪl/
wildlife (n) ★★ /'waɪldˌlaɪf/

GEOGRAPHICAL FEATURES

bank (of river) (n) ★★★ /bæŋk/
coral reef (n) /'kɒrəl ˌriːf/
desert (n) ★★ /'dezə(r)t/
falls (n) /fɔːlz/
forest (n) ★★★ /'fɒrɪst/
grassland (n) /'grɑːsˌlænd/
ice (n) ★★★ /aɪs/
interior (n) ★★ /ɪn'tɪəriə(r)/
jungle (n) ★ /'dʒʌŋg(ə)l/
mountain (range) (n) ★★★ /'maʊntɪn/
oasis (n) /əʊ'eɪsɪs/
outback (n) /'aʊtˌbæk/
plain (n) ★★ /pleɪn/
polar ice cap (n) /ˌpəʊlər 'aɪs kæp/
prairie (n) /'preəri/
rainforest (n) ★ /'reɪnˌfɒrɪst/
river (n) ★★★ /'rɪvə(r)/
semi-desert (n) /ˌsemi'dezət/
tundra (n) /'tʌndrə/

waterfall (n) ★ /'wɔːtə(r)ˌfɔːl/

ILLNESSES AND AILMENTS

cold (n) ★★ /kəʊld/
cough (n) ★ /kɒf/
headache (n) ★ /'hedeɪk/
hiccoughs (n) /'hɪkʌps/
sore throat (n) /ˌsɔː 'θrəʊt/
toothache (n) /'tuːθeɪk/

SURVIVAL KIT

candle (n) ★★ /'kænd(ə)l/
compass (n) ★ /'kʌmpəs/
first aid kit (n) /ˌfɜːst 'eɪd kɪt/
insect spray (n) /'ɪnsekt ˌspreɪ/
magnifying glass (n) /'mægnɪfaɪɪŋ ˌglɑːs/
map (n) ★★★ /mæp/
matches (n pl) ★★★ /'mætʃəz/
mirror (n) ★★★ /'mɪrə(r)/
needle and thread (n) /ˌniːd(ə)l ən 'θred/
penknife (n) /'penˌnaɪf/
safety pin (n) /'seɪfti ˌpɪn/
sun cream (n) /'sʌn ˌkriːm/
torch (n) ★ /tɔː(r)tʃ/
whistle (n & v) ★ /'wɪs(ə)l/

WATER

dam (n) /dæm/
downstream (adv) /ˌdaʊn'striːm/
fresh water (n) /'freʃ ˌwɔːtə/
frozen (adj) ★ /'frəʊz(ə)n/
flood (v) ★★ /flʌd/
hosepipe (n) /'həʊzˌpaɪp/
rainwater (n) /'reɪnˌwɔːtə(r)/
salt water (n) /'sɔːlt ˌwɔːtə/
tap (n) ★★ /tæp/
upstream (adv) /ʌp'striːm/
water (v) ★★★ /'wɔːtə(r)/
watering can (n) /'wɔːt(ə)rɪŋ ˌkæn/

WEATHER AND CLIMATE

cyclone (n) /'saɪˌkləʊn/
drought (n) /draʊt/
hurricane (n) /'hʌrɪkən, 'hʌrɪkeɪn/
lightning (n) ★ /'laɪtnɪŋ/
minus (temperature) (adj) ★★ /'maɪnəs/
monsoon (n) /mɒn'suːn/
rainfall (n) /'reɪnˌfɔːl/
snow (n) ★★★ /snəʊ/
sunshine (n) ★★ /'sʌnˌʃaɪn/
temperature (n) ★★★ /'temprɪtʃə(r)/
thunderstorm (n) /'θʌndə(r)ˌstɔː(r)m/
tropical (adj) ★★ /'trɒpɪk(ə)l/
wind (n) /waɪnd/

EXPRESSIONS

count sheep /ˌkaʊnt 'ʃiːp/
in other words /ɪn ˌʌðə ˌwɜːdz/
take a deep breath /ˌteɪk ə diːp 'breθ/

IRREGULAR VERBS

Infinitive	Simple past	Past participle
be	was, were	been
become	became	become
begin	began	begun
bend	bent	bent
bet	bet	bet
bite	bit	bitten
blow	blew	blown
break	broke	broken
bring	brought	brought
broadcast	broadcast	broadcast
build	built	built
burn	burnt/burned	burnt/burned
buy	bought	bought
catch	caught	caught
choose	chose	chosen
come	came	come
cost	cost	cost
cut	cut	cut
dig	dug	dug
do	did	done
draw	drew	drawn
dream	dreamt/dreamed	dreamt/dreamed
drink	drank	drunk
drive	drove	driven
eat	ate	eaten
fall	fell	fallen
feed	fed	fed
feel	felt	felt
fight	fought	fought
find	found	found
fit	fit/fitted	fit/fitted
fly	flew	flown
forbid	forbad(e)	forbidden
forget	forgot	forgotten
freeze	froze	frozen
get	got	got
give	gave	given
go	went	gone/been
grow	grew	grown
have	had	had
hear	heard	heard
hide	hid	hidden
hit	hit	hit
hold	held	held
hurt	hurt	hurt
keep	kept	kept
know	knew	known
lay	laid	laid
learn	learnt/learned	learnt/learned
leave	left	left
lend	lent	lent

Infinitive	Simple past	Past participle
let	let	let
lie	lay	lain
light	lit	lit
lose	lost	lost
make	made	made
mean	meant	meant
meet	met	met
pay	paid	paid
put	put	put
read /riːd/	read /red/	read /red/
retell	retold	retold
rewrite	rewrote	rewritten
ride	rode	ridden
ring	rang	rung
rise	rose	risen
run	ran	run
say	said	said
see	saw	seen
sell	sold	sold
send	sent	sent
set	set	set
shake	shook	shaken
shine	shone	shone
shoot	shot	shot
show	showed	shown
shut	shut	shut
sing	sang	sung
sink	sank	sunk
sit	sat	sat
sleep	slept	slept
slide	slid	slid
smell	smelt/smelled	smelt/smelled
speak	spoke	spoken
speed	sped/speeded	sped/speeded
spell	spelt/spelled	spelt/spelled
spend	spent	spent
spread	spread	spread
stand	stood	stood
steal	stole	stolen
stick	stuck	stuck
swim	swam	swum
take	took	taken
teach	taught	taught
tell	told	told
think	thought	thought
throw	threw	thrown
understand	understood	understood
wake	woke	woken
wear	wore	worn
win	won	won
write	wrote	written

PRONUNCIATION GUIDE

Vowels

/ɑː/	arm, large
/æ/	cap, bad
/aɪ/	ride, fly
/aɪə/	diary, science
/aʊ/	how, mouth
/aʊə/	our, shower
/e/	bed, head
/eɪ/	day, grey
/eə/	hair, there
/ɪ/	give, did
/i/	happy, honeymoon
/iː/	we, heat
/ɪə/	ear, here
/ɒ/	not, watch
/əʊ/	cold, boat
/ɔː/	door, talk
/ɔɪ/	point, boy
/ʊ/	foot, could
/u/	annual
/uː/	two, food
/ʊə/	sure, tourist
/ɜː/	bird, heard
/ʌ/	fun, come
/ə/	mother, actor

Consonants

/b/	bag, rubbish
/d/	desk, cold
/f/	fill, laugh
/g/	girl, big
/h/	hand, home
/j/	yes, young
/k/	cook, back
/l/	like, fill
/m/	mean, climb
/n/	new, want
/p/	park, happy
/r/	ring, borrow
/s/	say, this
/t/	town, city
/v/	very, live
/w/	water, away
/z/	zoo, his
/ʃ/	shop, machine
/ʒ/	usually, television
/ŋ/	thank, doing
/tʃ/	cheese, match
/θ/	thing, north
/ð/	that, clothes
/dʒ/	jeans, bridge

Macmillan Education
Between Towns Road, Oxford OX4 3PP
A division of Macmillan Publishers Limited
Companies and representatives throughout the world

ISBN 978-0-230-40849-4

Text © Judy Garton-Sprenger and Philip Prowse 2012
Design and illustration © Macmillan Publishers Limited 2012

This edition published 2012
First edition published 2006

Original design by Giles Davies Design Ltd
Page make-up by Giles Davies Design Ltd
Illustrated by Ilias Arahovitis (Beehive Illustration) p48; Andrew Bock (Beehive Illustration)
pp51, 54 and 55; Emmanuel Cerisier (Beehive Illustration) pp102 and 103; Mark Duffin p74;
Maria Cristina Pritelli (Beehive Illustration) p81; Mark Ruffle pp52, 53 and 101*b*; David
Semple p89; Kate Sheppard pp18, 44, 70 and 96; Nadine Wickenden p101*a*; and Gary Wing
pp36, 49, 60, 69, 77 and 95).
Cover design by Designers Collective
Cover photos by **Art Directors & Trip**/NASA; **Corbis**/Scott Markewitz/Aurora Photos,
Corbis/Carlos Villoch/Specialist Stock; **Getty**/ASP; **Photolibrary**/Yvette Cardozo; **Rex**/KPA/
Zuma; **Superstock**/Photoalto.

Authors' acknowledgements
The authors would like to thank all the team at Macmillan Education in the UK and
worldwide for everything they have done to create *New Inspiration*. We are most grateful to
Celia Bingham for editing the Student's Book, to Helena Gomm for revising the Workbook,
and to Tim Bowen for the Teacher's Book. We would also like to thank James Richardson
for his usual great skill in producing the recorded material, and the actors who appear on the
recordings and bring the book to life.

We owe an enormous debt of gratitude to teenage students and their teachers in many
different countries who welcomed us into their classrooms and contributed so much to the
formation of *New Inspiration*. In particular we would like to thank teachers and classes in
Argentina, Greece, Italy, Poland, Spain, Switzerland, Turkey and Uruguay. We are equally
indebted to all those participants on teacher training courses in Europe, South America and
elsewhere from whom we have learnt so much, in particular British Council courses in the UK
and overseas, and courses at the University of Durham and NILE in Norwich.

The authors and publishers would like to express their great thanks to all those who
commented on syllabus and materials for *New Inspiration* and provided feedback on their
use of *Inspiration*, in particular: Fatiha Ajaoui, Mª Angeles Ramiro Alvarez, Alejandro De
Angelis, Asun Armendáriz, Roseli Franco Babora, Cristina Ceratti Bo, Monika Bucher,
Barbara Chuck, Bilsev Demir, Anastasia Egorova, Yolanda Elsener-Fischer, Pia Ettlin, Nadine
Fesseler, Katharina Fischer, Joe Hediger, Lisbeth Heinzer-Föhn, Alda Heloisa Santoyo Garcia,
Anna Häfliger-Schmidlin, Mgr.Jana Hanesova, Katharina Hofmann, Corinna Iaizzo, Daniela
Iskerková, Estrella Gómez Jiménez-Tusset, Bulent Karababa, Figen Kılıçarslan, Antonia
Köppel, Svetlana Korostelyova, Lycia Lourenço Lacerda, Carmelia Loher, Pilar García
López-Tello, Zuzana Lovasova, Monika Mižáková, Fabiane R. Montanari, Andrea Cristina
Neiger, Clara González O'Sullivan, Ingrid Rizzi Razente, Brigitte Reber, Peach Richmond,
Alfonsa Pliego Romera, Jean Rüdiger-Harper, Karl Russi, Monica Cristina Sales, Susanna
Schwab, Adilson Geraldo Da Silva, Monica Dolores Sosa, Geraldo de Souza Jr, Janine Strub-
Dittli, Maria Vertiletskaya, Mª Rosa Pradilla Vicente, Maria Luisa Villarruel, Menekşe Yildiz,
Andrea Zeiger.

The authors and publishers would like to thank the following for permission to reproduce
their photographic material:
AKG/20th Century Fox/Album p22(tr); **Alamy**/AF archive p22(br), Alamy/Alvey & Towers
Picture Library p38(tr), Alamy/Blend Images p25(br), Alamy/Andy Day p64(cl), Alamy/
Dbphots p50(t), Alamy/dmac p17(c), Alamy/James Fairclough p50(c), Alamy/Foodfolio
p27(cr), Alamy/Tim Gainey p98(t), Alamy/Mike Goldwater p42, Alamy/Blaine Harrington
III p72(l), Alamy/Hemis p108(tr), Alamy/Imagerymajestic p24(r), Alamy/isifa Image Service
s.r.o/© DACS 2011 p104(br), Alamy/John Warburton-Lee Photography p108(br), Alamy/
Marion Kaplan p68(b), Alamy/June Morrissey p108(ct), Alamy/Moviestore Collection Ltd
p22(ct), Alamy/Outdoor-Archiv p64(tr), Alamy/Chris Rout p6(br, tr), Alamy/RT Images
p87(cr), Alamy/Rubber Ball p6(tl), Alamy/Image Source p67, Alamy/Masa Ushioda p107(b),
Alamy/Ann and Steve Toon p15, Alamy/Barry Turner p94(t); **Art Directors & Trip**/NASA
p37(bl), Art Directors & Trip/Constance Toms p17(r); **Bananastock** p100(b); **Bookcrossing
Inc** p26(logo); **Brand X Pictures** p34(c), 38(l); **Comstock Images** p27(bl, cb); **Corbis**
p82(bl), Corbis/Diego Azubel p104(cl), Corbis/Elvis Barukcic p86(t), 100(background),
Corbis/Bettmann p78(t), Corbis/David Buffington/Blend Images p46(cbl), Corbis/Dallas
and John Heaton/Free Agents Limited p106(br), Corbis/Stephen Frink p64(br), Corbis/Edith
Held p7(tl, bcr), Corbis/Historical Picture Archive p80(b), Corbis/Tiara Hobbs p24(cl),
Corbis/Hulton-Deutsch Collection p79(l), Corbis/Justin Lane p82(tl), Corbis/I Love Images
p6(tl, tcl), Corbis/Yuji Kaneko/Aflo Relax p37(bl), Corbis/Bob Krist p68(t), Corbis/Wayne
Lynch/All Canada Photos p56(r), Corbis/Simon Marcus p6(bl), Corbis/Scott Markewitz/
Aurora Photos p62(l), Corbis/Olivier Matthys p106(c), Corbis/Nyein Chan Naing/epa p20(bl),
Corbis/NASA - digital version copyright/Science Faction pp37(tl), 45, Corbis/Thierry Orban
p21(bl), Corbis/Jose L Pelaez p25(bl), Corbis/William Philpott p16(l), Corbis/Hugh Sitton
p72-73, Corbis/Stapleton Collection pp80-81(t), Corbis/Atsuko Tanaka p46(tl), Corbis/©
The Estate of Roy Lichtenstein/DACS 2011 p28(br), Corbis/The Gallery Collection p79(c),
Corbis/John Van Hasselt p20(cr), Corbis/Carlos Villoch/Specialist Stock p106(bl), Corbis/
Jake Warga p104(tr), Corbis/Chris Whitehead/Cultura p9(br); **Creatas** p107(t); **David Hertz
Architects, inc** p76(t); **Isabelle Dubois** p104(ct); **Elixir Films**/(c) Long Way Round 2004 pp60,
63; **Eyevine**/2011 Jeff Topping/The New York Times Syndicate /Redux p88(t), 105(r); **Fotolibra**/
Mark Harris p62(tr), Fotolibra/Nikhilesh Haval pp37(c), 87(tr), Fotolibra/Nick Jenkins p50(b),
Fotolibra/Dan Wragg p38(c); **Getty** pp21(br), 25(tr), 61(t), 78(l), Getty/ASP pp9(t), 14, 105(l),
Getty/Tim Graham p21(tc), Getty/Jamie Grill p76(cr), Getty/Tom Grill p24(l), Getty/Amanda
Hall p110, Getty/Image Source pp8(b), 24(cr), Getty/Ruth Jenkinson p62(cr), Getty/Ken
Kaminesky p8(c), 11, Getty/Bernhard Limberger p64(tl), Getty/Alex Mares-Manton p98(b),
Getty/Javier Pierini p46(bl), Getty/Rosebud Pictures p34(t), Getty/Stock4B-RF p61(r); **Grand
Resort Lagonissi** pp86(c), 104(bl); **Image Source** p27(c); **Macmillan Publishers Ltd**/Paul
Bricknell pp27(tr), 87(ct), Macmillan Publishers Ltd/David Tolley p27(tl); **Macmillan Readers**
p30, Macmillan Reader/Corbis/Bettmann p46(t), Macmillan Reader/Alamy/Masa Ushioda
p46(b), Macmillan Reader/Rex Features/ITV p47(t), Macmillan Reader/Alamy p47(b); **Rachel
Mahlke**/giddyspinster.etsy.com p76(cb); **Kathy Morlan**/Massachusetts Institute of Technology
p74(bl); **Photodisc** pp17(l), 27(tc); **Photolibrary**/Ableimages p62(br), Photolibrary/Yvette
Cardozo p108(tl), Photolibrary/Jim Craigmyle p46(cbl), Photolibrary/Design Pics Inc p32,
Photolibrary/Fancy p91(r), Photolibrary/Imagebroker.net p87(cb), Photolibrary/Image Source
p84, Photolibrary/Arthur Morris pp72-73(background), Photolibrary/Peter Arnold Images p52,
Photolibrary/Radius Images p91(l); **Raytheon BBN Technologies** pp86(b), 90; **Remarkable
Pencils Ltd**/www.remarkable.co.uk p76(br); **Rex Features** p82(tr), Rex Features/20th Century
Fox/Everett p79(r), Rex Features/Back Page Images p75, Rex Features/Chris Martin Bahr
p56(l), Rex Features/Canadian Press p37(ct), Rex Features/Everett Collection p16(r), Rex
Features/Francesco Guidicini p20(br), Rex Features/KPA/Zuma p20(t), Rex Features/Monkey
Business Images p7(bl, br), Rex Features/Tim Rooke p21(tl), Rex Features/Sipa Press pp21(tr),
66, 105(c), Rex Features/TOM p78(b), Rex Features/WestEnd61 p37(tr); **Richard Smith &
Luke Bateman**/'You Can Get Arrested for That' p39; **Rossparry.co.uk** pp61(b), 74(cb); **Ryan
Patterson**/National Institute on Deafness and other communications Disorders p74(br);
Science Photo Library/Lynette Cook pp35(tl), 36; **Splash News** pp87(tl), 88(b); **Stockbyte**
pp35(b), 40; **Studio 8** p27(cl, br); **Superstock** p94(b), Superstock/Corbis pp12-13(b), 38(br),
Superstock/Glow Images pp12(t), 19, Superstock/Hemis.fr p99, Superstock/Kablonk p35(tr),
Superstock/Phillips Collection, Washington D.C., USA p28(tr), Superstock/Succession Picasso/
DACS, London, 2011 p28(bl); **The Kobal Collection**/20th Century-Fox Film Corporation
pp8(t), 23, The Kobal Collection/The Disney Channel p22(tl), The Kobal Collection/Walt
Disney Productions p30(r); **Tom Rielly**/Moving Windmills Project p87(br), 92; **Topfoto**/
RIA Novosti p20(cl); **Torpedo Factory Art Center**/Chance B. Liscomb 'Biblio File' p76(l);
www.apple.com p87(br).

Commissioned Photography by Lisa Payne pp9(tl&bl), 10, 26.

The author and publishers are grateful for permission to reprint the following copyright material:
Page 96: Material from 'Laundry Systems: Relay & Slave Units' copyright © Brightwell
Dispensers Ltd 2011, reprinted by permission of the publisher;
Page 70: Material from 'Cambridge Encyclopaedia of Language' by David Crystal (1987),
copyright © Cambridge University Press 1997, reprinted by permission of the publisher;
Page 18: Material from 'First Person: Ziad Fazah' by Ed Hammond, copyright © Ed Hammond
2008, first published in *The Financial Times* 21.06.08, reprinted by permission of the publisher.
All rights reserved;
Page 76: Material taken from 'Imaginative Recycling' by Oliver Heath, taken from
www.foe.co.uk, reprinted by permission of Friends of the Earth (England, Wales & Northern
Ireland);
Page 66: Material from 'Usain Bolt: 9.58' by Usain Bolt (2010), copyright © Usain St Leo Bolt
2010, reprinted by permission of HarperCollins Publishers Ltd;
Page 46: LIVE AND LET DIE copyright © Glidrose Productions Ltd 1954. Reprinted with the
permission of Ian Fleming Publications Ltd. www.ianflemingpublications.com. All the James
Bond books by Ian Fleming are currently available through Penguin Books. www.penguin.co.uk;
Page 47: Material from 'Persuasion by Jane Austen' retold by Rachel Bladon for Macmillan
Readers, copyright © Rachel Bladon 2011, reprinted by permission of Macmillan Education;
Page 46: Material from 'Ghandi' by Rachel Bladon for Macmillan Readers, copyright © Rachel
Bladon 2011, reprinted by permission of Macmillan Education;
Page 72: Material from 'The Tourists are Coming' from WICKED WORLD by Benjamin
Zephaniah (Puffin, 2000), text copyright © Benjamin Zephaniah, 2000, reprinted by
permission of the publisher;
Page 14: Material from 'SOUL SURFER' by Bethany Hamilton. Copyright © 2004 by Pocket
Books. Reprinted with the permission of Simon & Schuster, Inc.and Simon & Schuster UK. All
Rights Reserved;
Page 36: Material from 'We Are Not Alone: one in four stars "may have earth-like planets in
orbit around them"' by David Derbyshire, first published in *The Daily Mail* 29.10.10, and
'Teenage girl on stairlift to millions after stumbling on handrail idea for GCSE project' by
Claire Ellicott, first published in *The Daily Mail* 14.11.09, both reprinted by permission of the
publisher;
Page 78: Material from 'She's A Lovely Little Car – one owner, 526 years old, runs like
clockwork' by Georgina Littlejohn, first published in *The London Metro* 26.04.04, reprinted by
permission of the publisher;
Page 72: The Tourists are Coming' by Benjamin Zephaniah. (Copyright ©Benjamin Zephaniah)
is reproduced by permission of United Agents (www.unitedagents.co.uk) on behalf of Benjamin
Zephaniah.

Definitiosn adapted from the *Macmillan English Dictionary 2nd Edition* © Macmillan Publishers
Limited 2007

Printed and bound in Thailand

2016 2015 2014 2013 2012
10 9 8 7 6 5 4 3 2 1